Better Health in Africa

Experience and Lessons Learned

THE WORLD BANK
WASHINGTON, D.C.

The Development in Practice series publishes reviews of
the World Bank's activities in different regions and sectors. It
lays particular emphasis on the progress that is being made
and on the policies and practices that hold the most promise
of success in the effort to reduce poverty in the developing
world.

The findings, interpretations, and conclusions expressed in
this study are entirely those of the authors and should not be
attributed in any manner to the World Bank, to its affiliated
organizations, or to members of its Board of Executive
Directors or the countries they represent. The boundaries,
colors, denominations, and other information shown on any
map in this volume do not imply on the part of the World
Bank Group any judgment on the legal status of any territory
or the endorsement or acceptance of such boundaries.

Cover photo: Curt Carnemark, World Bank staff

Library of Congress Cataloging-in-Publication Data

   Better health in Africa : experience and lessons learned.
      p.   cm.—(Development in practice)
   Includes bibliographical references (p.   ).
   ISBN 0-8213-2817-4
   1. Public health—Africa.   2. Health planning—
Africa.   3. Medical policy—Africa.   4. Medical
economies—Africa.   I. International Bank for Reconstruc-
tion and Development.   II. Title.   III. Series: Development in practice (Washington, D.C.)
RA545.B48   1994
362.1'096—dc20   94-18249
                                                CIP

DEVELOPMENT

IN   PRACTICE

Better Health
in Africa

microinfo ltd

P.O. Box 3
Omega Park

Contents

Boxes

Text Tables

Figures

Statistical Appendix Tables

Foreword

HIGH rates of disease and premature mortality in Sub-Saharan Africa are costing the continent dearly. Poor health causes pain and suffering, reduces human energies, and makes millions of Africans less able to cope with life, let alone enjoy it. The economic consequences are immense. Poor health shackles human capital, reduces returns to learning, impedes entrepreneurial activities, and holds back growth of gross national product (GNP).

Better Health in Africa presents African countries and their external partners with positive ideas on how to improve health. It argues that despite tight financial constraints, significant improvements in health are within reach in many countries. Experiences in countries as diverse as Benin, Botswana, Kenya, Mauritius, and Zimbabwe testify to this claim. This report documents lessons learned and "best practices" in four major areas.

First, to achieve better health, African households and communities need the knowledge and resources to recognize and respond effectively to health problems. Publicly sponsored programs that inform households and communities about threats to health and the services that can respond to them are essential. Formal and nonformal education play a major role, providing information and practical guidance on self-care, cleanliness, food preparation, and nutrition. The central position of women in household management and reproductive health must be emphasized. Intersectoral interventions to complement and sustain health improvements, such as the provision of safe water, are important. So too is local and community participation in the management of health services. These factors, this report argues, make crucial contributions to an "enabling environment for health." They are as important to health as improving income. Without them, the efficacy of medical interventions is greatly reduced.

Second, *Better Health in Africa* shows that much health improvement can be achieved by reforming health care systems to use available human and financial resources more productively. Correcting the many sources of waste and inefficiency takes top priority. Inefficiencies in the procurement, storage, prescribing, and use of drugs are so extensive, for example, that consumers in some countries get the benefits of only $12 dollars' worth of drugs for each $100 spent on drugs by the public sector. Inequities prevail to the extent that poor households in many countries have no access to quality care at times of serious illness or injury.

Critically important to health system reform is better management of pharmaceuticals, health sector personnel, and health infrastructure and equipment. Ministries of health are working on this in a number of countries. By giving more attention to the formulation and implementation of national policies and devolving responsibilities for health care provision to decentralized entities and the nongovernment sector, they can spur reform. In many countries, private voluntary organizations already assume a large share of the responsibility for providing health care, and can do more. Legal and regulatory environments are becoming increasingly conducive to the provision of health services by the private sector.

Third, this report shows that cost-effective packages of basic health services—delivered through networks of local health centers and small hospitals in rural and periurban areas—can go a long way to respond to the needs of households and reduce the burden of disease in Africa. Experience suggests that a package of such services can be provided in a typical low-income African country for as little as $13 per capita per year. This compares with average per capita expenditures on health from all sources in Sub-Saharan Africa of $14, ranging from $10 or less per capita in countries like Nigeria and Zaire to more than $100 per capita in Botswana and Gabon. The key to improving the use of resources is to reallocate funds to the most cost-effective services.

Fourth, *Better Health in Africa* envisions that with about $1.6 billion per year in additional funds, those living in Africa's low-income areas can obtain basic health services. Cost-sharing can make an important contribution to health equity and the sustainability of health services. It can also stimulate the provision of quality services in rural and urban areas. User fees and health insurance are now a reality in many countries and merit increasing roles. Evidence in this report shows that African households are willing and able to pay for quality services.

Larger commitments of domestic resources from government, nongovernment partners, and households can also lead to more financial support from donors. According to a scenario presented in this report, Africa's low-income countries would increase their total annual spending on health by $1 billion—a goal within reach through gradual increases in government financing and rising participation by households. For their part, donors might be expected to con-

tribute somewhat over $600 million, representing a 50 percent increase in exter-
nal assistance for health in Africa today. Donor support would be directed
chiefly to low-income countries that are implementing the actions necessary for
better health.

The transition to better health will obviously vary from country to country
and no one formula would apply to all. At the same time, however, no country
should delay committing itself to the task. The first step on the agenda is to
establish an action plan and yardsticks to measure progress. Indicative actions
and yardsticks are provided in this report.

At the international level, a consultative group of Africans and donors
could be formed to review progress and ensure coordinated support for international training programs, operational research, and other aspects of follow-up.
A consultative group could further serve as a forum to exchange experiences
among African health leaders, and to strengthen mutual support in addressing
difficult issues. A ministerial meeting could help to launch the consultative
group, determine an initial action agenda, and establish monitoring and evaluation benchmarks. Such a meeting could bring African ministers of health and
senior personnel from ministries of finance and planning together with senior
staff from donors and other international agencies.

Initiatives in these areas have already commenced with the participation of
African health experts in the review of this study and discussions with health
officials from countries like Cameroon, Central African Republic, Congo, Côte
d'Ivoire, Gabon, Guinea, Kenya, Sierra Leone, Tanzania, Uganda, and Zambia.
An Independent African Expert Panel on Health Improvement in Africa has
also reviewed the report and made important suggestions for improvement. The
panel, co-sponsored by the African Development Bank, the Swedish International Development Agency, The United Nations Children's Fund (UNICEF),
the World Health Organization (WHO), and the World Bank, is chaired by Pro-
fessor O. Ransome-Kuti, former Nigerian Minister of Health and former Chairman of the WHO Executive Board. Some major health commitments have already been made at the 1990 World Summit for Children and in the Consensus
of Dakar, where African governments and international donors agreed in November 1992 on a core of mid-decade health goals and reiterated support for the
year 2000 goals.

Better Health in Africa was written by World Bank staff, in close cooperation with many other individuals and institutions. It complements *World Development Report 1993: Investing in Health* by emphasizing operationally oriented strategies. In so doing, it draws on important initiatives by the World
Health Organization, such as its Three-Phase Scenario for Health Development
and its support for district health systems, and the National Plans of Action to
implement goals of UNICEF's 1990 World Summit for Children. Staff from the

WHO Regional Office for Africa, from WHO Headquarters, and from UNICEF Headquarters and its Regional Offices for Africa assisted in the conception, preparation, and review of the study. The analyses and messages also reflect the views of these three organizations, which will work together in helping African countries adapt the report's recommendations to local circumstances and carry them out.

G. L. Monekosso, M.D.	E. V. K. Jaycox	James P. Grant
Regional Director for Africa	Vice President	Executive Director
World Health Organization	Africa Region	United Nations
	The World Bank	Children's Fund

Acknowledgments

Better Health in Africa was written by R. Paul Shaw and A. Edward Elmendorf. The study team was managed by A. Edward Elmendorf and Jean-Louis Lamboray, under the general direction of Ishrat Z. Husain. Pierre Landell-Mills and Kevin M. Cleaver provided management support. Jean-Louis Lamboray and Reiko Niimi contributed to the conceptual design of the study, the preparation of initial drafts of Chapters 3, 4, and 8, and coordinated a review of inputs of external partners. Zia Yusuf contributed to the design of the costing and financing framework used in Chapter 9. My Vu and Ali Sy prepared the statistical appendix, and James Shafer had principal responsibility for processing the text.

Consultations and workshops with many African health leaders, including policymakers, analysts and health care providers, contributed to the final product. The Regional Director of WHO for Africa provided invaluable advice and moral support in the task. His African Advisory Committee on Health Development, the WHO/African Regional Office "Health for All" team, WHO Headquarters International Cooperation Division (ICO) personnel, and UNICEF staff members at Headquarters and in the field made substantial contributions at the design, writing, and review stages.

Donors to health improvement in Africa, and nongovernment organizations aiding health in Africa, were consulted on the study. Preparation of the study was also aided by a series of background papers, as well as the contributions and comments of many other people inside and outside the World Bank.

WHO/ICO contributed to the financing of the study. FINNIDA financed the workshops held in Africa, and the Swedish International Development Agency financed the African expert review panel. The governments of Belgium, Finland, Japan, and the Netherlands contributed consultant support. Support was also received from the Center for Health and Development at The George Washington University and the International Organization Fellows Program of the United Nations Association/National Capital Area.

Acronyms

AACHD	African Advisory Committee on Health Development (WHO)
AIDS	Acquired immune deficiency syndrome
AMA	Accra Metropolitan Area
APAC	African Population Advisory Committee
ARI	Acute respiratory infection
BCG	Bacillus of Calmette and Guérin vaccine (to prevent tuberculosis)
CHW	Community health worker
CIESPAC	Centre Inter-Etats d'Enseignement Superieur en Santé Publique d'Afrique Centrale
DALY	Disability-adjusted life year
DANIDA	Danish International Development Agency
DHT	District health team
DPT	Diphtheria, pertussis, tetanus vaccine
EPI	Expanded Programme of Immunization
FAO	Food and Agriculture Organization of the United Nations
FINNIDA	Finnish International Development Agency
GDP	Gross domestic product
GNP	Gross national product
HIV	Human immunodeficiency virus
IEC	Information, education, and communication
IHPP	International Health Policy Program
IMF	International Monetary Fund
IPRES	Institut de Prevoyance et Retraites du Senegal
MIS	Management information system
MR	Most recent year for which data are available
MRI	Magnetic resonance imaging

MSH	Management Sciences for Health
MSP	Ministère de la Santé Publique (Benin)
MSPAS	Ministère de la Santé Publique et des Affairs Sociales (Guinea)
NCHS	National Center for Health Statistics
NGO	Non government organization
NHIF	National Hospital Insurance Fund
NPA	National plan of action
ODA	Overseas Development Administration
OECD	Organization for Economic Cooperation and Development
ORS	Oral rehydration salts
ORT	Oral rehydration therapy
PHC	Primary health care
PHN	Population, Health, and Nutrition
PMIS	Personnel management information system
PRHETIH	Primary Health Training for Indigenous Healers
SANRU	Santé rurale (Zaire)
SAP	Structural adjustment program
SIDA	Swedish International Development Agency
STD	Sexually transmitted disease
UNDP	United Nations Development Programme
UNICEF	United Nations Children's Fund
USAID	United States Agency for International Development
VHW	Village health worker
VIP	Ventilated improved pit (latrine)
WHO	World Health Organization
WHO/AFRO	World Health Organization African Region Office
WHO/ICO	World Health Organization International Cooperation Division (Headquarters)

CHAPTER ONE

Introduction and Overview

GOOD HEALTH is basic to human welfare and a fundamental objective of social and economic development. Yet most of Africa's forty-five countries lag far behind other developing countries in the vital task of improving health.[1] Infant mortality is 55 percent higher and average life expectancy is eleven years less in Sub-Saharan Africa than in the rest of the world's low-income developing countries. Maternal mortality, at 700 women per 100,000 live births, is almost double that of other low- and middle-income developing countries and more than forty times greater than in the industrial nations. Tens of millions of Africans suffer from malaria each year, an estimated 170 million are afflicted by tuberculosis, and the AIDS epidemic seriously threatens several of the continent's countries.

It is no surprise therefore that ill health has a powerful effect on the region's economic progress. Productivity in some countries could increase by up to 15 percent were illness and disability attacked more strenuously. A substantial reduction in maternal illness and deaths would greatly increase women's contribution to economic development. Better control of disease would allow expansion of agriculture into lands previously uninhabitable. Investments in education would yield a greater return because of longer life expectancy. Greater control over reproductive health outcomes, through reduced infant mortality, for example, would pave the way for the demographic transition that

---

[1] The terms Africa and Sub-Saharan Africa are used synonymously in this book. Because health and socioeconomic conditions in South Africa differ so greatly from those in the rest of Sub-Saharan Africa, that country is not discussed explicitly in this study, and data presented as (Sub-Saharan) Africa-wide averages do not include South Africa.

is essential to economic progress. And pressures on households to borrow and use up savings during times of illness would be greatly reduced.

The challenge facing African societies today is to empower households and communities with the knowledge and practical support needed to reduce suffering, illness, and mortality more effectively than in the past. The health of household members is affected (among other things) by the nutritional value of the food they eat, the safety of their drinking water, their habitual self-care practices, their purchase and use of pharmaceuticals, and their visits to traditional healers and providers of modern health care. These behaviors are profoundly influenced by the "enabling environment" for health (Box 1-1).

Some African countries are already taking important steps toward creating an "enabling environment" for health, and these successes play a prominent part in the lessons learned and recommendations of this report. But in many other countries, progress has been hampered by weak political commitment to health reform and mismanagement of national health systems. In some cases, these problems have been compounded by political instability, macroeconomic shocks, civil war, and natural disasters. Nonetheless, this study proposes that the health of Africa can be dramatically improved despite serious socioeconomic and financial constraints.

The rest of this chapter provides a brief overview of obstacles to better health in Africa, a cost-effective approach to combating effects of illness and disease, options for financing an action agenda, and the role of government in encouraging change.

Obstacles to Better Health

The obstacles to better health in Africa are not limited to such shattering but nonetheless transient events as civil conflict, drought, and falling commodity prices. If these factors alone mattered, Africa would have made more progress in improving the health of its people. Rather, an enabling environment for good health has been impeded by more deep-seated problems, which are only touched on here and are discussed in greater detail in subsequent chapters.

One obstacle has been the weakness of political commitment to better health. Although African countries over the last two decades have made numerous promises to adopt one of the prime elements of an enabling environment—namely, better primary and preventive health care—they have seldom made the institutional and financial changes necessary to bring it about. In most countries governments still devote most of their attention and funding for health to high-priced curative care and relatively cost-ineffective services provided through hospitals. Such services not only consume a large share of ministry of health resources but tend to benefit a small share of the population.

BOX 1-1. THE ENABLING ENVIRONMENT FOR HEALTH

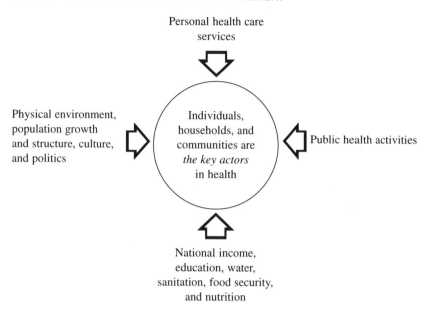

Personal health care
services

Physical environment,
population growth
and structure, culture,
and politics

Individuals,
households, and
communities are
the key actors
in health

Public health activities

National income,
education, water,
sanitation, food security,
and nutrition

Better health in Sub-Saharan Africa hinges on the ability of households and communities to obtain quality health services at less cost and to use them more effectively. This requires:

■ A strong political commitment to improving health, as reflected in preferential government spending

■ An intersectoral perspective in planning and operating systems of health care, including provisions for safe drinking water, sanitation, and health education

■ An appropriate organizational framework and managerial process

■ An equitable distribution of health resources

■ Community involvement at all levels.

Another sign of insufficient political commitment has been a general disinclination to appropriate a larger share of government funds to health purposes. Poor economic conditions clearly play some role, but they do not totally explain the often-observed tendency to give health services short shrift in funding. As a result, publicly owned and operated infrastructure and equipment are visibly aging in many countries. Stock-outs of drugs are frequent, especially at publicly run urban health centers and village health posts. Inefficiency and waste in the procurement, storage, prescribing, and use of drugs are so extensive that consumers in some countries get the benefits of only $12 worth of drugs for each $100 spent on drugs by the public sector.

To some extent, donor funding has compensated for low funding of health in national budgets. And, in some countries donor-funded projects have been the driving force in health planning, even when these projects have not truly addressed the country's dominant health problems. An unwelcome side effect, however, has been the fragmentation of systems of health care and lack of government leadership.

Another deep-seated obstacle is the hierarchical and centralized structure of ministry of health programs and policies. Several African countries have made notable progress in recent years toward devolving responsibilities for program development and implementation, but an entrenched opposition to the decentralization of authority often prevails. A chief argument of this report is that better health in Africa depends on an overall decentralization that encourages African households and communities to become more responsible for their own health and more capable of achieving it.

The consequences of all these obstacles are frequently compounded by other encumbrances that are no less significant—for example, rapid population growth, gender inequalities, and pervasive poverty. In combination with poor economic performance, rapid population growth has contributed to negligible rates of growth in gross national product per capita in more than half of the African countries over the past two decades. As better health in Africa cannot be divorced from the implications of rapid population growth, the benefits of spacing and limiting of births for the healthy mother and child are stressed throughout this report.

Underpinnings of a Cost-Effective Approach to Health

Africa's households and communities could become much healthier through three mutually reinforcing improvements that would enhance the effectiveness of each dollar spent on health. The first requires broad use of cost-effective "packages" of services designed to deal with the most common health problems (Chapter 4). The second involves decentralization of health care delivery, especially through expansion of district-based health care networks composed of health centers and first-referral hospitals (Chapter 8). The third requires improved management of the essential inputs to health care—pharmaceuticals (Chapter 5), health sector personnel (Chapter 6), and health sector infrastructure and equipment (Chapter 7).

The purpose of the cost-effective package is to provide better health at the lowest cost. Emphasis in the package is on *basic personal health care* (Box 1-1). This includes prenatal and delivery care, management of high-risk pregnancies, postpartum care, well-baby services, family planning, outpatient care for such common afflictions as diarrhea, and ongoing care of certain chronic illnesses.

Each of these inputs is relevant to the demographic and epidemiological profile of most African countries. People at greatest risk tend to be members of vulnerable groups, including newborns, infants, toddlers, and women of reproductive age. High-risk groups tend to be afflicted disproportionately by infectious and parasitic diseases.

Basic health care would also cover vaccinations, oral rehydration therapy, administration of drugs to malaria victims, prevention of iron deficiency, and treatment of common urinary and gynecological infections. Essential drugs to be used would be those that are effective against Africa's chief afflictions, including malaria, tuberculosis, diarrhea, respiratory infections, measles, polio, and sexually transmitted diseases.

These basic health care inputs would be supplemented by much greater attention to providing *supporting services* to enhance the value of contacts between health care providers and patients. A broad range of information, communication, and education services would be included, as noted in Box 1-2. Thus a woman who brings her child to a health center for treatment of chronic diarrhea would be expected to leave not only with an oral rehydration salt but also with information on better nutrition and on the advantages of family planning methods. Such supporting services help maximize the value of personal health care.

Basic health care and stronger supporting services, in turn, would be supplemented by much greater attention to *intersectoral interventions.* These would include in particular the construction and operation of safe water and sanitation facilities in the many regions of Africa that now lack them. In this report, intersectoral interventions constitute improvements to the enabling environment for health (Chapter 3).

The effectiveness of basic health care inputs, supporting services, and intersectoral interventions depends largely on the degree to which all of the parts—private as well as public health activities—come together at the community level. What counts most is the geographic proximity of services and system responsiveness to households and the community. That is why Box 1-2 is titled "Maximizing Community Effectiveness."

When offered by well-functioning health centers, the aforementioned package has reduced total hospital admissions in some communities in Africa by up to 50 percent and has cut hospital admissions for such illnesses as measles, tetanus, and diarrhea by up to 80 percent.

BOX 1-2. MAXIMIZING COMMUNITY EFFECTIVENESS

Maximizing community effectiveness	$= A + B + C$
A. Basic package of health care inputs	EPI, ante- and postnatal care, treatment of maternal morbidity, family planning outpatient care, and so on
	+
B. Supporting services	Information, education, and communication to improve screening and diagnostic accuracy, provider compliance, and patient compliance
	+
C. Intersectoral interventions	Safe drinking water and sanitation

---

The Cost of the Package

A major goal of this study has been to determine the indicative cost of such a package in low-income, low-wage African countries. The cost framework presented in Chapter 9 describes the *process* by which decisions were made about the right inputs for a cost-effective approach. The framework is also used to illustrate how costs would change (probably upward) for African countries that enjoy higher levels of income.

This study estimates that a package of basic health care inputs, important supporting services, and intersectoral interventions could be provided for approximately $13 per capita per year in low-income African countries. This has been disaggregated into health care costs ($7.74 per capita), intersectoral interventions ($3.98 per capita), and supporting services ($1.50 per capita). No pretense is made, however, that it is possible to calculate a single, universally applicable cost. One reason is that the cost will be highly conditioned by differences among countries in wage and price levels, technologies in use, per capita incomes, and health aspirations. Another reason is that socioeconomic change modifies the age structure of the population, epidemiological conditions, and societal priorities to the extent that the burden of disease and cost to combat it may change. Thus, a parallel exercise for an African country with a higher income, also presented in Chapter 9, suggests that the approximate cost would be about 20 to 25 percent higher, or about $16 per capita per year.

Establishing the indicative figure of $13 per capita is valuable as a means of prompting reflection on what people in African countries are getting now for what they pay (which varies greatly from country to country), how resources might be reallocated to usher in a more cost-effective approach, and the additional resources needed to ensure that the poorest countries and the poorest groups within each country can pay for the package. For example, per capita expenditures on health from all sources are $14, on average, in Sub-Saharan Africa. They range from $10 or less per capita in countries like Nigeria and Zaire, to more than $100 per capita in countries like Botswana and Gabon. Accordingly, Chapter 9 also discusses how to finance the package in countries that differ in terms of gross national product and per capita expenditures on health. Assuming that, with active household support, the entire public sector—that is, all of the African governments and the donors—was willing to increase its commitments in ways suggested in Chapter 9, an additional $1.6 billion per year could be mobilized for better health in low-income Africa. The donor share, at about $650 million a year, would be about double the amount now provided by external sources.

Resource Mobilization

All countries (including the rich industrial countries) face serious financial constraints in their efforts to mobilize and sustain additional resources for health. Many African countries trail other developing countries in expenditures on health as a share of GNP. Equally if not more important, many African governments have reduced their per capita health sector expenditures. This trend should be reversed.

This study finds, moreover, that large percentages of public funds committed to the health sector are not being used for cost-effective goods and services. Action must therefore be taken to match symbolic pledges to preventive and primary care with actual allocations and use of funds, along with reductions in public funds for expensive and urban-based curative care. Such care, whatever its virtues, is not cost-effective.

User fees and other types of cost recovery are important to ensure the financial sustainability of publicly provided health services. This study reports considerable scope for expanding user fees. Revenue generated may be modest at first, but it can be expected to increase when quality of services are improved, and households perceive the benefits of paying. Research reveals that even low-income African households are prepared to pay what is necessary to obtain basic curative services, especially if the quality of the services is good. The retention of fees at the point of collection, moreover, is an incentive to hospital and health center managers to strengthen revenue collection and service quality. Moreover, and purely on equity grounds, patients from African households with higher incomes (some of which have health insurance) should be required to pay for the health care they receive. In particular, charging better-off patients at publicly financed or operated hospitals (as discussed in Chapter 10) affords ministries of health the opportunity of freeing up scarce resources for reallocation to primary and preventive care.

Furthermore, governments can create conditions that will lead to the expansion of both public and private insurance programs, generating increased revenues for the health sector in general and stimulating expansion in the number of nongovernment providers of health care. This study found that the prospects for expanding health insurance are promising, especially at the community level. One possible approach is for governments to mandate compulsory insurance for salaried workers and to encourage expansion of private insurance programs.

Another possibility is for governments to promote greater collaboration between the public and nongovernment sectors as a means of increasing efficiency and fostering the expansion of private providers and especially of private voluntary organizations. Subsidizing health services provided by religious missions, for example, has worked effectively to provide such services to indigents and serve areas where public and private-for-profit health facilities are scarce. Fostering community control and ownership of health facilities and financing mechanisms—such as prepaid community-based insurance—has also worked to mobilize revenues in rural areas.

Finally, African governments can reap far greater sustainable benefits through better use of available external funding. This study argues that donor initiatives and lending, while no doubt valuable, have produced few permanent successes thus far and have sometimes caused counterproductive imbalances in the operation of health systems without significantly enlarging national capacities.

The Role of Government

Government's first priority should be to use its comparative advantage to finance cost-effective public health activities and other public goods and services. The figure in Box 1-3 provides a visual depiction of ideal expenditure priorities in the public sector and serves as a framework for this report. Broadly speaking, this means financing public goods known to have an immense impact on the enabling environment for health, such as safe drinking water, sanitation, and health education. Such expenditures are less likely to be mobilized by the private sector. Rather, they are usually financed and sometimes undertaken by governments because collective action is required to make investments beyond the capacity of individuals alone. These expenditures are called public goods because they tend to benefit the community as a whole, and no individual can be excluded from their benefits.

Government also enjoys a comparative advantage in such tasks as health system planning, health education, regulating the health professions, collecting epidemiological data, and preventing communicable diseases. If national demographic and health surveys had not been carried out in several African countries, for example, it would not be known that 70 to 75 percent of deaths in the youngest age groups are caused by problems at or soon after birth, and by preventable infectious and parasitic diseases. Such information is crucial in setting health targets.

Globally, government's primary role should be leadership—identifying and promoting cost-effective approaches to health and facilitating the activities of public and nongovernment providers. This is not to say that governments should be the main providers of health care. Rather, priorities for action by African governments include the following:

- Establishing appropriate programs of public health services, and financing them before supporting other health services
- Determining which package of health services, if adequately used, would be the most cost-effective
- Reducing direct government engagement in provision of health care where nongovernment providers show potential for an increasing role, and reallocating public financial support for health care from relatively cost-ineffective curative care interventions to the basic package
- Subsidizing the package of services for the poor and, in the absence of nongovernment willingness to provide services on acceptable terms, directly providing these services to the poor
- Subsidizing those components of the package that result in the largest number of direct and indirect benefits for the largest number of people (e.g. immunizations)
- Providing information to the public that will stimulate demand for the basic package, empower citizens to choose wisely among providers, and assist households to make sound use of the package.

A Call to Action

Who stands to benefit and who will be motivated to take action in keeping with the major themes of this report? Obviously, African households and communities will benefit in their quest to alleviate pain, suffering, and disease, through greater access to, and use of, quality health care. Public health officials are likely to be supportive because the cost-effective approaches emphasized here provide a framework for organizing their work more efficiently, equitably, and

BOX 1-3.   PRIORITIES FOR PUBLIC AND PRIVATE EXPENDITURE ON HEALTH

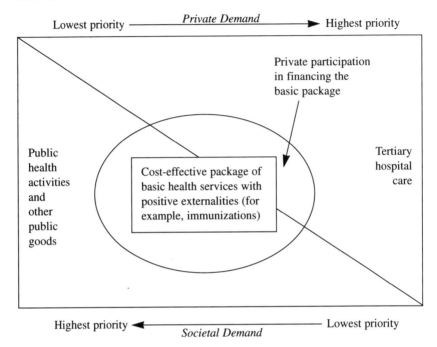

The war on disease in Sub-Saharan Africa cannot be won by individually oriented health care services alone. It must involve interventions to control the transmission of disease and disease vectors in the physical environment where they thrive. These interventions, such as health education and information and the eradication of malaria from swamp areas, are usually supported and some-

sustainably. Policy analysts associated with professional health associations, universities, and think tanks can benefit in their endeavors to devise strategies for better health in Africa. Core agencies, such as ministries of planning and finance stand to benefit given their interest in restructuring health care systems, as well as increasing efficiency and equity, in ways that countries can afford without compromising progress to better health. And the donor community can be counted on to play a supporting role given the promise that domestic health expenditures will be used far more cost-effectively than in the past.

Hard decisions on health are needed now, to convert the vision set forth in this study and other declarations for better health into realistic plans of action,

Box 1-3, continued

times undertaken by governments because collective action is required to make investments beyond the capacity of individuals alone. They are called *public goods* because they tend to benefit the community as a whole and no individual can be excluded from their benefits. It is equally important to finance and, where necessary, provide other *public health services,* such as epidemiological data collection and analysis, health system planning, provision of health information to health care providers and consumers, health education, regulation, licensing, and prevention of communicable disease. As depicted in the figure, expenditures on public health activities and other public goods should be a high priority of governments, reflecting a high level of societal demand. Indeed, without commitment to public health improvements and an enabling environment for better health, high levels of per capita income cannot ensure good health.

Governments also have a critical role to play in supporting activities that sometimes benefit individuals directly (thus qualifying them more as private goods) but also construe large benefits to society at large. These include family planning, maternal and child health, infant nutrition, immunization and treatment of communicable diseases. In the endeavor to assist the poorest households, government support for cost-effective packages of basic health care will almost certainly include such services. In the figure, this is conveyed by the large circle, suggesting that governments have a strong interest in identifying and partially financing cost-effective packages of health care.

Finally, the lowest public priority, and, conversely, the highest private priority, is to allocate funds to tertiary care services, and hospital "hotel" services. An implication is that charging fees and full cost recovery are most feasible at central hospitals because such tertiary-level services benefit individuals and people are most willing to pay for them.

and to move from planning to implementation. Governments have a responsibility, as well as the mandate, to take action to reduce unnecessary suffering, increase human resource potential, and contribute to a major foundation of sustainable development. Chapter 11 of this report offers an agenda of the actions needed for better health and a timetable for the probable sequence of actions.

CHAPTER TWO

Health and Development

AFRICA is host to a number of major disease vectors. Their transmission is aided by a warm, tropical climate and variable rainy seasons. The mean number of infective malaria bites per person can be ten times higher in the forest or savannah areas than in the Sahel or more mountainous areas. In agricultural communities, exposure to infection, especially diarrhea, malaria, and guinea worm, tends to be greatest during the wet season, when food is in shortest supply and high prices prevail. This chapter describes the main epidemiological and demographic conditions affecting health in Africa, and the economic losses caused by these conditions.

Health Status

Africa's struggle to overcome illness and disease over the past quarter century has had mixed results. On the positive side, the infant mortality rate has been cut by more than one-third, and average life expectancy has increased by more than ten years. At the beginning of the period, only one in seven Africans was supplied with safe drinking water, whereas twenty-five years later about 40 percent of the African population was obtaining drinking water from a safe source. By the end of the 1980s, around half of all Africans were able to travel to a health care facility within one hour (UNICEF 1992b).

On the negative side, however, life expectancy in Africa in 1991 was only fifty-one years, compared with sixty-two years for all low-income developing countries and seventy-seven years for the industrial countries. Africa's infant mortality rate is almost 50 percent higher than the average for all low-income countries and at least ten times higher than the rate in the industrial countries. Maternal mortality in Africa is twice as high as in all low-income developing countries and six times higher than in the middle-income developing countries (Table 2-1).

Mortality differentials among African countries are no less striking. The mortality of children under five ranges from more than 200 deaths per 1,000 live births in Mali, Angola, and Mozambique to fewer than 100 in Botswana and Zimbabwe (Figure 2-1). Maternal deaths per 100,000 live births have been estimated to range from 83 in Zimbabwe to more than 2,000 in Mali. Adult mortality—the risk of dying between ages fifteen and sixty—has been estimated to range from 18 percent in Northern Sudan to as high as 58 percent in Sierra Leone (Feachem and others 1992). In many countries, more than 30 percent of females and 40 percent of males of working age will die before age sixty.

Mortality also varies widely within countries, revealing inequalities in health status between urban and rural residents as well as between socio-economic groups. In Zimbabwe, for example, childhood mortality in urban areas is 45 percent less than the rate in rural areas and is up to 20 percent less among urban dwellers in Sudan, Togo, and Uganda. The children of married women with a secondary education are 25 to 50 percent less likely to die before age five than are the children of women with no education. Differentials between residential areas with higher and lower incomes have given rise to the so-called "ten to twenty" rule of thumb, meaning that in most settings the life expectancy of the richest 10 to 20 percent of the population is somewhere on the order of ten to twenty years higher than that of the poorest 10 to 20 percent (Gwatkin 1991).

Ethnicity also ranks as a powerful correlate of infant and child mortality differentials, even after education and occupation are taken into account (Akoto and Tabutin 1989). In Cameroon, for example, the mortality of children less than two years of age between 1968 and 1978 ranged from 116 per 1,000 live births in one ethnic group to 251 in another. In Kenya, child death rates ranged from 74 for one ethnic group to 194 for another, while in Ghana they ranged

Table 2-1. Key Health Indicators, Sub-Saharan Africa and Other Countries, 1991

	Country group			
Indicator	High-income	Middle-income	Low-income	Sub-Saharan Africa
Life expectancy at birth (years)	77	68	62	51
Infant mortality (per 1,000 live births)	8	38	71	104
Maternal mortality (per 100,000 live births)	—	107	308	686

— Not available.
Source: World Bank 1993e.

Figure 2-1. Geographic Variations in Under-five Mortality Rate, Sub-Saharan Africa, 1991

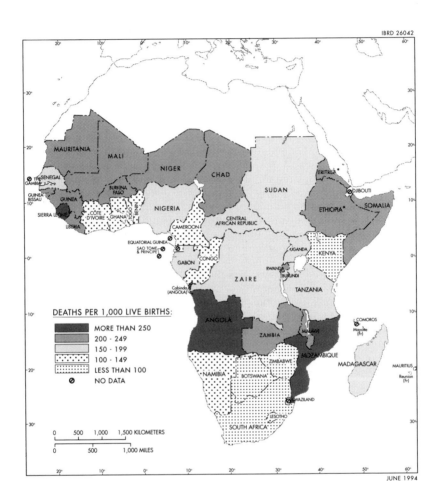

* Data prior to the creation of the independent country of Eritrea.
Note: Under-five mortality is the probability of dying between birth and age 5, expressed per 1,000 live births. The term "child mortality" is also used.
Source: UNICEF 1993.

from 74 to 158, and in Senegal from 261 to 452 (Akoto and Tabutin 1989). These ethnic differentials may be attributable in part to different attitudes concerning illness and nutritional practices, access to and use of modern health services, and dependence on modern versus traditional healers. But they are also due to schisms among ethnic groups that produce unequal access to social and economic opportunities.

Causes of Death and Illness

Although the major causes of death and illness vary by age group, certain health problems affect Africans at every age (Table 2-2). Perinatal, infectious, and parasitic illnesses are responsible for 75 percent of infant deaths. Infectious diseases and parasitic afflictions are also responsible for 71 percent of the deaths of children age one to four and 62 percent of the deaths of children ages five to fourteen. Child health in Africa is threatened particularly by diarrhea, acute respiratory infections, malaria, and measles (Table 2-3).

The incidence of disease among children can be profiled as follows (Feachem, Kjellstrom, and Murray 1992):

■ The typical African child under five has five episodes of diarrhea per year, a 10 percent risk of suffering from diarrhea on any given day, and a 14 percent risk of dying from a severe episode. Diarrhea accounts for 25 percent of all illness in childhood and 15 percent of admissions to health facilities. The World Health Organization (WHO) estimates that 37 percent of all cases of diarrhea in the world occur in Sub-Saharan Africa, where only 50 percent of children benefit from oral rehydration therapy, compared with 70 percent in Asia and North Africa (WHO 1990).

■ The typical child appears to have approximately ten acute respiratory infections (ARI) per year and a 25 percent chance of suffering from ARI on any particular day. It is estimated that such infections are responsible for 25 to 66 percent of childhood illness, and for about 17 to 41 percent of visits and admissions of children to a health facility.

■ Vaccine-preventable diseases are implicated in the deaths of 20 percent of all children.

In 1985, before AIDS began to affect adult mortality, about half of all deaths of adults age fourteen to forty-four were also due to infectious and parasitic diseases. Now, according to WHO, one in every forty Sub-Saharan African adults is infected with the human immunodeficiency virus (HIV), which causes AIDS. In many hard-hit African countries, AIDS is the major cause of adult deaths in this age group (see below). Among older adults (those over forty-

Table 2-2. Distribution of Causes of Death within Age Groups in Africa, 1985

Cause of death	Proportion of total deaths within age category (percent)						Total deaths (thousands)	Deaths (percentage of total)
	<1	1–4	5–14	14–44	45–64	65+		
Perinatal	30.0	0.0	0.0	0.0	0.0	0.0	627	9.3
Infection and parasitic	45.0	71.0	62.0	53.0	28.0	19.0	3,403	47.2
Cancer	0.1	0.3	1.0	3.0	14.0	9.0	42	3.4
Circulatory system	1.0	2.0	6.0	12.0	34.0	41.0	909	12.6
Maternal	0.0	0.0	0.0	4.0	0.2	0.0	48	0.7
Injury and poisoning	1.0	3.0	6.0	12.0	5.0	2.0	294	4.1
Other	23.0	24.0	24.0	16.0	18.0	28.0	1,635	22.7
Total	100.0	100.0	100.0	100.0	100.0	100.0	7,203	100.0

Source: Bulatao and Stephens 1992.

Table 2-3.   Child Morbidity by Selected Socioeconomic Characteristics, Selected African Countries

(percentage of children ill)

Disease and country	Sex		Residence		Education		
	Male	Female	Urban	Rural	None	Primary	Secondary or higher
Diarrhea[a]							
Ghana	40.8	41.9	44.0	40.3	39.6	43.7	29.3
Senegal	55.2	52.0	48.2	56.7	55.4	51.9	31.9
Zimbabwe	39.5	33.5	29.0	38.9	37.2	34.7	39.4
Fever[b]							
Ghana	37.4	35.4	33.1	37.6	34.5	38.5	31.6
Senegal[c]	61.9	60.1	46.6	68.9	64.8	48.1	33.3
Zimbabwe	7.1	7.0	5.7	7.5	8.0	6.8	6.9
Respiratory problems[c]							
Ghana[d]	20.8	20.4	18.6	21.4	18.9	21.9	21.5
Senegal	—	—	—	—	—	—	—
Zimbabwe[e]	51.5	47.6	47.0	50.4	48.6	49.8	49.6

— Not available.

a. Children less than two years old with diarrhea in the two weeks preceding the survey.

b. Children less than five years old with fever in the four weeks preceding the survey.

c. Data refer to malaria during the last cold season, zero to six months preceding the survey.

d. Severe cough or difficult breathing.

e. Rapid or difficult breathing.

Source: Boerma, Sommerfelt, and Rutstein 1991.

five), circulatory system diseases are the most important causes of mortality. Surprisingly, injuries appear to be an unimportant cause of death, although the accuracy of the data is doubtful. A large proportion of deaths in all age groups (23 percent) is lumped under "other causes" in Table 2-2, reflecting the weakness of the data.

Maternal mortality rates in Africa are higher than anywhere else in the world due to a number of afflictions, including hemorrhage, infections, obstructed labor, anaemia, hypertensive disorders of pregnancy, unsafe abortions, and violence (Box 2-1). These problems are exacerbated by substandard prenatal care, patient tardiness in seeking treatment when infection occurs, and a higher risk of sexually transmitted diseases due to multiple sexual partners. In Angola the national rate of maternal mortality was 570 per 100,000 live births; in areas like Kuando Hubango and Huamb in the early 1990s, the rate exceeded 1,600 per 100,000 live births. Although comprehensive data on abortion in Africa are lacking, a recent study estimated that there were approximately 75,000 abortions in Kenya in 1990. Extrapolation to Sub-Saharan Africa suggests that there are up to 1.5 million abortions each year in the region as a whole (Rogo 1991). Studies on Ethiopia and Nigeria have indicated that almost 50 percent of maternal deaths result from complications due to flawed abortions (Rogo 1991).

African countries have some of the highest adolescent pregnancy rates in the world. By age eighteen, more than 40 percent of girls give birth in Côte d'Ivoire, Nigeria, and Mauritania. (Population Reference Bureau 1992). Large shares of pregnancies among unmarried women age fifteen to nineteen are un-intended: 87 percent in Botswana, 77 percent in Kenya, 74 percent in Togo, and 63 percent in Uganda (Senderowitz 1993). A survey of fifteen- to twenty-four-year-old females in Uganda revealed that 7 percent had had an abortion (Ageyi and Epema 1992). Early entry into reproductive life increases the risk of such health problems as anaemia, malnutrition, and sexually transmitted diseases (Wasserheit 1989).

Persistent and New Health Threats

Malaria is Africa's largest and most persistent disease problem (Table 2-4). Pregnant women, fetuses, and young children are particularly susceptible to malarial infection. WHO estimates the global number of malaria cases per year at 110 million, with nearly 80 percent of them occurring in Sub-Saharan Africa and only 1,000 cases in North Africa. A review of more than 400 studies on the subject suggests that malaria accounts for 20 to 50 percent of all admissions to African health services per year, although only an estimated 8 to 25 per-

---

BOX 2-1. VIOLENCE AGAINST WOMEN AS A GLOBAL HEALTH ISSUE

Violence against women is a significant cause of female morbidity and mortality in Africa and elsewhere. Such violence includes sexual abuse of children, physical and sexual assaults, and certain culture-bound practices, such as female genital mutilation. A study in Kenya found that 42 percent of women were "beaten regularly" (Raikes 1990). Women are often beaten or otherwise abused if they do not comply with men's sexual and childbearing demands. Where spousal consent is required before contraceptives can be obtained, women can be at increased risk of violence. In Kenya, women have been known to forge their partner's signature rather than risk violence or abandonment. When family planning clinics in Ethiopia removed their requirement for spousal consent, clinic use rose 26 percent in just a few months (Cook and Maine 1987).

cent of persons with malaria visit health services (Brinkman and Brinkman 1991).

Malaria now appears to be worsening in much of Africa as malaria parasites become more resistant to chloroquine and other malarial drugs. Annual growth rates of the disease by country include 7 percent for Zambia, 10 percent for Togo, and 21 percent for Rwanda. The data for Burkina Faso show a downward trend of 15 percent during the period from 1973 to 1981 but an 11 percent increase each year since then. Hospital data from Zambia indicate that mortality from malaria is rising 5 percent a year among children and almost 10 percent among adults (Brinkman and Brinkman 1991).

The incidence of tuberculosis is also rising in Africa, due in part to the interaction between TB and AIDS and in part to a breakdown in surveillance and management of cases. By some estimates there are approximately 171 million TB carriers in Africa, and 10 percent of all deaths from tuberculosis occur in children under age five (WHO 1991b).

AIDS is the most dramatic new threat to health in Africa. More than 8 million African adults are estimated to be infected with the AIDS virus, HIV, with more than 1.5 million estimated to have full-fledged AIDS, although only 210,000 adult and pediatric AIDS cases have been officially reported to WHO.

Table 2-4.   Rank and Share of Malaria, AIDS, and Other Diseases in the Total Burden of Disease and Injury, Africa, 1990

Female		*Male*	
Occurrence by rank order	*Share (percent)*	*Occurrence by rank order*	*Share (percent)*
1 Malaria	11	1 Injuries	13
2 Respiratory infections	11	2 Respiratory infections	11
3 Diarrheal diseases	10	3 Malaria	11
4 Childhood cluster[a]	9	4 Diarrheal diseases	10
5 HIV/AIDS	6	5 Childhood cluster[a]	10
6 Perinatal	6	6 Perinatal	9
7 Maternal	6	7 HIV/AIDS	6
8 Injuries	6	8 Tuberculosis	5
9 Tuberculosis	4	9 Other STDs	2
10 Other STDs	3	Other causes	23
Other causes	28		
Total	100	Total	100

a. Pertussis, polio, diphtheria, measles, and tetanus.
Source: World Bank 1993e.

There are large geographic variations in the prevalence of HIV (Figure 2-2). Approximately one-half to two-thirds of HIV infections have occurred in East and Central Africa, an area that has only one-sixth of the total population of Sub-Saharan Africa. Infection rates in men and women are close to equal. Young girls and commercial sex workers are particularly vulnerable. Moreover, and in contrast to malaria and many other causes of excess adult mortality in Africa, AIDS does not spare the elite.

High levels of other sexually transmitted diseases, such as chancroid, syphilis, and gonorrhea, and the high rates at which new and unprotected sexual encounters occur in Africa appear to be important factors in HIV transmission. Thus, the prevalence rates of STDs other than AIDS are probably good indicators of the potential spread of HIV in countries where HIV infection rates are still low.

Recent data suggest that the HIV pandemic has continued to spread, particularly in Southern and Western Africa. More than 600,000 people are estimated to be infected in Zimbabwe alone. In the major urban areas of Botswana, HIV prevalence exceeds 18 percent among adults. In Côte d'Ivoire the prevalence of HIV among pregnant women in Abidjan is reported to have risen from 3.0 percent in 1986 to 14.8 percent in 1992. Sentinel surveillance from Nigeria shows that the epidemic has spread throughout the country. In nine of the eleven states in which sentinel surveillance has been instituted among people attending STD clinics, HIV prevalence is reported to range from less than 1 percent to 22 percent.

Combating Demographic Pressures

Rapid population growth exacerbates critical gaps in basic health services, especially when economies are growing slowly or per capita incomes are in decline. This conjunction of factors produced negative average annual growth rates per capita for almost one-half of all African countries between 1965 and 1990. This is one reason why the ratio of people per doctor in Africa increased at only half the rate of other low- and middle-income countries over the past twenty-five years.

Africa is a continent of exceptionally high fertility and very low contraceptive use. In 1992 the total fertility rate (average number of children ever born to women of reproductive ages) was approximately 6.5, compared with about 3.6 for all developing countries. Contraceptive use rates were only 11 percent on average, compared with approximately 51 percent for all developing countries and 71 percent for the industrial countries.

Low rates of contraceptive use deprive couples of the health benefits associated with family planning. Good spacing of births and the integration of fam-

Figure 2-2.   Estimated HIV Infections, Sub-Saharan Africa, 1990

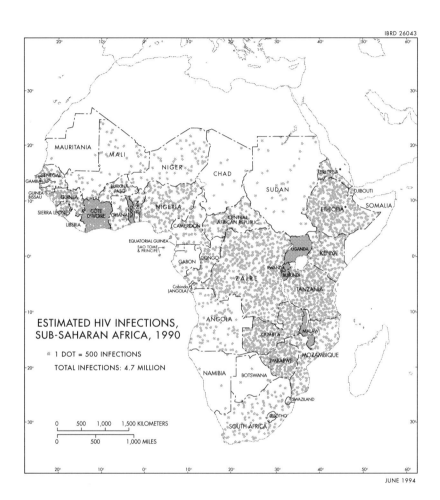

* Data prior to creation of the independent country of Eritrea. Data for Liberia, Somalia, and Madagascar were unavailable.

Source: Reproduced from Chin 1991.

ily planning services with maternal and child health care lead to reduced infant, child, and maternal mortality (Box 2-2).

The AIDS epidemic provides an additional reason for including family planning and STD services as part of a cost-effective set of interventions. Women with sexually transmitted diseases (STDs) are estimated to be ten to fifty times more likely to contract the AIDS virus than those without STDs. According to a recent World Bank/WHO study of women at a prenatal clinic at Malago Hospital in Kampala, Uganda, syphilis and gonorrhea were found in 11 percent, chlamydia in 5 percent, and trichomoniasis vaginalis in 37 percent.

High fertility rates also mean that growth in the numbers of particularly vulnerable demographic groups is likely to outstrip the capacity of private and

---

BOX 2-2.   HEALTH BENEFITS OF FAMILY PLANNING

The most widely confirmed health benefits of family planning derive from more efficient birth spacing. This can be achieved through modern methods of family planning, helping women to improve their health and to increase chances that children will survive. To illustrate, infant mortality rates are 69 percent higher among women in Uganda who have a child less than two years after a previous birth, than among those who wait two to three years. The same survey shows that child deaths before five years of age are 27 percent higher among women who had their first birth before age twenty, than those aged twenty to twenty-nine. Inadequate birth spacing also places women at risk of death themselves.

That women want such services, yet do not have sufficient access to them, is apparent from national demographic and health surveys in nine Sub-Saharan African countries, which reveal unmet need for such services, ranging from 22 to 40 percent of married women. Closing these gaps will clearly enhance the critical role women have to play as agents of change for better health.

Fortunately, awareness regarding the hazards of rapid population growth has risen greatly among African policymakers. Twenty-five African countries have developed, or are in the process of developing, national population policies, and most African government leaders are signatories of seminal declarations by parliamentarians in support of slowing rapid population growth. The Report of the South Commission, written by leaders from Nigeria, Côte d'Ivoire, Mozambique, Zimbabwe, and Senegal, took a particularly strong stand on population (South Commission and Nyerere 1987). Chaired by Julius K. Nyerere of Tanzania, the commission concluded that not only do high rates of population growth reduce the resources available per capita, making it difficult in some countries to maintain subsistence levels, but they also limit the ability to raise productivity.

public health care providers. Between 1990 and 1995, approximately 75 million newborns will have joined Africa's population, or 14 million each year. Assuming "business as usual," World Bank projections indicate that the population of Africa will grow from 502 million in 1992 to 634 million by the end of the decade and to more than 1.2 billion by 2025. More optimistic projections, involving a rapid fertility decline scenario, suggest substantially reduced numbers (Figure 2-3).

Some countries have shown considerable awareness of the problems posed by high fertility rates. As of 1993, the governments of seventeen Sub-Saharan Africa countries had adopted official population policies, nine having done so since 1990 (African Population Advisory Committee 1993b).

Figure 2-3.   The Specter of 1.2 Billion People by 2025

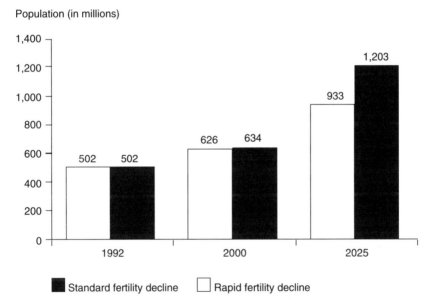

Population (in millions)

Note: Rapid fertility decline: under the right circumstances, Africa's population could grow far more slowly, with approximately 88 million fewer births by the end of this century and 270 million fewer by 2025. This would imply a decline in Africa's population growth rate from its current level of 3.0 percent per year to 1.3 percent per year by 2025. To accomplish this rapid fertility decline, family planning would have to become an integral part of health care delivery, with contraceptive prevalence rates rising from about 11 percent to about 45 percent by the end of the decade and to 75 percent by 2025 (McNamara 1992). More than half of this increase could be achieved by accommodating the unmet needs of the 20 to 40 percent of sexually active women who want to limit their fertility but who lack access to family planning.
Source: Statistical appendix in this volume.

The importance of raising contraceptive use rates sharply throughout Africa, especially over the next ten years, cannot be overstated. Reduced fertility would hold back population momentum and improve the age distribution of the population. Some countries, such as Botswana, Kenya, Mauritius, and Zimbabwe, are moving aggressively in this area. Such actions would help provide breathing space to governments currently unable to meet gaps in the demand for basic health services.

Impact on Economic Development

The effects of poor health go far beyond physical pain and suffering. Learning is compromised, returns to human capital diminish, and environments for entrepreneurial and productive activities are constrained. And, in view of the demonstrated importance of human capital to economic progress, it comes as little surprise that no country has attained a high level of economic development with a population crippled by high infant and maternal mortality, pervasive illness of its work force, and low life expectancy.

Evidence showing that poor health imposes immense economic costs on individuals, households, and society at large is strong worldwide. A selection of findings makes a compelling case that better health can contribute positively to economic outcomes in Africa.

■ Household surveys in eight developing countries show that the economic effects of adult illness are substantial; three of the four study countries with the highest incidence of adult illness are in Africa—Côte d'Ivoire, Ghana, and Mauritania (King and Yan Wang 1993). In Côte d'Ivoire, 24 percent of the adult labor force experienced an illness or injury during the month prior to the survey, and 15 percent became at least temporarily inactive. These workers lost nine full days of work, on average, and the cost of treating them amounted to about 11 percent of their normal monthly earnings. Given the costs of treatment and the adjustments made elsewhere in society, the total cost of illness equaled almost 15 percent of per capita GDP. Similar losses occurred in Ghana and Mauritania (Table 2-5).

■ Studies of malaria in Rwanda, Burkina Faso, Chad, and Congo suggest that the direct and indirect costs of an average case were equivalent to about twelve days' output. Accordingly, the annual economic burden of malaria in 1987 was estimated at $800 million and was projected to rise to $1.7 billion by 1995. The economic costs of malaria represented about 0.6 percent of GDP in 1987, and were projected to rise to 1 percent by 1995 (Shepard and others 1991). The latter figure exceeds average government expenditures on health in several Sub-Saharan African countries during the mid-1980s.

Table 2.5. Economic Burden of Illness, Three African Countries

	Côte d'Ivoire (1987)	Ghana (1988–89)	Mauritania (1988)
Burden for labor force ages 20–59 years			
Workers experiencing illness/injury (percent)	24.1	44.4	18.4
Workers inactive due to illness/injury (percent)	14.8	26.4	17.2
Average work days lost to ill or injured workers	8.6	4.8	9.4
Share of normal monthly earnings used to treat illness/injury (percent)	10.9	6.7	17.6
Costs of illness or injury averaged across all workers			
Income losses due to illness as a share of total income of all adult labor force members (percent)	6.4	6.4	6.5
Income loss as a share of per capita GDP (percent)[a]	15.3	13.5	16.1

a. Income loss as a percentage of per capita GDP is higher than income loss averaged across all adult labor force members because in the former measure, GDP per capita is reduced by pooling workers and nonworking dependents.
Source: King and Wang 1993.

■ In Nigeria, Guinea worm disease temporarily incapacitated 2.5 million Nigerians in 1987. A cost/benefit study in one area revealed that, apart from shortages of financing for agricultural activities, the disease was the chief impediment to rice production. It was estimated that the net effect of the disease was to reduce rice production by $50 million. It was also estimated that the benefits of a worm control program would exceed its costs after only four years (UNICEF 1987).

■ Diseases such as onchocerciasis and malaria are location-specific and have been shown to discourage settlement on and development of fertile land. By some accounts, trypanosomiasis has made one-third of Africa unsuitable for cattle raising, which in turn has aggravated protein deficiency problems (Kamarck and World Bank 1976; Wells and Klees 1980). Onchocerciasis contributed heavily to the depopulation of river valleys in Nigeria (Bradley 1976) and Ghana (Hunter 1966). Malaria and trypanosomiasis are inhibiting migration and resettlement of new lands in Uganda.

■ AIDS will have immense economic consequences in Africa as the years pass because it is fatal and primarily strikes adults in their most productive years. The deaths of parents from AIDS will lower the incomes and well-being of their households, thus reducing the consumption level of survivors (Over and others 1991). Household savings and productive assets often have to be liquidated to pay for medical care and funerals. The rise in mortality caused by AIDS will have particularly harsh effects on women, who in many African societies are not entitled to inherit the property of their deceased husbands. The children of AIDS victims will often be forced to leave school early and go to work, thus weakening their economic prospects. The elderly will also suffer. Thus, the AIDS epidemic threatens to create large new pockets of poverty.

Figure 2-4.   Potential AIDS Treatment Cost as Share of Total and Government Health Expenditures, Various African Countries, 1987–89

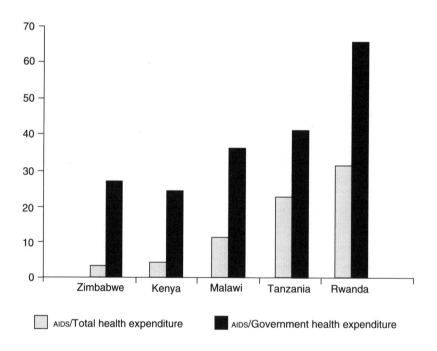

Source: Ainsworth and Over 1992.

AIDS will also have a broad and negative impact on African economies. Figure 2-4 shows the potential cost of treating all persons infected by AIDS in five selected countries in the late 1980s. The cost of treating AIDS cases in Rwanda, for example, was potentially the equivalent of 60 percent of the public health budget.

In severely affected countries, the work force is likely to become younger, less skilled, and less experienced. In Tanzania and Uganda, for example, AIDS has already increased absenteeism and lowered productivity. Most models of the macroeconomic impact of the disease suggest that adult deaths from AIDS will cause per capita economic growth to be lower than it would have been otherwise. (Ainsworth and Over 1992; World Bank 1991a; African Population Advisory Committee 1993c).

■ Using up savings and borrowing often take place during illness to finance medical care and maintain consumption. West African households with family members suffering from onchocerciasis, for example, used assets like bridewealth to finance medical care (Evans 1989). In Côte d'Ivoire, average medical expenditures by households at the time of illness exceeded the loss of full-time employment earnings (at the local minimum wage) during illness (Corbett 1988). Sales of livestock and land are also frequently cited as a coping response to illness (Over and others 1991). One study of coastal Kenya found that ill health was the reason for a fourth of all land transactions (Chambers 1982).

■ Other mechanisms for coping with illness produce other economic effects. A study of 250 Sudanese tenant families (Nur and Mahram 1986) found that healthy family members took time away from their other activities to maintain farm production by performing the work of family members suffering from malaria and schistosomiasis. Other studies of malaria have found that a loss in work days by the affected individuals was partly compensated for by work by other members of agricultural households (Conly 1975; Castro and Mokate 1988). In urban areas, companies with high absenteeism due to employee health problems have lost many of the benefits of mass production (Over and others 1991).

The negative effect of poor health on economic activity is unambiguous. By extension, improved health can be expected to have a positive impact on the economic well-being of families by lowering the costs of treatment for disease and easing demands on family members to care for the ill or for their survivors. Better health also helps employers by minimizing the absence of workers with key skills and experience.

Conclusion

This chapter has provided an overview of the epidemiological, demographic, and socioeconomic conditions affecting health in Africa. It has identified important links between health and development.

High levels of mortality and morbidity cost Africa dearly in the quality of life and the capacity of its human resources. Poor health increases suffering and reduces people's alertness and their ability to cope with and enjoy life. Poor health shackles human capital and undermines socioeconomic environments conducive to entrepreneurial activities.

CHAPTER THREE

Creating an Enabling Environment for Health

$\mathbf{A}$ CURSORY inspection of the world health picture suggests that the single most important factor determining survival is income. Yet a central message of this study is that even within existing levels of per capita income, health in Sub-Saharan Africa can be dramatically improved by strategies that create an enabling environment for health.

That income is not the sole determining factor in health status is apparent from an analysis of cross-country variations in life expectancy that simultaneously assesses the effects of income and other influences. Only one-half of the total gain in life expectancy over the thirty-year period from 1940 to 1970 could be accounted for in terms of changes in per capita income, adult literacy, and calorie intake (Preston 1980, 1983). It is equally important to realize that wealth does not necessarily bring health. Figure 3-1 shows that the mortality rate of males under age five in Zimbabwe is approximately one-half that in Côte d'Ivoire, even though Zimbabwe's per capita income is lower. And in Kenya, with a per capita income one-half that of Côte d'Ivoire, the male child mortality rate is again lower, at 112 per thousand, compared with 144 for Côte d'Ivoire.

Almost a decade ago, the Rockefeller Foundation sponsored a concerted effort to determine why health in China, Costa Rica, Sri Lanka, and the State of Kerala in India had improved so markedly despite very low annual per capita incomes. The conclusion was that poor countries could achieve good health through a political commitment to equity that took the form of policies and programs assuring wide access to food, education, and basic health services. Case studies of the three countries and Kerala showed that their governments had managed to overcome the social and economic barriers that prevented the

Figure 3-1   Per Capita Income and Under-five Male Mortality in Eight Countries, 1990

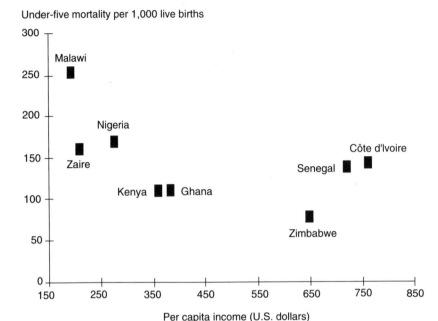

Under-five mortality per 1,000 live births

Per capita income (U.S. dollars)

Source: World Bank data.

disadvantaged from obtaining those essential elements of health. With reference to specific widespread physical ailments, such as diarrhea, the studies found that a multifaceted approach had been put into place that included social and environmental interventions as well as widespread access to a modern and well-managed system of health care (Halstead, Walsh, and Warren 1985).

Figure 3-2 places the commitment to health in perspective as it relates to the simultaneous use of other inputs known to affect health at the household and community level. The kinds of benefits from creating an enabling environment for health can be illustrated with regard to safe water and sanitation, food security and nutrition, education, the special roles and status of women, and culture.

Safe Water and Sanitation

Safe water is an essential pillar of health. Yet large shares of Sub-Saharan African populations are deprived of safe drinking water. Poor sanitation and dis-

Figure 3-2   Services Contributing to Health of Households

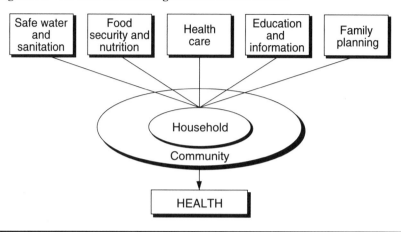

posal of fecal matter complicate matters, particularly in rural areas and periurban slums where seepage and runoff can contaminate ponds, streams, rivers, and wells (Box 3-1).

A review (Esrey and others 1991) of findings from 144 studies revealed that improved water supply and sanitation often reduces child diarrheal mortality by 50 percent, and sometimes as much as 80 percent, depending on the type of intervention and on the presence of risk factors such as poor feeding practices and maternal illiteracy. Improvements in the rural water supply in Africa have resulted in a remarkable reduction in the number of cases of Guinea worm. In Nigeria, for example, 640,000 cases were reported in 1989; this number declined to 282,000 in 1991 as a result of a combination of improved water supply and treatment and education.

It is also evident that improved excreta disposal has a major impact on health, as does improved personal, domestic, and food hygiene. According to one study, improvements in excreta disposal reduced diarrhea morbidity by 22 percent compared with improvements in water quality (16 percent) and water availability (25 percent) or both together (37 percent). Studies in Lesotho recorded a 36 percent reduction in diarrhea related to improved excreta disposal (Daniels and others 1990). The study concluded that interventions to improve excreta disposal would have a greater impact than improvements in water quality, particularly in highly contaminated environments where the prevalence of diarrhea is high.

Fecal-oral transmission of disease becomes a more serious problem as population densities increase. A study (Bradley and others 1992) comparing

BOX 3-1. THE ENVIRONMENTAL DIMENSION OF HEALTH: THE CASE OF ACCRA

The Accra Metropolitan Area (AMA) had an estimated 1990 population of 1.6 million, which is expected to grow to more than 4 million by the year 2020. Accra is characterized by overcrowding, inadequate municipal services, and substandard housing. Almost half of the population have incomes below the World Bank's absolute poverty threshold. In this environment cholera cases are increasing steadily: between July and September 1990, 113 cases were reported; in November, another 354; and, within the first two weeks of December alone, 239.

Almost half of the significant diseases that are reported in Accra (malaria, measles, enteric fever, food poisoning, tuberculosis, diarrhea, leprosy, polio, guinea worm, typhus, and cholera) can be linked to the following problems:

■ Overcrowding in economically depressed neighborhoods—e.g., with average occupancy rates of 4.4 persons per room in the low-income residential area of James Town—facilitates the spread of communicable disease and puts enormous pressure on shared resources such as kitchens, bathrooms, and laundries. Poor drainage forces sullage, or wastewater discharge, to flow through holes in household walls onto the ground outside and gives rise to stagnant pools for mosquitos and moist soils in which hookworm ova readily develop. Malaria is the single most widespread disease, with 92,046 reported cases in the AMA, or more than 40 percent of disease reports at outpatient facilities (Leitmann 1992).

■ Where excreta disposal systems are poorly developed—especially in slums, squatter settlements, and peri-urban areas without convenient access to public facilities—defecation in public space, beaches, and watercourses is common.

infection with helminths in an urban slum in Lagos, Nigeria, with infection in a rural district showed that 95 percent of school children in the urban study area were infected, compared with 52 percent in the rural area. Differences were attributed to the urban area's higher population density, lower level of hygiene, inferior drainage, and absence of excreta disposal facilities.

Food and Nutrition

Malnutrition underlies more than one-third of infant and child mortality in rural and urban districts of many African countries (McGuire and Austin 1986) and 20 to 80 percent of maternal mortality. Protein-energy malnutrition, nutritional anemia, vitamin A deficiency, and iodine deficiency disorders have been iden-

Box 3-1, continued

- In slum areas where water is frequently purchased or the water supply is irregular or both, daily per capita consumption is about 60 liters, or less than half of middle-income neighborhoods. While water quality is generally good at the source, its risk of contamination during transport, and low likelihood of being boiled for sterilization, raise the incidence of water-borne diseases.
- Until recently, illegal garbage dumps have choked the roadside, drains, and open spaces around households and provided breeding grounds for insects and rodents. Incinerating refuse has resulted in air pollution and acute respiratory diseases within the community.
- Poor hygienic food preparation and handling in Accra lead to higher prevalence of communicable diseases, as noted in (a) a 36 percent prevalence of diarrhea among children in households where their hands were not washed prior to eating; (b) swarms of disease-spreading flies around street food vendors and small restaurants (chop bars); and (c) the absence of enforceable legislation on food quality and hygiene.
- Accra's high temperatures and considerable rainfall also favor disease vectors, of which the most problematic are malaria-transmitting mosquitos, houseflies, cockroaches, bed bugs, and lice; rodents are also prevalent. Unfortunately, toxic pesticides can also have negative health consequences.

These environmental health problems arise from a combination of inadequate infrastructure and services, lack of settlements planning, and cultural practices. The result: 70 percent of the economic cost of health problems in Ghana has been attributed to environmentally related diseases—taking account of lost labor and the cost of resources (doctors, nurses, technicians, administration, equipment, and drugs).

---

tified as the most serious problems. Inadequate quality and quantity of food intake (including breastmilk) cause growth failure, decreased immunity, learning disabilities, poor reproductive outcome, and reduced productivity (Box 3-2). Nutritional rehabilitation can be effectively undertaken as part of a district-based basic package of health services. In Tanzania, for example, the Iringa Nutrition Program and child survival and development programs in other regions succeeded in reducing severe malnutrition from a preprogram level of about 6 percent to a postprogram level of 2 percent.

According to FAO estimates, the average per capita dietary energy supply worldwide reached 2,600 calories per day in 1985, but currently only 2,100 calories are available to each person every day in Sub-Saharan Africa (FAO 1991). Though increases in incomes of the poor may lead to increases in calorie

BOX 3-2. NUTRITION DEFICIENCIES
AND STUNTING

Nutritional deficiencies represent an extremely serious health problem in Africa. Stunting, which reflects chronic, long-standing undernutrition, is more widely prevalent than wasting, which reflects acute nutritional crisis. A series of demographic and households surveys in the 1980s revealed more than 20 percent of children from three months to thirty-six months old to be stunted, compared with only 2 percent in a reference population.

Poor feeding practices are at the heart of child nutrition issues, reflecting once again the importance of household behavior for health improvement. WHO recommends that all infants be breastfed exclusively until they are four to six months old, but in Nigeria, for example, only 1 percent of such infants are exclusively breastfed. In contrast, in Uganda, 70 percent of the children age four to six months were exclusively breastfed during this period, despite the fact that older infants and young children are widely undernourished. Similarly, WHO recommends that, by the age of six months, all infants should receive solid foods in addition to breast milk. Yet, only 45 percent of infants from six to nine months old in Mali, and 57 percent in Ghana, receive breastmilk and solid foods.

Source: U.S. Agency for International Development 1993, Figure 2, p. 5.

consumption over and above the general population, improved income alone cannot be expected to raise calorie intake. Nutrition policy can make a difference by: offering nutrition education parallel to income-generating activities to influence purchasing and feeding practices, providing women with functional literacy classes using nutritional themes, and targeting food subsidies.

In addition to stressing household food security, intervention could emphasize the immunological and nutritional benefits of breastmilk in African countries, where the proportion of infants three months of age and under, exclusively breastfed, varies from about 2 percent to 89 percent. A breastfed baby is only one-twentieth as likely to die from diarrheal diseases and one-quarter as likely to die from pneumonia as a baby who is bottle-fed (UNICEF 1992a).

Female Education

The education of females is so important to health improvement that it merits special attention in any reformulation of health policies that aim to improve health outcomes rather than solely improving the delivery of health care services. Women with more education marry and start having children later, make better use of health services, and make better use of information that will improve personal hygiene and the health of their children. Household surveys in Ghana, Nigeria, and Sudan show that the single most important influence on child survival is the level of a mother's education (Figure 3-3). Data for thirteen African countries between 1975 and 1985 show that a 10 percent increase in female literacy rates reduced child mortality by 10 percent, whereas changes in male literacy had little influence (World Bank 1993e). The effect of a mother having attained secondary-level education may contribute to lowering the infant mortality in a given family by as much as 50 percent. Finally, having an educated adult female population can significantly increase the effectiveness of government expenditures on health; without an educated female population, the impact of government expenditures on health appears to fall dramatically (Bhargava and Yu 1992; Stomberg and Stomberg 1992).

Female participation in primary and secondary schools has improved significantly in Africa over the past thirty years, but it has a long way to go to deliver the kinds of health benefits reviewed above. At the primary level, fe-

Figure 3-3.   Under-five Mortality and Level of Female Education, Selected African Countries, 1985–90

Under-five mortality rate per 1,000 live births

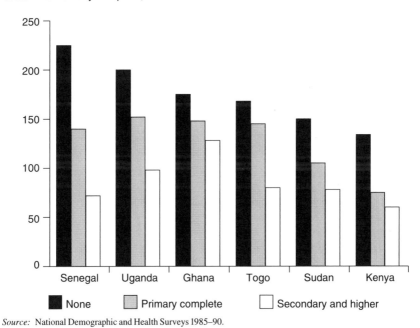

Source: National Demographic and Health Surveys 1985–90.

male participation rose from 24 percent in 1960 to 61 percent in 1990. At the secondary level, it increased from 1 percent in 1960 to 16 percent in 1990. (Over the same period, male participation rose in primary education from 46 to 83 percent and in secondary education from 4 to 32 percent.) These levels compare poorly with the rest of the world. In 1985, for example, female primary enrollment in Africa was 58 percent, compared with 92 percent for low-income economies as a whole. Furthermore, the chances for girls to pursue higher levels of schooling worsen as they progress from grade to grade. Seventy-six percent of girls start school, compared with 86 percent of boys, but only 36 percent of the girls finish primary school, compared to 44 percent of the boys. Of the girls who finish primary school, only 41 percent continue to secondary school, and—of this group—only 18 percent finish secondary school. These low levels of education are further reflected in the median literacy rates among Sub-Saharan African countries, which were only 38 percent for females in 1990, compared with 50 percent for all adults.

Special Roles and Status of Women

Women occupy a special place in efforts to improve health because they participate in, and often manage, many activities that affect the health and well-being of their families. Women perform an estimated 60 to 80 percent of all agricultural labor in Africa, thus placing them in an important position to contribute to food security and nutrition. Women are also largely responsible for fetching water and fuelwood, thus placing them in an important position to ensure safe drinking water and adequate cooking and preparation of food. In Kenya, for example, 89 percent of rural women over age fourteen, but only 5 percent of the men, report fetching water and fuelwood as one of their normal tasks (Cleaver and Schreiber 1993).

Research on the determinants of infant mortality further shows that "the mother is the most important health worker for her children" (Schultz 1989). This conclusion not only reflects the strong correlation between female literacy and lower infant mortality, but agrees with studies of government expenditures on health showing that their effects are likely to be greater when they interface with an educated female population (Bhargava and Yu 1992; Stomberg and Stomberg 1992).

Time availability is one of the most important constraints affecting the ability of women to produce healthy children. Surveys in Central African Republic, Côte d'Ivoire, Sudan, Tanzania, and Zambia show that rural women in Africa work more than ten hours a day, even without counting child care and health care responsibilities (Leslie 1987). Policymakers need to bear in mind that the supply of health care services, or even pharmaceuticals, may not lead to use if their availability does not respond to women's sense of priorities and imposes unacceptable time costs for travel or time away from work.

Culture

Africans have long placed a high value on health care because good health is seen as the basis for development and societal growth. Traditional notions of disease and their origins are well established and can determine when, where, how, or even if treatment will be sought. Traditional African societies categorize some diseases and illnesses as man-made or "spiritually" induced. For instance, in the Groun and Yoruba regions of Benin and Nigeria, respectively, smallpox was considered to be the manifestation of a supernatural power, Segbata—a punishment inflicted by the goddess on those who had incurred her anger. Instead of being isolated, the sick person was taken from one place of worship to another in an effort to appease the goddess and, being in constant contact with the worshippers of Segbata, spread the disease unnecessarily to a greater number of people. In contrast, smallpox among some communities in Burkina Faso, Niger, and Chad was considered natural in origin and not the result of sacred or supernatural sources. As a result, people practiced a combination of vaccinations and isolation of the sick. Yaws is not considered a disease in some parts of Cameroon, and goiter, which is an indication of a malfunctioning thyroid gland, is not regarded as an illness in many traditional Nigerian and other African communities.

So important are culture and ethnicity to health outcomes, that *even* if structural constraints are removed in the health sector, desired results are unlikely to be achieved unless the cultures of communities, health policymakers and planners, and providers of health care are taken into consideration. Indeed, increased attention by policymakers to these issues increases the chances of success in implementing policy. If this is done, providers will be less likely to display an ambivalence toward the use of traditional medicine; and users will be less likely to vacillate between modern and traditional medicine (Amadi 1992).

Households at the Center

The health benefits of policies to promote safe drinking water and sanitation, increasing levels of education, improved food security and nutrition, family planning, and health care depend on efforts by the individual and the household. For drinking water to be safe and beneficial, households must be able to distinguish safe from nonpotable water, filter water when necessary, and ensure that their members rely exclusively on these supplies for consumption. Addressing malnutrition requires appropriate storage, preparation, and sharing of food. The management of individual food supplies and use of food resources can only be undertaken at the household level, occasionally with community support.

Self-care for illness can only be promoted by ensuring that households have access to sound health information and, in schools, suitable health education. The importance of self-care is indicated by a study in a Nigerian town that revealed that more than 80 percent of the illness episodes over a twelve-month period had been managed by the household (Brieger, Ramakrishna, and Adeniyi 1986). Finally, without the active involvement of households in identifying symptoms of illness, providing information on the history of the illness to health care providers, and complying with treatment plans, even the best individual health care will have no impact on illness.

Engaging households and communities in health, and responding to the health-related demands of the public, must therefore be central to the concerns of Sub-Saharan African governments for health improvement (Box 3-3). There are important implications for health in Africa:

BOX 3-3. INFORMATION, EDUCATION, AND COMMUNICATION AND THE HEALTH BEHAVIOR OF INDIVIDUALS AND HOUSEHOLDS

Information, education, and communication (IEC) programs for health have begun to receive increasing attention in Africa as a means of improving knowledge about individual self-care and best practices. This is a two-way street, however. Effective IEC programs also aim to establish what sorts of health activities will engage the cooperation, or lack of it, of households. A few examples of success:

■ The Happy Baby lottery campaign in The Gambia taught mothers the proper mixing and administration of oral rehydration salts (ORS), to reduce child mortality caused by dehydration from diarrheal disease. An independent evaluation after two years showed that, in diarrhea cases treated at home, the share treated with ORS increased by 22 percent to 94 percent (Rasmuson 1985).

■ The Man Is Health program to educate villagers in Tanzania on disease control led to the construction of hundreds of thousands of latrines and to significant increases in sales of mosquito nets. Approximately two million adults followed the Man Is Health radio program (Hall 1978).

■ The importance of changing behavior also has gained greater attention in health circles as a result of the HIV pandemic. Social marketing, using commercial marketing techniques to sell socially desirable products and services below their full cost, shows promise for expansion beyond population, family planning, and condom promotion for AIDS prevention, into other health areas. A pilot project to demon-

- Provision of sound health information, in forms that are readily comprehensible by and credible to households, is a central responsibility of African governments.
- The impact of improved health care services on health outcomes of households and communities will be either greatly facilitated or constrained, depending on conditions in the socioeconomic and cultural enabling environment.

Setting the Stage for Health Reform

The international conference sponsored by the Rockefeller Foundation in 1985 proved that commitments to create an enabling environment for health are integral to successful health strategy. The application of that model to all African countries would go a long way toward bringing Sub-Saharan Africa's health up to the level of health in the more prosperous countries. To do so means setting the stage for health reforms that would include the following elements:

Box 3-3, continued

strate its feasibility to treat and prevent sexually transmitted diseases has been underway in Cameroon since 1991.

Consulting beneficiaries and taking their views into account is an especially important aspect of efforts to promote changes in health-related behavior. Program planners too often operate within their own paradigms and make unrealistic assumptions about the values and desires of people whom they intend to help. Contrary to the frequent desire of health professionals to keep the modern and traditional systems of care separate, a beneficiary assessment in Lesotho led to decisions to bring traditional healers into the national health system and to give them basic health courses. It also led to a decision to provide almost

untrained village health workers with aspirin and other simple remedies to facilitate their interactions with beneficiaries (Hall and Malesha 1991).

Analysis is needed to formulate and test effective IEC strategies and messages. An essential tool for changing behavior is media-disseminated information—as distinct from formal classroom learning—provided in ways that are comprehensible and acceptable to the varied audiences in Africa, and backed by social science research on the cost-effectiveness of different messages. And, despite the evident importance of reaching people in their own language, a survey of twelve countries in eastern and southern Africa revealed that none possessed subnational or regionally based local-language radio stations that were geared to community programming (Johnston and de Zeeuw 1990).

BOX 3-4. THE WORLD SUMMIT FOR
CHILDREN: HEALTH GOALS FOR 1995
AND 2000

The Declaration and Plan of Action adopted at the 1990 World Summit for Children incorporate priority health goals for children and women. Some forty African countries have prepared national plans of action (NPAS) adopting and adapting these goals to their national situation. Implementation is a major problem in most countries, requiring ranking of national resources and sustained international support.

At the Organization of African Unity (OAU) International Conference on Assistance to African Children in 1992, African governments presented their NPAS and reaffirmed their commitment to mobilize national resources for implementation, including thorough restructuring of existing public expenditures. They also committed themselves to a set of intermediate goals by the end of 1995.

The mid-decade health goals adopted by African governments commit them to:
- Raise immunization coverage to 80 percent against diphtheria, pertussis, tetanus, poliomyelitis, and tuberculosis
- Ensure 90 percent immunization against measles as well as against tetanus for women of childbearing age

---

Strong Political Commitment to Better Health

Since the pivotal Alma Ata Declaration of 1978, representatives of African countries have attended a number of international conferences, which, like the one at Alma Ata, were designed to stir action to improve the environment for health. All of the conferences ended in agreement that action was necessary, and pledges to act were made. Generally speaking, however, those agreements and pledges have remained mere symbols of good intentions.

Prior to 1990 only seventeen African governments had prepared health policy statements that could be called comprehensive and operationally relevant. Only five of the seventeen—those of Botswana, Mali, Nigeria, Swaziland, and Tanzania—discussed problems in the enabling environment and outlined programs to correct them.

Following the 1990 World Summit for Children, sponsored by UNICEF, many African countries began preparing national plans of action (NPAS) covering many aspects of the enabling environment. According to WHO (Monekosso 1993), twenty-nine African countries had adopted policies on the provision of basic health care by the middle of 1993. However, these policies ignore many elements of the enabling environment.

Box 3-4 continued

■ Achieve 80 percent use of oral rehydration therapy

■ Virtually eliminate iodine deficiency disorders and vitamin A deficiency

■ Encourage exclusive breastfeeding for four to six months following childbirth and sustain breastfeeding for up to two years of age and beyond.

The goals for the year 2000 include:

■ A reduction to 70 per 1,000 in the mortality of children less than five years old, or by a third of the 1990 level if it is already lower than 70

■ A 50 percent reduction in child deaths caused by diarrhea and a reduction by one-third in child deaths caused by acute respiratory infections

■ Achievement of at least 90 percent immunization coverage of one-year-old children, as well as universal tetanus immunization for women of childbearing age

■ Access for all women to prenatal care, trained attendants during childbirth, referral for high-risk pregnancies and obstetric emergencies, and halving of maternal mortality rates

■ Elimination of dracunculiasis and eradication of polio.

In the process of building basic health systems that lead to improvements in health, the challenge is to use goals such as those of the World Summit for Children to set priorities and ensure accountability.

To demonstrate a real commitment to the creation of an enabling environment for health, governments need to formulate comprehensive, operationally oriented health policies that include explicit health goals and targets, statements on how all the elements of the enabling environment will be strengthened, and specific arrangements for monitoring and evaluating progress.

More Cost-Effective and Equitable Use of Public Funds

Public spending on health needs to be guided more stringently by cost-effectiveness and equity criteria. Correcting the most obvious inequity—the overfinancing of curative medical care and the underfinancing of primary and preventive care—would also go a long way toward correcting inefficiencies in the allocation of public spending for health. Redirecting spending away from curative care to combat the majority of diseases and illnesses that are preventable or relatively easily treated has obvious appeal on cost-effectiveness grounds. The argument for greater equity in health spending is a particularly strong one, given the widespread poverty and the many political and economic conditions that make for unstable household incomes.

Just as important to good health are the public services known to have an immense impact on health such as safe water, sanitation, and prevention of communicable diseases. Such services benefit the community at large but the investments are frequently so costly that people are unlikely to be motivated to provide them for themselves on an individual basis.

Thus, if these services are to be provided, local or national governments will be the only agents capable of ensuring that they are provided. Moreover, national and local governments are often the only institutions that have the necessary legal authority to do so.

Public services targeted to those who have not previously benefited from them have redistributive effects. Hence commitments to provide such services are in accord with the goal of health equity. In most African countries, equity and efficiency considerations are fully consistent.

More Effective Incentives.   Households and health service providers need financial and other incentives to encourage increased efficiency in using health resources. When the cost to households of using hospital-based services is no greater than using local health centers, as discussed in detail in subsequent chapters, people will naturally turn to hospitals. Yet the cost to society of providing care in hospitals is usually much higher than at health centers. Appropriate price signals combined with quality care at health centers can create the right incentives for households to use services where they can be provided most cost-effectively.

Health service providers also need to face incentives to provide high-quality services at low cost. Transparency, local accountability, and local retention of revenues from fees can establish incentives among public sector, private voluntary, and private for-profit providers, to furnish high-quality and low-cost services.

More Pluralistic Decisionmaking.   One of the chief elements of any strategy to improve health in Sub-Saharan Africa must be a commitment to recognize and encourage the decisionmaking on health issues of households and communities. Put another way, the tradition of hierarchical decisionmaking in matters affecting health must give way to more pluralistic decisionmaking.

This is not a new concept with respect to African health. As long ago as the Alma Ata Declaration of 1978, the notion of greater community involvement in decisionmaking was proclaimed as one of the antidotes to illness and disease. As time has passed, more and more evidence has accumulated that the participation of local community groups in the design and implementation of health and health-related activities has a significant impact on success and sustainability. Success and sustainability, in turn, arise in part from the recognition that tradition is an important factor in community life and must be taken into account. But tradition is hardly the only reason for greater community involvement. Those who live in local communities have a good view of their own health problems and, therefore, can make valuable contributions to solving them.

Moreover, local communities themselves have become more assertive because of poor delivery of publicly financed and publicly provided services. This assertiveness has been accompanied by stronger demands for control of public resources at the provincial and local levels.

Given that hierarchical decisionmaking is also a tradition in Africa, such impulses toward greater pluralism in health have encountered resistance from many in established political and medical circles. Nonetheless, this report is based in large part on the belief that households and communities, because they are the heart of the health system, must be not only recipients of medical services but also active participants in determining, funding, and managing the wide range of health interventions. The most important prerequisites for achieving these goals are a sustained political commitment to them and (where necessary) retraining of civil servants (WHO 1988a). Medical officers at the local level, for example, often fail to appreciate the value of community participation. Even when they understand its importance, they often lack the training needed to facilitate community involvement.

Greater recognition of the voice of the public will be enhanced by administrative decentralization—that is, giving public officials at the regional and local levels greater authority in decisionmaking. Overly centralized public administration in many African countries has meant failure to provide the organizational framework, managerial processes, and financial and human resources needed to make longlasting successful attacks on health problems. The organizational structure of Benin's ministry of health, for example, has been characterized as overcentralized and managerially weak. Under Côte d'Ivoire's health care system, decisionmaking used to be the exclusive responsibility of the state. Although various methods of health service decentralization have been attempted in a number of Sub-Saharan African countries, success has often been undermined by unclear linkages among the various levels of government and by inadequate authority at the local level to make expenditures. These and other aspects of institutional decentralization are discussed in greater detail in Chapter 8.

Better Use of Donor Funding to Build National Capabilities

Donor funds now account for about one-fifth of the spending on health in Africa. This eases the financial burden for countries often hard-pressed by factors beyond their control. Unfortunately, however, donor funding in too many instances has been a case of the tail wagging the dog. The donors—mainly multilateral and international institutions, and national governments in the industrial world—have sometimes had their own agendas, and in carrying out these agendas the donors' wishes have tended to dominate the health agendas of the recipient countries or else complicated the implementation of national agendas by setting up projects and programs outside national purview. In many cases donors' actions have tended to fragment the health sectors of the African countries. In other words, the frequent failure to integrate donor-financed activities as part of comprehensive national policy has resulted in duplication, overlap, lack of consistency in standards and procedures, and inconsistent or disjointed policy recommendations.

The time has come for Sub-Saharan African countries to put donor funding to work in sustainable ways to make dynamic improvements in health. In the long run, only African countries themselves can make the right decisions about their health goals and the means necessary to achieve them.

CHAPTER FOUR

Revitalizing National Systems of Health Care

WHEN PEOPLE are struck by serious illness, effective use of the health care system plays a large role in their recovery. Yet it is equally true that recovery—or, in many cases, the ability of people to obtain preventive care that forestalls illness—depends on whether existing health care systems are operating efficiently and equitably. But many health care systems in Africa are unable to provide preventive and primary care near where a majority of their people live and work, which is in rural and periurban areas. The need, therefore, is to expand health care services and to provide care in more cost-effective ways. And to promote equity, the use of public resources for health care must produce greater benefits for the poor.

This chapter describes Africa's current health care systems and identifies ways to revitalize their lagging performance. A careful look at recent experience in several African countries strongly suggests that household welfare and the cost-effectiveness of health care improve when preventive and primary services are offered by well-functioning health centers working in coordination with small first-referral hospitals in rural and periurban areas.

African Health Care Systems Today

The health care systems inherited by African countries at independence were equipped to provide personal care to only a small fraction of the population. During colonial rule, control of endemic diseases was the main concern of the French and British regimes. The French made serious efforts to deal with vector-borne diseases through programs organized on a paramilitary basis, while the British placed greater stress on controlling fecal contamination of food and water. Hospitals were built principally for the benefit of colonial administrators and settlers, and rural clinics were usually the by-product of missionary activities. From time to time, a few elite Africans were invited to use the modern facilities established for outsiders, but such matters as health education, mass immunizations, screening of populations for disease, and good nutrition played only a small part in colonial policies.

Progress since independence has varied greatly from country to country. When access to personal care, for instance, is defined as the patient being no more than an hour away from a health facility by local means of transportation, only 11 percent of the rural population in Côte d'Ivoire, 15 percent in Somalia, 25 percent in Rwanda, and 30 percent in Liberia, Niger, and Nigeria have such access. Some African countries, however, have made a concerted effort to improve access by emphasizing the delivery of primary health care in rural areas. WHO reports that some 99 percent of the rural residents of Mauritius have such access, as do 85 percent in Botswana, 73 percent in Tanzania, and 70 percent in Congo.

Within most African countries, though, access to personal health care tends to be highly unequal across administrative districts and between rural and urban areas. Among thirty states in Nigeria, the number of health facilities ranges from one per 200 people in Lagos State to one per 129,000 in Benue State. Three-fourths of the country's public and private health facilities are located in urban areas, which contain only 30 percent of the population. In Angola the supply of hospital beds ranges from 4 per 10,000 people in the province of Malage to 42 per 10,000 in Luanda Norte. In Kenya there is one doctor on average per 500 people in Nairobi, compared with one per 160,000 people in the rural Turkana district. Periurban areas are also underserved, especially squatter-type settlements, which also lack basic water and sanitation services.

The geographic imbalance in access to health care is reflected by the imbalance in public spending on health care. Major urban hospitals (so-called tertiary facilities) often receive half or more of the public funds spent on health and commonly account for 50 to 80 percent of recurrent health sector expenditures by the government. In the mid-1980s, for example, the major hospitals' share of public recurrent health expenditures was 74 percent in Lesotho, 70 percent in Somalia, 66 percent in Burundi, 54 percent in Zimbabwe, and 49 percent in Botswana (Barnum and Kutzin 1993).

In addition, major urban hospitals often employ the largest proportions of highly trained health personnel. In Kenya, for example, 60 percent of all physicians and 80 percent of all nurses are assigned to such hospitals (Bloom, Segall, and Thube 1986).

Inpatient spending at major hospitals, however, is often devoted mainly to paying the costs of treating conditions that could have been managed or even prevented by primary care. These include malaria, tuberculosis, unwanted pregnancies, digestive ailments, ill-defined fevers, respiratory infections, and skin infections. Among the ten leading causes of admission to hospitals in Malawi and Nigeria in the mid-1980s, for example, parasitic and infectious diseases ranked first. It would appear that at least a third of all hospital expenditures in Africa could be avoided if more cost-effective strategies than remedial care— such as vector control, environmental protection measures, and construction of household sanitation facilities—were used to reduce the incidence of infectious and parasitic diseases.

The disproportionate assignment of professional medical personnel to major urban hospitals, the use of more expensive inputs in outpatient services, and their more reliable supply of drugs often means that such hospitals compete with, rather than complement, health centers and small rural hospitals (Box 4-1).

The Multitiered System of Health Care

Health sector problems in Africa can be traced in large part to the continued hierarchical organization of health care. In most African countries, personal health care facilities reflect the country's administrative hierarchy, which operates from the top down. In theory, village health posts, local dispensaries, health centers, and small rural hospitals are intended to provide the preventive and primary care needed by the people living in rural and periurban areas. This is where the bulk of Africa's population lives, it is where demand is greatest, and it is where preventive and primary care would have the greatest positive impact

---

BOX 4-1. WHY PRIMARY AND PREVENTIVE CARE SHOULD NOT BE PROVIDED BY HOSPITALS

■ Provision of primary and preventive care by hospitals is uneconomical; treatment cost per illness is much more expensive than at a health center or dispensary. By some estimates it can be ten to twenty-five times as much.

■ Provision of primary care distorts a hospital's functions. Many of the apparent shortcomings of hospitals are linked to congested outpatient departments and overworked laboratories performing hundreds of so-called routine tests.

■ The pressure of primary care on hospital facilities also distorts health program development at the community level because it fixes attention on the distressed hospital, creating the impression that further extension and development is required, when the real need is for a very large increase in the number of effectively functioning health centers.

on national health. But at these lower levels of the health care hierarchy, bureaucratic authority is weakest and spending is lowest. Neither private providers nor private voluntary organizations have filled the resulting gaps in the provision of health care. Although private voluntary organizations, such as mission hospitals and clinics, often are effective providers in local areas, they account for only 5 to 10 percent of all health expenditures in most African countries.

The poor quality of care in many rural and periurban areas is often the result of shortages of qualified staff, lack of essential supplies (such as effective generic drugs), unreliable health data, and insufficient numbers of health facilities. In some cases, though, administrative weaknesses become apparent because facilities are underused and overstaffed. Some rural health centers in Tanzania, for example, were found to employ twenty health workers who treated only three or four patients a day. Lack of standards for facilities and procedures complicates matters. As a result of lax building standards, basic health facilities in Sahelian countries range anywhere from 46 to 1,734 square meters in floor space, thus contributing to an uneven infrastructure across communities (Abeillé and others 1991).

Given the absence or inadequacy of many village clinics, health care centers, and small rural hospitals, they often are bypassed by potential clients who decide to seek better care at full-fledged urban hospitals (Bocar 1989). As a result, overqualified staff and expensive facilities are used in ways their planners did not contemplate. Most major hospitals in Sub-Saharan Africa now commonly provide primary and preventive health care services, such as vaccinations, growth monitoring, and prenatal care (Van Lerberghe, Van Balen, and Kegels 1989), becoming in effect direct competitors with lesser facilities. While the quality of care provided by large hospitals may be quite good, the social costs are high. In addition to longer travel time to and longer waiting time at these hospitals, clients from rural and periurban areas are deprived of the personal attention and the more frequent follow-up visits that could be provided by a local facility.

The Performance of Major African Hospitals

Major African hospitals, often referred to as central or tertiary level hospitals, are at the top of the personal health care system in most African countries. They are often associated with a medical school and are designed to offer clinical services highly differentiated by function, technical capacity, and skills—for example, cardiological services and magnetic resonance imaging (MRI) units. The number of beds in these hospitals ranges from 300 to more than 1,500.

The greater complexity of the cases that these hospitals were designed to handle and their more expensive inputs commonly translate into much higher operating costs than at lower levels of the medical care hierarchy. However, the extent to which resources are concentrated in these hospitals often goes beyond what they need to fulfill their curative functions (Barnum and Kutzin 1993). In Zambia, for instance, the country's three large central hospitals used 30 percent of all Ministry of Health resources and an estimated 45 percent of the ministry's total hospital resources in the 1980s. The remaining 55 percent was spread among thirty-nine lower-level hospitals. In Kenya, the Kenyatta National Hospital accounted for almost 20 percent of the ministry's recurrent financial spending in 1986–87, and Kenya's provincial hospitals used another 24 percent. In Zimbabwe, 45 percent of the ministry's allocations were used for recurrent expenditures at four central hospitals.

But upper-level hospitals are less cost-effective in reducing mortality or morbidity than facilities lower in the hierarchy. In Ghana, for example, the leading causes of morbidity are upper respiratory tract infections, diarrhea, parasitic diseases, and accidents. The leading causes of mortality are vaccine-preventable diseases, respiratory diseases, malnutrition, diarrhea, and accidents. Hospitals do not play a significant role in reducing years of life lost due to any of these causes except accidents (Barnum and Kutzin 1993).

Africa's major hospitals, as noted earlier, are usually located in metropolitan areas. Thus, even when their stated purpose is to provide tertiary care (that is, specialized, second-referral care) for a broad population base, they actually provide large amounts of primary and first-referral care to a disproportionately urban clientele. Moreover, urban residents in Africa generally have higher incomes than those living in rural areas. Surveys of patients at Niamey National Hospital in Niger, for example, showed that outpatients had a higher median income than inpatients, whose median income was comparable to or slightly higher than that of other urban residents. Urban residents, in turn, had higher incomes than rural residents (Weaver, Handou, and Mohamed 1990).

The concentration of resources at the tertiary level in urban areas, with benefits going disproportionately to households with higher incomes, defeats the objective of providing equitable and cost-effective care throughout the country to people at every income level. This does *not* mean that tertiary hospitals should be disregarded. They play a necessary role in curing illnesses whose successful treatment requires specialized medical procedures. The point, rather, is that tertiary hospitals should play this role within a larger system designed to meet the health needs of the entire population.

A Brief History of Primary Health Care Strategies in Africa

The 1978 Alma Ata Declaration stressed the importance of providing primary health care for everyone in the developing countries and the need for strong community participation in achieving that goal. In subsequent years, however, efforts to provide primary health care have taken the form of either highly selective, "vertical" programs designed to deal separately with specific health problems, or broader programs involving community or village health workers (CHWs or VHWs). In most African countries, neither of these strategies has done much to persuade policymakers to shift resources away from curative care to a well-defined package of cost-effective primary and preventive care services.

Usually developed with the strong support of international and multilateral donors, vertical programs have focused on specific problems, such as controlling outbreaks of contagious childhood diseases through mass immunizations, or encouraging greater use of family planning measures. Narrow targets and assured funding made it possible to use many means (including mobile teams) to provide quality care and to gain community acceptance of these specific interventions.

Some of the vertical programs have proved worthwhile. The most striking success was the eradication of smallpox in 1977, after the world's last known case showed up in Somalia. Vertical programs also appear to have been cost-effective when crises have occurred in the form of threatened epidemics following earthquakes and floods.

But these highly selective programs have had minuses as well as pluses. To administer these programs, vertical administrative entities have been set up that often had little contact with the national agencies or local officials charged with responsibility for health care administration. Because of minimal coordination between separate vertical programs in the same country or region and little integration with the rest of the health care system, selective, single-purpose interventions have sometimes proved disappointing (Table 4-1). Reviews of programs in Burkina Faso, Mali, Niger, and Central African Republic have uncovered various problems:

■ District health teams have sometimes included as many as ten coordinators for ten different vertical programs, each supervising health personnel and reporting to a different administrator, when one or two coordinators would have been enough.

■ AIDS screening kits and EPI vaccines have been transported in separate "cold chains" (refrigeration facilities) when both could have been distributed through the same chain.

■ Administration of Zaire's family planning program was artificially split between two national agencies, and the ensuing competition between them did little to increase contraceptive prevalence rates.

Table 4-1.   Single-Purpose Interventions: A Review of Studies

Study design	Intervention	Conclusion
Longitudinal with control group	Measles vaccination (Kasongo, Zaire)	Reduction in measles deaths partly wiped out by delayed excess mortality from other causes in vaccinated group
Before/after	Oral rehydration (Several studies)	Impact on under-five mortality lower than expected from reduction of diarrhea deaths
Time series	Community-based nutrition (Iringa, Tanzania)	Under-five mortality gains reversed due to malaria
Before/after	Malaria control and measles vaccination (Saradidi, Kenya)	Reduction in under-five mortality attributed to measles vaccination, not malaria control
Before/after	Measles vaccination (Mvumi, Tanzania)	Impact on under-five mortality wiped out by malaria

Source: Knippenberg, Ofosu-Amaah, and Parker 1990.

■ Some vertical programs have attracted large amounts of resources from donors and governments, while other causes of mortality and morbidity have been largely ignored. One study found that up to 15 percent of the women in some regions where vertical AIDS programs were in operation were suffering from untreated syphilis, a disease that creates a particularly receptive environment for HIV.

■ Routine health care can be disrupted and national capacity weakened when vertical programs temporarily or permanently lure away specialists from national health systems.

On a more positive note, selective PHC programs have enjoyed positive and robust results in situations where health centers and under-five clinics offer integrated child care. High levels of immunization have been sustained and significant reductions in infant and child mortality rates achieved by integrating maternal and child health care services in health facilities in Guinea and Benin.

The principal shortcoming of vertical programs is that they are not intended to and cannot provide steady and ongoing care. A child born after a mobile team spends a week in a community to vaccinate children against an immunizable disease may not be immunized until another team comes along six months later. Meanwhile, the child may get the disease. What is needed are health facilities that give vaccinations regularly. The Expanded Programme of Immunization (EPI) in Togo, Senegal, Ivory Coast, and Congo (UNICEF 1990a) only temporarily increased the number of children vaccinated because vaccinations were not a part of the daily responsibilities of health centers (Figure 4-1, upper panel A). In Zimbabwe (Cornea, Jolly, and Stewart 1987), Botswana, and Cape Verde (UNICEF 1990a), in contrast, immunization coverage was high and significant reductions in infant and child mortality were achieved when immunization and maternal and child health services became the ongoing responsibility of permanent health facilities. In Benin, a strategy of simultaneously improving health care service and immunization coverage led to a steady and sustained increase in EPI coverage (Figure 4-1, B).

Village Health Workers

Attempts have also been made to expand primary health care by establishing networks of village or community health workers (VHW or CHW) modeled on China's success in using "barefoot doctors" to enlarge the geographic scope of health care. VHW programs are aimed at extending health care to unserved regions, while CHW programs are principally intended to be catalysts for community development and involve a more holistic approach to health that includes such tasks as developing safe water supplies.

These programs have performed relatively well when their role as intermediaries between the community and the health care system is clear, and when they receive visible support from health centers. This has been the case in Lesotho, where more than 4,000 trained village health workers are supported by local development councils; in Zimbabwe, where more than 6,000 CHWs receive stipends as general development workers; and in Zaire, where CHWs are persons selected by their communities to act as liaisons to the health establishment (Reynders and others 1992). The contribution of VHW or CHW workers to community involvement in the planning and management of health services has also been documented in Kenya, Tanzania, Zaire, and Somalia (Beza and others 1987; Leneman and Fowkes 1986, 4; Vaughn, Mills, and Smith 1984).

VHW and CHW programs have not worked well when their links to the health system and to communities have been weak. In Burkina Faso, Gambia, Ghana, Niger, and Tanzania, community health workers were trained on a massive scale in the 1980s to be the principal providers of primary health care. Because of their limited training and nebulous connection to the formal system of health care, these CHWs were forced to rely on support and supervision from cadres of specialized coordinators, often organized by nongovernmental organ-

Figure 4-1. Performance of Expanded Programme of Immunization (EPI) under Different Conditions

A. EPI through campaign or mobile strategies

Percent coverage

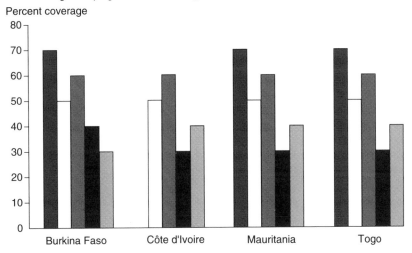

B. EPI through strong network of health centers

Percent coverage

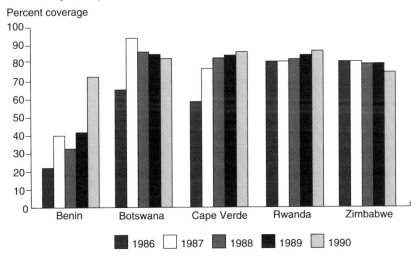

Source: WHO Information System 1993.

izations (NGOs) or externally funded projects. The potential contribution of community health workers has been blunted by lack of constant support and supervision (Sauerborn, Nougtara, and Diesfeld 1989; Walt 1988; Walt, Perera, and Heggenhougen 1989).

Table 4-2 summarizes the findings of a number of studies that reveal that VHW and CHW programs have produced mixed results. If they have no clear connection to the existing health system, community health workers are often bypassed by household members who consult providers at the first level of the formal system. Their presence may even delay access to professional care rather than deter unnecessary consultations. High attrition rates among CHW workers, exacerbated by dwindling donor support for the programs, suggest that the value of these programs should be reexamined.

Health Care System Realities

The reality in many African countries is that health care systems are not providing cost-effective services in ways that would have the greatest impact on the major causes of illness and death. For households, this means low confidence in the health system and barely marginal improvements in health. For governments, this means that a large share of public expenditures on health is wasted. For private providers, this often means trying to deal with a vast number of unmet needs with little guidance, assistance, or even competition from the public sector.

Chronic shortages of drugs, infrequent equipment maintenance, inadequate logistical support, and weak supervision further contribute to inefficiency. Also lacking are procedures or systems to monitor and evaluate the quality of health care and to ensure that providers are accountable to clients. National standards that would make it possible to ascertain progress in resolving health problems across communities, districts, and countries do not exist (Smith and Bryant 1988; Pangu 1988). Thus, it is difficult to know whether a particular health intervention is having a discernible impact on major health problems.

It might seem obvious that first-referral hospitals should be a vital part of an effective health care system. In the years after Alma Ata, however, many policymakers seemed to think that district hospitals were irrelevant. In Tanzania, for example, the Essential Drugs Program provided donor-funded drug kits to dispensaries in rural areas but not to first-referral hospitals. PHC policies have done little to divert public resources away from major urban and teaching hospitals, while severely weakening peripheral and rural hospitals.

Table 4-2. Review of VHW and CHW Programs

Country or region	Method	Findings
Africa	Review of 1,000 publications	Problems in all aspects of the functioning of VHWs (tasks, selection, recruitment, training, remuneration, and, most seriously, support).
West African countries	Desk review	Same observations.
Senegal and other West African countries	Case studies	Same observations; questioned relevance and sustainability.
Tanzania	Multiplicity of methods used to gather information on the acceptability, quality, and cost of the CHW program	Below a certain level of support the quality of community-based health services is very questionable.
Niger	Systems analysis combined questionnaires from VHWs, mothers, supervisors, and community representatives; structured observations of service delivery and support activities, and focus group discussions with villagers	Training of more than 13,000 VHWs provided additional access to primary health care in 45 percent of the villages of Niger, but low quality of care was linked to weak support.
Burkina Faso	Representative household survey on MCH	Presence of village health posts did not increase use of MCH care.
The Gambia	Mortality surveys to assess the impact of a TBA program on maternal mortality	No impact of TBAs on maternal mortality.
Ghana	Study of community clinic attendants (VHWs) in nine of the ten regions of the country	Problems related to the selection, training, abuse of functions, lack of remuneration, shortage of drugs, and supervision; the program generally failed to achieve its objectives.

Note: CHW, community health worker; MCH, maternal and child health; TBA, trained birth attendant; VHW, village health worker.
Source: Knippenberg, Ofosu-Amaah, and Parker 1991.

Underpinnings of a Cost-Effective Approach

Well-functioning health centers, working in conjunction with first-referral hospitals, have the capacity to manage more than 90 percent of health care demands. Experience in a number of African countries shows that the most fundamental element of such an approach is a limited and flexible, cost-effective package of basic services that can be delivered at the community level. The first element of the package is a basic set of health care inputs. The second is a battery of supporting services that aim to ensure that households make the most effective use of such inputs. The third consists of multisectoral inputs to better health.

The basic services emphasized in this report are those needed largely in countries that have not yet passed through the "health transition." This means a shift in the demographic and epidemiological makeup of a country, and associated social conditions and attitudes, from an environment dominated by high fertility, high mortality, infectious disease, and malnutrition to a low-mortality, low-fertility environment with a disease profile increasingly weighted toward noncommunicable conditions of adults and the elderly. Although some population groups within individual African countries, particularly among the elite, have entered or passed the health transition, the package concept still applies to all countries and populations. Both the content and the cost of a basic package

---

BOX 4-2. COST-EFFECTIVE HEALTH INTERVENTIONS

The cost-effectiveness of many of the health interventions recommended in this study has been substantiated in the World Bank's *World Development Report 1993: Investing in Health.* Given a common currency for measuring cost and a unit for measuring health effects, the *World Development Report* compares the costs required for different interventions to achieve one additional year of healthy life. Outcomes are expressed in terms of disability-adjusted life years (DALYs). The ratio of cost and effect, or the unit cost of a DALY, is called the cost-effectiveness of the intervention. The lower the unit cost to gain one DALY, the greater the value for money offered by the intervention.

Only a small number of the thousands of known medical procedures have been assessed using the cost-effectiveness criteria described above, but the approximately fifty studied would be able to deal with more than half the world's disease burden. Just implementing the twenty most cost-effective interventions could eliminate more than 40 percent of the total burden and fully three-quarters of the health loss among children.

Several public health activities stand out as being particularly cost-effective: the cost of gaining one DALY can be remarkably low—sometimes

will vary according to a country's epidemiological profile, social priorities, and income levels.

A number of public health interventions have been documented to be particularly cost-effective, and include health and nutritional education aimed at personal behavior change, control of environmental hazards, immunization, and screening and referral for selected infectious diseases and high-risk pregnancies. A review of disease control priorities in developing countries includes the following among the most cost-effective interventions: breastfeeding promotion, DPT plus polio immunization; measles immunization; smoking prevention; antibiotic treatment of acute respiratory infection in children; and supporting therapy, including vitamin A (Box 4-2).

Health facilities may be publicly operated; private, for-profit; or private voluntary organizations, such as mission facilities. When they function well, they respond to local health and economic conditions by "bundling" services into basic care packages.

Packages may change over time to adapt to evolving epidemiology or changing resource availability. For example, oral rehydration therapy (ORT) has been strongly promoted in well-functioning health centers as a low-cost technology to manage cases of diarrhea. As the incidence of diarrhea decreases, more people learn to use ORT at home, or clean drinking water becomes more

---

Box 4-2, continued

less than $25 and often between $50 and $150. Activities in this category include immunizations; school-based health services; information and selected services for family planning; programs to reduce tobacco and alcohol consumption; regulatory action, information, and limited public investments to improve the household environment; and AIDS prevention.

Although the cost-effectiveness of clinical services will vary from country to country, depending on local health needs and the level of income, five groups of interventions are highly cost-effective and address very large disease burdens. These include ser-

vices to ensure pregnancy-related care (prenatal, childbirth, and postpartum); family planning services; control of sexually transmitted diseases; tuberculosis control; and care for the common serious illnesses of children—diarrheal disease, acute respiratory infection, measles, malaria, and acute malnutrition.

These interventions form the core of the package of health care services recommended in this study. Provided by well-functioning health centers and first-referral hospitals, they have the capacity to (a) manage more than 90 percent of health care demands and (b) reduce the national burden of disease by up to 30 percent.

Source: World Bank 1993e.

accessible, health workers will spend less time on treatment and more on prevention. As coverage rates for immunization increase—through sustained understanding and demand by the population—vaccinations will continue to be important, but their place in the health worker's daily caseload will be reduced.

To combat frequently occurring illnesses and health conditions, such as malaria, hypertension, diarrhea, respiratory infections, measles, polio, STDs, and malnutrition, a regular supply of essential drugs is also needed.

Making drugs, contraceptives, and vaccines more available to the community is not enough, however. It is also important to ensure that clients' ills are diagnosed correctly, that providers prescribe or apply the right services, and that clients use the drug or service correctly. While these caveats may sound obvious, problems of diagnosis, drug prescription, and client use of drugs or other treatment regimens are sufficiently prevalent in Africa that the effectiveness of potentially good solutions can be reduced by up to 50 percent (Box 4-3).

Bringing these services together in well-functioning health facilities can benefit households in a number of important ways:

BOX 4-3. COMPARATIVE ADVANTAGES OF HEALTH CENTERS

Most health problems, ranging from common illness to measles, malnutrition, tuberculosis, or sexually transmitted diseases, can be treated with the technology and competence available to well-functioning health centers. And in 80 to 90 percent of preventive work and for most curative cases, the health center can outperform hospitals in terms of continuity, comprehensiveness, integration, and cost of care.

The small scale of the health center also favors integration of various programs. Major gains in vaccination coverage or family planning can be made when the health center staff consults a sick child's growth monitoring chart and vaccination record. Conversely, at a hospital, outpatient care is a service separate from vaccination, growth monitoring, or family planning.

Overprescription is also less common in health centers than in hospitals. In Ghana, for example, a study found that the average cost of drugs per person, per episode was $.20 at hospitals compared with $.07 at health centers, with the lower costs explained by less sophisticated prescription and better management of drug stocks (Hogerzeil and Lamberts 1984).

The health center's comparative advantage lies in its accessibility and potential for communication with the community. Its scale of operations permits nurses to become acquainted with the households and their social environment, thus preventing dropout and facilitating reestablishment of contact if the patient stops treatment. The small scale of the health center cannot guarantee greater interpersonal communication and empathy toward clients, but it makes it possible.

■ *Comprehensive care.* This means that the health care provider deals not only with the immediate illness but also its underlying causes. For example, a battered child will receive more than a painkiller or a cast for a broken leg. His family situation will become a matter of concern to the health care provider as well. For a child suffering from micronutrient deficiencies, the health care provider will not only provide vitamin supplements but also look into the child's daily diet.

■ *Continuity of care.* This means that a specific health care provider will interact with household members as long as such interaction is necessary to have a longlasting impact on health. A tuberculosis patient, for example, will not only receive a drug prescription but will be asked to discuss her work and family situation so that an appropriate long-term treatment program can be established for her. If she stops treatment prematurely, the health service will try to reestablish contact by visiting her home or contacting other members of the household. Continuity of care also implies that community health workers and health care providers will make sure that cost-effective preventive and primary care services are made available at opportune times. For example, children less than one year old are identified during home visits, a practice in well-functioning health facilities in Ghana (Ofosu-Amaah and others 1978), Zaire (Niimi 1991), Benin (Alihonou and others 1988), and Nigeria (Ransome-Kuti and others 1990).

■ *Integrated care.* By moving from project-based to program-based approaches, the health care provider is able to perform several tasks concurrently, cognizant of the household's time constraints and cultural background. The provider may link preventive and curative care so that a pregnant woman who arrives at a health center to be treated for malaria will have a prenatal consultation before going home. And her children's immunization records will be checked so that vaccination can be given if necessary. In Kenya, integrated care resulted in increased use of clinics, fewer consultations, a more balanced use of health staff, a reduction in unmet demand, and a striking increase in immunization rates (Dissevelt 1978).

The Role of the Health Center

The concept of the health center as a necessary part of health care was well articulated in the 1960s (Fendall 1963; King 1966; Roemer 1972). During the 1970s and 1980s, health centers with community outreach began to appear in Africa, launched with donor assistance in Danfa (Ghana), Pahou (Benin), Machakos (Kenya), Pikine (Senegal), Kasongo (Zaire), Kinshasa, and Lagos. To make health centers more effective, planners have developed ways to tackle the problems of accessibility (Van Lerberghe, Pangu, and Vandenbroek 1988), acceptability, intensity of use and compliance with medical instructions, quality of care (Kasongo Project Team 1982), recurrent costs (Pangu and Van Lerberghe 1988), and community ownership (Jacobson 1989; Kaseje and others 1989; Matomora 1989).

In many African countries, the health center (sometimes known as health post or dispensary) is a physical entity at the hub of community life and is the first level of contact with the formal health care system. Community participation, and especially the participation of women, in deciding the location and operation of health centers is critical to their success. By serving communities of 5,000 to 15,000 people, health centers justify the employment of a critical mass of personnel and services, thus providing a strong underpinning for cost-effective health care. Health centers have also gained attention because they have performed more effectively and at less cost than hospitals in providing primary care.

BOX 4-4. PROTOTYPICAL HEALTH CENTER

Demographic profile of community served

Total population	10,000
Children <1 year (4 percent of the population)	400
Women ages 15–49 years (20 percent of the population)	2,000
Children <15 years (50 percent of the population)	5,000

Package of care and services provided

Maternal services
- Predelivery care, delivery care and postdelivery care
- Breastfeeding IEC
- Micronutrient supplements (iodine for pregnant women)
- Supplementary feeding (pregnant and lactating women)

Well-baby services
- Expanded Programme of Immunization (EPI)
- Micronutrient supplements (iron, iodine, and vitamin A)
- Nutritional rehabilitation (children ages 0–5)
- Supplementary feeding programs (children ages 0–2)

School health
- Antihelminthic treatment (children ages 5–14)
- Vitamin A plus iodine, as required

Curative care (especially children 0–5)
- Basic trauma
- Malaria

An essential precondition for well-functioning health centers is that the communities they serve be well-defined. For example, when a given health center serves about 10,000 people in an area with a high fertility rate, the staff can safely estimate that about 400 babies are likely to be born in the community each year (Box 4-4). To meet the objective of universal immunization, EPI planning can therefore be based on serving roughly thirty-five new children a month. When district-based health systems are in place, health centers can obtain information useful for patient management. Though largely ignored for such purposes by national health systems, household files can be used by health center nurses to contact individual households, to make a profile of the community to be served, and to measure the impact of health care within the district.

Nutrition services targeted toward malnourished children and feeding programs for preschool children, pregnant women, and lactating mothers can also be organized effectively at the district level. Information available to this study

---

Box 4-4, continued

- Diarrhea
- Other local infections

Limited chronic care
- Tuberculosis treatment

STDS and AIDS
- STD testing, treatment, and IEC
- AIDS prevention (provision of condoms and IEC for high-risk groups)

Family planning
- Family planning IEC
- Provision of contraceptives

Staff profile
- Doctor on visiting basis from District Health Management Team
- One registered nurse; two assistant nurse/midwives, one community service (FP/nutrition) assistant; one clerk

Infrastructure profile
- One building (approximately 125m^2; includes sanitation facilities); one housing unit for staff
- Two bicycles, one refrigerator, and other medical and office equipment

Note: IEC includes ongoing dialogue during consultation and outreach visits to villages and groups served by the health center.
Source: Adapted from World Bank 1993a.

---

suggests that nutritional services of this kind can be provided for about $1.30 per capita a year (World Bank 1993a).

Health centers are also in a position to generate their own information on community coverage and use. When combined with in-house assessments of staff work load and costs, a balance can be established to ensure reliability, accuracy, and affordability of services (Imboden 1980; DeSweemer and others 1982; Jagdish 1985; King 1984). For example, a low-cost health management information system (MIS) in Zaire has been developed to trigger timely management decisions and actions by health centers and communities (Beza and others 1987). In Guinea and Benin, the entire MIS was revamped and simplified so that health center staff could use it to integrate and manage their own services. Forms, files, and registers were redesigned first to serve supervisors and local monitoring needs (including feedback to communities) and second for reporting to agencies at the provincial and national level (Knippenberg and others 1990). Although registering information and performing periodic analysis are time-consuming tasks, most health center staff consider them an important responsibility and do not suggest a reduction in the quantity of forms and files (Ministère de la Santé Publique [MSP], Benin 1990; Ministère de la Santé Publique et des Affaires Sociales [MSPAS], Guinea 1990).

Any attempt to generalize about the characteristics of well-functioning health centers must, of course, take into account different conditions, resources, and needs among and within countries. At the same time, however, it is helpful to visualize what may be involved. A prototypical health center is depicted in Box 4-4 in terms of demographics of the community serviced, care and services provided, staff profile, and infrastructure.

The Role of the First-Referral Hospital

The first level of referral for problems beyond the scope of a health center is typically a district hospital. Health care systems with these two tiers have demonstrated the capacity to provide comprehensive and effective care (WHO 1992b; Hamel and Janssen 1988; Van Lerberghe, Van Balen, and Kegels 1989; Barnum and Kutzin 1993; Mills 1991; Van Lerberghe and Lafort 1991). In Kasongo (Zaire), for example, the network that provides comprehensive primary care clearly reduces hospitalization rates. Rural dwellers' hospital admission rates were 50 percent lower in areas with health centers than in areas without. Treatment for illnesses targeted in the past by selective programs, such as measles, tetanus, and diarrhea, dropped by 86 percent when health centers provided vaccinations, oral rehydration therapy, and chloroquine as well as general outpatient care for amoebiasis, skin diseases, and accidents. Conversely, patients who needed hospitalization benefited from easier access to hospital care (Van Lerberghe and Pangu 1988).

Judging from the performance of a number of rural hospitals in central Africa, a staff composed of three physicians, perhaps one surgeon, and a support staff of about fifteen can provide the following services at an affordable cost and with reasonably good results:

- Outpatient care: treatment of emergency cases and patients referred from health centers. A nurse may provide primary care equivalent to what can be obtained at a district health center, but such care would carry a high consultation fee to discourage patients from bypassing the health center.

BOX 4-5. PROTOTYPICAL FIRST-REFERRAL HOSPITAL

Demographic profile of community to be served

Inhabitants served by the 15 health centers	150,000
Children <1 year (4 percent of the population)	6,000
Women ages 15–49 (20 percent of the population)	30,000
Children <15 years (50 percent of the population)	75,000

Package of care and services offered

Inpatient care
- Obstetrics and Gynecology
- Pediatrics
- Medicine: infectious diseases
- Medicine: limited surgery

Outpatient care
- Emergencies
- Referred patients

Other services
- Basic laboratory
- Blood bank

Staff profile
- Three medical doctors; ten registered nurses; twenty-five assistant nurses; three medical technicians
- Two management staff (including accountant)
- Fifteen support staff (including driver); two clerks

Infrastructure profile
- One building (approximately 4,000m^2; 140 beds)
- Three vehicles (including two ambulances)
- Cold storage facilities
- Medical equipment
- Other equipment (including beds, furniture, and so on)

Source: Adapted from World Bank 1993a.

■ Inpatient care: wards for pediatric patients, patients with standard serious diseases, surgery, gynecological cases, and delivery of babies.

■ Laboratory services: blood microscopy, direct examination of cerebrospinal fluids, urine and faeces tests, vaginal smears, and blood grouping. The hospital produces its own intravenous fluids, has a blood bank, and performs blood transfusions. Also important is microscopy, primarily for the detection of tuberculosis.

■ Radiography and fluoroscopy of extremities, skull, chest, stomach, and bowel.

There is, of course, great variation in district size, infrastructure, and personnel, within and among countries. Based on the median of two surveys of eighty-nine and forty hospitals, and average figures from official sources, a "typical" rural district hospital serves 110,000 to 160,000 inhabitants and has 140 beds, 3 physicians, and 15 health centers in its district. It conducts about 1,000 deliveries and hospitalizes 4,000 to 5,000 patients a year on average. Size varies from as little as thirty to forty beds in Mozambique, for example, and catchment areas of tens of thousands, as in Lesotho, to hundreds of thousands, as in Ethiopia or Tanzania (Van Lerberghe, Van Balen, and Kegels 1989; Hamel and Janssen 1988). More important than the number of beds or staff size is that the first-referral hospital functions at full capacity and is neither underused (bypassed) nor overcrowded (because it competes for patients with health centers). A prototypical first-referral hospital is depicted in Box 4-5, again with the caveat that its community profile, services, staffing, and infrastructure are at best indicative.

Well-functioning health care centers and first-referral hospitals will also make it easier for African health care systems to cope with the otherwise unmanageable task of responding to the HIV epidemic (Box 4-6).

The Role of the Large Central Hospital

Central-level hospitals in urban areas would be expected to provide technical backup and support by training health personnel for service in district-based facilities and to perform relatively rare interventions, such as cataract operations. One such hospital might also be developed as a "center of excellence," as was done in Mozambique.

The challenge is to enlist central hospitals as partners in providing more efficient and equitable health care in Africa instead of enabling them to act as competitors with lower-level facilities. Their consumption of resources then jeopardizes the provision of basic care to the entire population. Since central hospitals have benefited from elitism in national systems of health care, their actual contribution should be reexamined so that their links with the rest of the

BOX 4-6. AIDS AND HEALTH CARE REFORM IN AFRICA

The burden of AIDS underscores the importance of reforming African health care systems. Despite the incurable character of the disease, AIDS patients have begun to overwhelm hospitals in a number of African capital cities, including Bujumbura, Harare, Kampala, Kigali, Kinshasa, and Lusaka. These patients displace others who can be cured, further reducing the effectiveness of the health care system. The development and introduction of guidelines for treatment and care of AIDS patients for use by health care personnel are critical. WHO's Global Program on AIDS has done important work on this subject to help developing countries.

An appropriate public policy response by African governments to the public outcry to combat HIV infection starts with prevention. The top priority is to use available public financial and human resources for carefully targeted public education and condom promotion campaigns, and for the detection and treatment of other sexually transmitted diseases. For those affected by the opportunistic infections associated with AIDS, the first point of contact in a well-functioning health care system will be health centers for drugs, counseling, and relief of suffering. As the afflicted develop full-blown AIDS, they may need referral to a hospital. In the final stages, they tend to become bedridden at home and are best served at the community level by family members and outreach from health centers. Making the health care system function as it should can be expected to reduce what would otherwise become an unbearable burden of AIDS patients on African hospitals.

system can be better articulated. Instead of being treated as special institutions qualifying for disproportionate shares of resources, central hospitals should be scrutinized to determine whether those who need specialized procedures are actually benefiting from them, and the costs at which these services are provided. Despite a dearth of studies on the subject, few administrators of large hospitals in Africa would deny that much of their staff's time is devoted to providing primary and first-referral care.

Governments need to consider ways to enforce the use of the referral system. One option is to issue bills for charges incurred by those who deliberately bypass the referral system, assuming that well-functioning health centers and first-referral hospitals are in place.

All African governments also need to consider imposing substantial user fees at central hospitals, or else—at least in part—privatizing them, to shift additional public resources to the primary health interventions that are most cost-effective. One hundred percent cost recovery at central hospitals would not be an unreasonable goal. A possible first step would be to freeze existing budget levels for tertiary care, instead of increasing them in parallel with population growth and inflation. Prospects and methods of cost recovery are taken up in Chapter 10, and it will suffice to say here that cost recovery from patients for care at central hospitals is quite defensible, given that (i) patients are generally willing to pay for hospital care for acute problems, (ii) the demand for such care tends to be price inelastic, meaning that higher prices do not deflate demand, (iii) the clients of tertiary-level hospitals tend to be from the middle- and upper-income echelons of society, and (iv) hospitals are more likely than health centers to have the administrative capacity to assess and collect fees.

Conclusion

Far greater headway is likely to be made in resolving Sub-Saharan Africa's health crisis if systems of health care feature cost-effective packages of basic services, well-functioning health centers and first-referral hospitals at the district level, and community participation. Emphasis on basic health care services is precisely what is needed given the demographic and epidemiological profile of African societies. Development of well-functioning health centers and first-referral hospitals is compatible with the goal of promoting equity by extending services to underserved households in rural and periurban communities. By improving efficiency of health care services at the first level of contact and getting the referral system working well, prospects of bringing down skyrocketing hospital costs improve. A distinctly community focus helps to overcome weaknesses in capacity at the national level and offers the opportunity of determining a locally relevant health care package, enhancing accountability between providers and clients of health care, and mobilizing resources for intersectoral inputs to health. Finally, support from public health services can play a critical role in building more effective communication between health care providers and consumers with regard to health legislation and regulation affecting facilities and services, and thus ensure provision of health information to the public.

CHAPTER FIVE

The Importance of Pharmaceuticals and Essential Drug Programs

MEDICINES offer a simple, cost-effective answer to many health problems in Africa, provided they are available, accessible, affordable, and properly used. From the household perspective, the availability of medicines is one of the most visible symbols of quality care. In Senegal between 1981 and 1989, for example, household expenditures for drugs accounted for half (48 percent) of all health expenditures.

Africa's health care providers also see a regular supply of drugs as a fundamental component of a well-functioning health system. At public and private health facilities in Africa, pharmaceutical expenditures typically make up 20 to 30 percent of total recurrent costs, ranking second only to personnel costs (World Bank 1992d). They also represent a sizable share of per capita expenditures on health.

The importance of drugs to consumers and health providers alike is also illustrated by what happens when drugs are unavailable: visits to health facilities decline precipitously. Studies in Nigeria, for example, showed that when health facilities ran out of commonly used drugs, visits by patients dropped by 50 to 75 percent.

Because pharmaceuticals are a highly marketable product and such a vital component of health care, and because more than 90 percent of the pharmaceuticals used in Sub-Saharan Africa are imported, African governments often intervene in drug markets. Their aim is to make sure that the pharmaceuticals used in their countries will be effective and are purchased at the lowest possible cost.

Some African governments have formulated national drug policies, created lists of essential drugs, and instituted quality controls. Since consumers seldom choose a particular drug themselves, relying instead on medical personnel or vendors of drugs, African governments also disseminate much information on drug safety and use.

This chapter begins by documenting problems that are undermining the potential contribution of pharmaceuticals to better health in Africa. Inefficiencies and waste in the management of pharmaceuticals are highlighted. This sets the stage for a discussion of more efficient, equitable, and sustainable drug practices. Broad guidelines for action are then suggested for inclusion in government programs of health care system reform.

The Performance of African Pharmaceutical Markets

In the mid-1980s, the World Health Organization conducted a survey of 104 developing countries to determine the domestic availability of essential drugs (WHO 1988d). In seventeen countries (including Nigeria), with a combined population of about 200 million people, about 70 percent had no regular access to essential drugs. In another fourteen countries, also accounting for about 200 million people, an estimated 40 to 70 percent of the population had no regular access. And in nine countries with a combined population of 50 million people, an estimated 10 to 30 percent had no regular access. These data, along with information from other sources, suggest that up to 60 percent of the inhabitants of Sub-Saharan Africa has no regular access to the drugs they need.

Shortages of appropriate drugs afflict public sector health facilities in many African countries, especially at the lower levels. Drug stock-outs due to management, logistical, and financial problems have been widely documented, especially in periurban and rural areas. In Angola, drug stock-outs are frequent, even at major hospitals. In seven provinces for which data are available, only 48 percent of the communities reported regular health staff visits (*controlo sanitario* visits) to resupply local health facilities with drugs and other supplies. In Tanzania, underfinancing of drug purchases by the Ministry of Health has led to shortages of medicines in hospitals and reliance on foreign aid to provide drugs for rural primary care.

Private-for-profit facilities in Africa experience fewer problems with drug shortages. They have the funds to buy for their limited (and hence high-cost) markets because their clients tend to be upper-income households in urban areas. Trained pharmacists are few, and they generally prefer to open retail pharmacies in urban areas and to trade largely in western specialty drugs. Wholesalers, and representatives of industrial country drug firms, thus also prefer to work with the private pharmacies in large cities. In Niger, for example, 46 percent of all private drug sales in 1986 took place in Niamey, the national capital, and another 35 percent were concentrated in the capital cities of smaller regions. Only about 20 percent occurred in rural areas, even though about 80 percent of the population lives in the countryside.

The organized private sector also benefits from a widespread belief that its products are superior and thus worth a much higher price. In Sierra Leone in 1983, for example, the markup on private sector sales of chloroquine ranged from 400 to 800 percent. Moreover, a common misconception among consumers (as well as prescribers) is that generic or low-cost drugs supplied through public agencies are inferior to those sold in the private sector. This is rarely the case, but the misconception often leads to wasteful drug decisions. In Kenya, for example, it was found that some patients traded in their free generic drugs at pharmacies to buy identical specialty drugs, which they believed were better (Ministry of Health, Kenya 1984).

The residents of periurban and rural areas generally find that irregular private suppliers are more accessible sources of drugs, but the quality of their services is often poor. Moreover, drugs sold by these suppliers have frequently been stolen from the public sector or imported from neighboring countries where quality control is absent (Whyte 1990). Irregular suppliers cannot be ignored, however. In Togo in 1989, for example, they were estimated to account for 35 percent of the supply of antimalarial drugs.

Medicines that do reach their destination are often inappropriately prescribed. A survey in Mali found that the average prescription called for ten drugs, sometimes including duplication of the same drug under different names. In many cases, it is likely that one or two drugs would have sufficed (Foster 1990). A study of the treatment of a large number of patients with diarrhea in Nigeria found that drug expenditures were some thirty times higher than necessary, largely because of the prescribing of specialty antibiotics that were more potent than necessary (Isenalumhe and Ovbiawe 1988). Although drug injections are standard treatment for only a minority of patients, a study in Ghana found that 96 percent of the patients were given at least one injection and then were given prescriptions that called, on average, for the use of four different drugs (Dabis and others 1988). Even essential drugs are often misused because limited understanding leads to poor compliance with prescribed regimens (Foster 1990).

Many developing countries have launched essential drug programs (EDPs) to improve availability, affordability, and proper use. To help facilitate these programs, the World Health Organization has prepared a model list of about 250 essential drugs that can effectively treat, at reasonable cost, a large majority of the ailments frequently experienced in Africa and other regions of the world. In Angola, an EDP was launched in 1987, supported by the Swedish International Development Agency (SIDA) in cooperation with UNICEF. An evaluation of Angola's EDP by SIDA and the Ministry of Health in 1990 revealed problems common to a number of African countries:

Table 5-1. Expenditures on Pharmaceuticals in Selected African Countries, Mid-1980s

Country	Year	Estimated public pharmaceutical expenditures (millions of U.S. dollars)	Estimated private pharmaceutical expenditures	Estimated total pharmaceutical expenditures	Estimated per capita pharmaceutical expenditures (U.S. dollars)	Pharmaceutical expenditures as share of GDP (estimate) (percent)
Burkina Faso	1981	5.5	10.1	15.6	2.19	1.38
Côte d'Ivoire	1985	2.7	81.5	84.2	8.63	0.57
Ethiopia	1986	8.7	33.8	42.5	0.95	0.86
Kenya	1986	16.0	34.0	50.0	2.36	0.84
Mozambique	1985	5.6	1.3	6.9	0.50	0.21
Niger	1989	5.9	18.3	24.2	3.20	1.03
Sudan	1988	5.5	49.5	55.0	2.31	0.49
Tanzania	1987	19.9	10.7	30.7	1.32	1.00
Zimbabwe	1988	15.1	6.5	21.5	2.42	0.38
Weighted average					2.10	0.76

Source: World Bank 1992d.

- The EDP was a vertical program with very little coordination with other programs.
- The EDP was not supplemented by a training program for health care providers.
- The information and feedback system on EDP performance was complicated and of little practical use, partially because the responsibilities and tasks of the National Pharmaceutical Directorate and the National Directorate of Public Health were poorly coordinated.
- The country did not have a well-defined pharmaceutical policy, although a National Drug Commission exists.

The experience of Ethiopia confirms that adoption of an essential drugs list is not enough. Such a list was adopted in 1985. Two years later, however, a complete selection of these essential drugs was found in only 7 percent of the country's health centers. A much more basic list of ten drugs was available at only 38 percent of the centers (Hodes and Kloos 1988).

Constraints and Opportunities

The performance of pharmaceutical markets is shaped by the interaction of a variety of demand and supply factors. Some of these present greater obstacles to resolving shortages of drugs than others and require coordinated action. In most African countries, private expenditures dominate pharmaceutical markets, as in Burkina Faso, Côte d'Ivoire, Ethiopia, Kenya, Niger, and the Sudan. A clear indication that private expenditures, consumer preferences, and ability to pay are important determining factors in the availability of medicines is apparent from Table 5-1. In six of nine countries for which data are available, private expenditures on drugs easily exceed public expenditures.

On the demand side, the most important factors are income, price, disease patterns, and the educational levels of consumers.

- *Income*. Differences in household expenditures on drugs closely follow differences in per capita GNP. In Ethiopia, where the average per capita GNP was about $130 in 1987, pharmaceutical expenditures at the time were about $0.95 per capita. In Sudan and Kenya, each with per capita GNP of about $330 in 1987, pharmaceutical expenditures were about $2.30 to $2.40 per capita. And in Côte d'Ivoire, with a per capita GNP of about $740, expenditures on drugs were about $8.60 per capita.

As might be expected, moreover, expenditures on drugs by high-income households greatly exceed those of the poor. Survey data on Ghana, for example, show that per capita household expenditures on medicines are several times larger in the highest income quintile than in the lowest (Table 5-2). Hence, effective demand for drugs is likely to be relatively weak among the poorest groups in periurban and rural areas. Because such groups tend to rely disproportionately on public sector health facilities, they suffer most from disruptions in the supply of medicines at government facilities.

As a rule of thumb, a 10 percent rise in GNP per capita means an 11 to 13 percent increase in per capita drug expenditures (Dunlop and Over 1988; Vogel and Stephens 1989; Gertler and van der Gaag 1990). And just as higher income tends to raise consumption of pharmaceuticals, a decline in per capita income can have the opposite effect. Since the per capita incomes and real purchasing power of African households generally declined during the 1980s, the implication is that falling incomes were at least partly responsible for changes in drug expenditures. Among the seven African countries for which time-trend data are available for at least four years, a drop in the share of pharmaceuticals in the recurrent expenditures of health facilities was apparent in Botswana, Kenya, Ethiopia, and Côte d'Ivoire.

■ *Price.* Available evidence suggests that demand for medicines is relatively inelastic with respect to price—that is, demand remains relatively steady even when prices go up (World Bank 1992d). An experiment in Cameroon showed that use of public sector health facilities by poor households actually grew when price increases were accompanied by improvements in health services, including greater drug supply reliability. There is also evidence to show, however, that demand falls more sharply with rising prices among the poor than among more affluent groups, as happened in Côte d'Ivoire (Gertler and van der Gaag 1990; Mwabu 1984).

Table 5-2.   Per Capita Household Expenditures on Medicines, Ghana, 1987–88
(U.S. dollars)

Household income quintile	Expenditures
1	1.45
2	2.21
3	3.32
4	4.24
5	8.50
Average	3.93

Source: Boateng and others 1989.

■ *Disease patterns.* Changes in patterns of disease and mortality have an effect on the kinds of drugs in greatest demand and, sometimes, the cost of particular kinds of drugs. Mortality and morbidity in Sub-Saharan Africa are dominated by perinatal, infectious, and parasitic health problems, which suggests that it is possible to create a standard package of essential drugs that can handle a sizable majority of the health problems in Africa. The World Health Organization has quantified drug costs on the basis of available morbidity data and information on past consumption in several African countries. The results, summarized in Table 5-3, show that a standard supply chest of thirty to forty drugs in a well-functioning health center results in a drug cost of about $0.31, on average, per treatment episode. Treatment of more complex illnesses with commensurate drug regimes is estimated to cost about $0.47 at a hospital outpatient department. WHO concluded that the range of drug costs portrayed in Table 5-3 is surprisingly low when compared with expenditure levels that prevail in many countries, although these average cost estimates assume a degree of supply efficiency that is rare in most Sub-Saharan countries (WHO 1988c).

■ *Educational levels.* Consumers with higher levels of education use over-the-counter medications more appropriately and seek care earlier than those with limited education (Haynes and others 1976). In view of the high levels of illiteracy in Africa, especially among females, this suggests that additional information, education, and communication programs could make an immense contribution to more efficient drug use.

Table 5-3.   Average Drug Costs Per Treatment Episode by Level of Care, Selected African Countries and Years, 1983–88
(U.S. dollars)

Country and year	Health center	Hospital outpatient department
Kenya	0.20[a]	0.50[b]
Sudan, 1985	0.32	0.59
Burundi, 1986	0.37	—
Gambia, The, 1987	0.35	0.50
Guinea-Bissau, 1987	0.31	—
Uganda, 1988	0.29	0.29
Average	0.31	0.47

— Not available.
a. 1984.
b. 1985.
Source: WHO 1988c.

A Supply-Side Perspective

It is frequently argued that shortages of drugs in Sub-Saharan Africa are the result of disincentives for domestic production and barriers to imports. Some analysts contend that local production would lead to savings of scarce foreign exchange, allow drugs to be produced at less cost (local labor being cheaper), and eliminate the risk of paying foreign companies for out-of-date drugs. These arguments are questionable, however. Although independent studies of local drug production costs are rare (especially by type of drug), expert opinion suggests that international drug makers typically realize full economies of scale with higher quality standards at non-African production facilities than would be possible in most African countries in the foreseeable future.

The extremely competitive world market for generic drugs makes it doubtful that production should be started now in countries without a pharmaceutical manufacturing tradition. The only exceptions would be products whose transport costs when imported are disproportionately high, as in the case of certain intravenous fluids. Where there is a nucleus of local production, a phased approach is likely to show the most promise, starting with the tableting and packaging of widely used items, such as aspirin and chloroquine. Intermediate phases involve increasingly complex production processes until, ultimately, local industry begins to create and produce pharmaceuticals (World Bank 1985). This pattern can be seen in such countries as Ethiopia, Sudan, Kenya, Ghana, and Zimbabwe, all countries where local companies were producing a growing share of total domestic consumption by 1992. In Kenya, for example, supplies of the first essential drug kit (composed of about twenty pharmaceuticals designed for rural health facilities) were imported, but supplies of the second (with twelve items) are largely produced locally (London School of Hygiene 1989). In Ethiopia, about 30 percent of domestic demand for drugs is now met by domestic production using imported raw materials. Thus, while the prospects are slim that economically competitive, large-scale domestic production can be relied on to meet shortfalls in essential drugs, many African countries should be able to expand the production and packaging of certain drugs over the next decade or so.

Given Africa's reliance on pharmaceutical imports, the availability of foreign exchange constitutes another important supply-side constraint. Because the accumulation of foreign exchange is contingent on export earnings and terms of trade, it is not surprising that external resources have been needed to sustain Africa's pharmaceutical imports. Major partners include DANIDA, SIDA, ODA, USAID, the World Bank, and the Drug Action Program of WHO. Total known assistance exceeds $160 million per year, though the actual amount may be several times higher.

Still, the level of international assistance is small when compared to the size of the African market, which was estimated at somewhere between $850 million and $1.5 billion for 1989 (World Bank 1992d). Moreover, foreign exchange can be squandered if the private sector imports expensive specialty drugs that are no better than generics. Assuming that the willingness of donors to provide support cannot always be foreseen, the availability of foreign currency resources, as well as their use for public and private sector drug imports, needs to be evaluated critically.

Inefficiency and Waste in Pharmaceutical Markets

Since pharmaceutical markets in Africa are heavily influenced by private and public expenditures, income levels, and drug prices, it is tempting to attribute shortages to insufficient funding, particularly in periods of economic decline. And because pharmaceutical markets will continue to rely heavily on imports, it is tempting to seek remedies in donations, loans, and the allocation of more public funds for drugs, especially in view of uncertainties over future economic growth. Yet studies published as far back as 1984 claim that full drug coverage could be achieved in Africa for less than $1 per person a year (Kasongo Project Team 1984; Steenstrup 1984; Jancloes and others 1985). These impressions are supported by evidence marshaled by WHO and shown in Table 5-3.

Although world commodity prices have risen since 1985, the $1 figure remains generally valid because international competition in the generic drug market has intensified and drug prices have actually gone down. And $1 per capita is clearly below the average per capita expenditure of about $2.10 computed for the nine countries in Table 5-1. This suggests that demand and supply constraints, as important as they may be, are *not* the main cause of drug shortages in Africa.

The most important problem is inefficiency and waste. In Nigeria, for example, technical reviews of public sector health facilities revealed that ineffectual and even dangerous drugs had frequently been procured, that brand-name rather than less expensive generic drugs are purchased, that drugs are often purchased locally in small quantities instead of in bulk from foreign producers, that many drugs become unusable because of faulty storage practices or disappear because of inadequate stock control procedures, and that health personnel tend to prescribe excessive numbers of drugs for patients in their attempt to treat a number of possible diseases simultaneously.

Because of widespread inefficiencies and waste, patients at public sector health facilities in Sub-Saharan Africa may be effectively receiving the benefits of only $12 worth of quality drugs for each $100 of tax money spent for them.

Figure 5-1. Inefficiency and Waste in the Supply of Drugs from Budget Allocation to Consumer

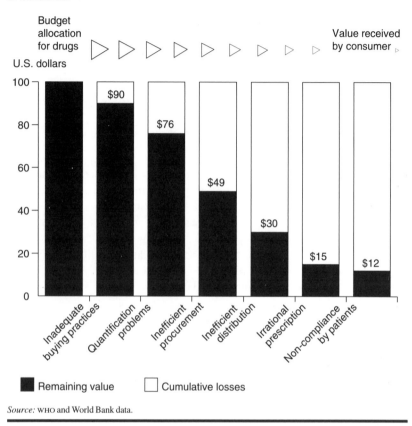

Source: WHO and World Bank data.

What follows is an explanation of the factors that produce this meager return on investment.

First, the selection of drugs tends not to be based on cost-effectiveness criteria. Prices for different drugs for the same condition commonly vary by as much as five to ten times and, in some cases, by as much as 130 to 150 times. Investigation of the drugs used in African countries in the 1980s, for example, reveals that high-cost drugs purchased for urinary tract infections, arthritis, and inflammation were six, eight, and twelve times more expensive, respectively, than their low-cost alternatives. An assessment of drug practices in Africa during the 1980s by WHO suggests that the absence of cost-effective selection was responsible for a 10 percent loss in spending power (WHO 1988c). As illustrated in Figure 5-1, this is equivalent to reducing the postulated $100 to $90.

Second, few attempts are made to quantify the amounts of any drug that will be needed over a given period (usually a year). When drug needs have been quantified on the basis of morbidity patterns, large quantities can be bought at substantial savings. It has been estimated, for example, that a system for calculating essential drug requirements could have reduced Gabon's drug expenditures in 1986–87 by up to 45 percent (Soeters and Bannenberg 1988). On average, failure to order on this basis can result in a loss of $13 for every $100 spent. In Figure 5-1, $77 now remains of the original $100 for drugs.

Third, procurement is rarely based on competitive bidding for generic drugs. Direct imports from high-priced sources tend to be "arranged." Yet astute buying on the world market has sometimes reduced the average cost of drugs imported by African countries by up to 40 percent (Marzagao and Segall 1983; Hogerzeil and Moore 1987; Yudkin 1980). A WHO study (1988c) of buying practices in Nigeria found that by shifting from brand name to generic drugs, costs could be reduced by another 25 percent. On average, losses from inefficient procurement of drugs have been estimated to amount to about $27 of every $100 spent. In Figure 5-1 the balance is now $49.

Fourth are poor storage and management practices. It has been estimated that 15 to 25 percent of the drugs imported by some countries remain unused until their shelf life ends (WHO 1986; Management Sciences for Health 1984). A study in Cameroon revealed that central medical stores lost 35 percent of their drugs because of poor storage and poor inventory control (Van der Geest, Sjaak, and Whyte 1982). In Uganda, a third of all drugs are thought to be lost to theft and corruption. In Cameroon, 30 to 40 percent may be "withdrawn for private use" by staff. In 1984 in Guinea, an estimated 70 percent of the government drug supply disappeared (Foster 1990). In Tanzania, the rate of pilferage for drugs not included in the essential drugs program was estimated at about 30 percent. On average, losses from poor storage and distribution have been estimated to amount to about $19 of every $100 spent. In Figure 5-1 the balance is now $30.

Fifth, irrational prescription of drugs contributes further to inefficiencies. A study conducted in the Kivu Region of Zaire found that a "typical" prescription filled by a private pharmacy for treatment of bronchitis in young children listed five or six drugs, including an antibiotic, cough syrup, a tranquilizer, vitamins, aspirin, and, if fever was present, antimalarials, for an average cost equal to approximately one month's per capita income. Studies in 1992 of health care facilities in Nigeria and Tanzania found, on average, 3.8 and 2.2 drugs, respectively, per prescription (WHO 1993b). On average, losses from irrational drug prescriptions have been estimated to reduce drugs effectively made available to patients by 50 percent. In Figure 5-1 the balance is now reduced from $30 to $15.

Sixth, incorrect use of drugs by patients reduces the proportion of drugs that are used effectively. Researchers in Zimbabwe concluded that self-medication with chloroquine for malaria prophylaxis was common but that the drug was often wrongly used, and that better public information was needed to make self-medication effective (Stein, Gora, and Macheka 1988). In other cases, essential drugs show poor results because patients failed to comply with the proper drug regimens (Foster 1990). On average, losses from poor compliance reduce drugs effectively used by 20 percent. This cuts the remaining amount in Figure 5-1 to just $12.

The Essential Problem

The reality in many African countries is that pharmaceutical markets are not efficient, equitable, or sustainable. Commitments to primary health care become merely symbolic when reliable supplies of medicines are not easily available in periurban and rural areas. This prompts households to buy medicines from itinerant traders or to travel to intermediate-level facilities and hospitals where they are available.

Cost-effective care is further compromised because chronic illnesses are not treated by relatively simple regimens of essential drugs that can be procured in bulk at far less cost than when individual consumers purchase them.

Because of inefficiencies and waste, far more is being spent on pharmaceuticals than is necessary, erroneously reinforcing the view that the answer to drug shortages in Africa is more money. Far greater headway is likely to be achieved through more effective use of existing resources. At the same time, though, ways must be found to sustain the revenues that are needed to pay for drug supplies, particularly those used by public sector health care providers, and to ensure that foreign exchange reserves are available to pay for imports.

Overcoming Obstacles

It has been estimated that the annual per capita cost of essential drugs at a well-functioning health center in Africa ranges from $0.10 to $0.25 (World Bank 1993a). When drug needs at the district hospital level are added, the cost rises to about $1 per person a year. This is enough to pay for the essential generic drugs needed to treat 85 percent of the illnesses most commonly found in Africa. Expanded diagnosis and treatment of sexually transmitted diseases, a need brought about by the AIDS epidemic, could reasonably be expected to raise the figure to about $1.60 per person (Chapter 8). This is less than the per capita expenditure on drugs in six of the nine countries in Table 5-1 and is also close to the amount spent by those in the lowest income quintiles in Ghana (Table 5-2).

To improve drug distribution in low-income areas, many African countries (Kenya, Tanzania, Uganda, Sierra Leone, Zambia) buy prepackaged drug kits assembled by wholesalers. The contents of the kits are determined by average patterns of use. The kits eliminate some of the managerial problems that now afflict centralized distribution systems. Care is needed, however, to make sure that the kits take into account differential patterns of morbidity by region. Government officials must also make sure that the kit system is not sabotaged by new forms of waste and corruption.

Drug distribution problems could also be reduced by estimating the quantities of basic pharmaceuticals needed at different levels of the referral system. Generally speaking, only twenty to forty pharmaceutical items are indispensable for primary care at health centers (Brudon-Jakobowicz 1987). Quantification of requirements is relatively easy at this level because demographic and epidemiological profiles can be readily determined and actual practices at health centers and district hospitals can be assessed. The limited range of products needed also increases the likelihood that prescription practices will be guided by standard treatment protocols.

In well-functioning health centers, one-to-one transmission of information to consumers by providers has been shown to improve compliance with drug regimens. As part of this process, prescribers at health centers can be held accountable by a community clientele that provides feedback on drug effectiveness, undesirable side effects, and so on.

In response to the declining availability of public resources for financing pharmaceuticals, a growing number of communities have adopted cost recovery and self-financing schemes. Many such schemes have evolved under the Bamako Initiative. In Benin, for example, attempts to resolve financial shortages produced an experimental scheme under which patients pay for the essential drugs they receive. The fee was set at three times the actual cost of the medications used and covers 85 percent of local operating costs, excluding salaries. Over a three-year period, fee receipts increased as the public gradually accepted the system and its generic products.

A popular form of community financing is the so-called drug revolving fund. This is begun with an initial stock of drugs donated by the community, the government, or some other donor. The drugs are then sold to community members at prices that allow for full cost recovery, and the revenues are used to replace stock and finance other operating and distribution costs. Drug revolving funds can be operated on a public, private-voluntary, or private, for-profit basis. Such funds have been introduced in Benin, Cameroon, the Central African Republic, Chad, Liberia, Mali, Niger, Nigeria, Senegal, Sierra Leone, Sudan, Tanzania, and Zaire.

Experience offers several lessons about the operation of drug revolving funds:

■ Sharp price increases should be avoided, especially in areas where the population is not accustomed to paying for public sector services (Blakney, Litvak, and Quick 1989). Gradual price increases over time, accompanied by service improvements, will be more successful. Another approach is to establish a set of declining subsidies over the years rather than carry out an immediate switch to full cost recovery.

■ A few experiments with revolving drug funds in Senegal, Niger, and Mali have run into problems because patient contributions were insufficient to maintain program momentum (Cross and others 1986; World Bank 1992d). These problems tend to reflect a failure to establish an effective scheme for the collection of payments or to provide realistically for the indigent. They may also be the result of an overambitious national program introduced without a period of testing through small pilot projects.

■ Cost recovery programs based on the amount of drugs sold may create incentives for overprescription and inappropriate use of drugs. Standard treatment protocols, external supervision, and payment by illness episode can help reduce these incentives (McPake and others 1992).

The Role of National Governments

Improving the impact of medicines on health in Africa requires a facilitating environment in which public officials, suppliers and distributors of drugs, and providers of health care act together to promote effective use of drugs. This means making them available and affordable. Governments have an especially important leadership role to play in instituting and maintaining quality controls, disseminating information on the proper use of drugs to prescribers and consumers, and monitoring drug reform (Box 5-1). Governments should also take the lead by establishing a *national drug policy*, overseeing the planning, programming and budgeting of national capacity in the pharmaceuticals area, and identifying suitably trained personnel to implement financial management and drug information systems.

National drug policies also need a *firm legal basis*. Existing laws and regulations tend to be concerned largely with quality control or new drug approval. A small but efficient drug authority, with a degree of autonomy and close links to government and nongovernment bodies involved with drugs, is likely to result in a more coordinated and consistent multisectoral effort. Much can be accomplished through information, persuasion, and incentives for all parties, coupled with a modicum of effective control to counter abuses. Least effective is to base policies on prohibition and repression. Unhealthy practices in the drug field are most effectively countered by offering acceptable alternatives. The case of drug peddlers in Kenya is typical. They largely lost their disreputable trade in malaria remedies once village health workers were adequately supplied with antimalarials (Mburu, Spenser, and Kaseje 1987; Whyte 1990).

Ongoing estimates of drug needs are required to ensure that the vast majority of the population has access to cost-effective medicines. Purchasing too much, or importing the wrong drugs, is obviously wasteful, but inadequate purchasing will result in shortages, which in turn can lead to emergency buying on the private market at inflated prices. Needs estimates are best made by a joint group of health professionals and resource managers convened by a drug authority (Box 5-2). The estimates can be published, and invited commentary by providers and users at national, regional, and community level can be constructive. Guidance on prices and sources of good-quality drugs is available from regularly updated drug price lists issued by the WHO Essential Drugs Programme, UNICEF, Management Sciences for Health (MSH), and the International Dispensary Association, a nonprofit wholesale procurement organization that purchases drugs and medical equipment for noncommercial health care projects.

Encouraging the development of the private noncommercial sector, including religious missions and such humanitarian bodies as Médecins sans Frontières and the Red Cross Pharmacies in Ethiopia, is another means of expanding drug coverage. Various religious missions in Africa are considering cooperating with one another to establish their own organizations for purchasing, warehousing, and distributing drugs, primarily to mission hospitals. In Zaire, concrete proposals were made in the early 1980s, and were widely endorsed in church circles, to establish a nonprofit pharmaceuticals purchasing group. These are often efficient operations, reflecting idealism and pragmatism. In several instances they have been guided into the essential drugs approach and use of generics to make better use of their resources (Hogerzeil and Lamberts 1984; Hogerzeil and Moore 1987).

Governments can also foster *the private commercial sector* by authorizing health services and hospitals to purchase drugs from private firms whose terms are more attractive and supplies more consistent than those of central medical stores. The private sector has the same access to the world generic market as the public sector, and is often capable of obtaining better prices through its international commercial contacts and profit-making incentives. The expansion of social marketing of essential pharmaceutical products, such as contraceptives, can further stimulate development of the private commercial sector.

Where there is no viable nongovernment alternative, African governments will need to continue to correct the principal defects of public sector phar-

---

---

maceutical entities while providing incentives for creating private sector bodies
to compete effectively with them. The ultimate balance between the public and
private sectors cannot be predicted, and will probably vary from country to
country. In some, the private sector may well develop to the point where it
entirely supplants public mechanisms. However, a public system to purchase
and distribute drugs should not simply be replaced by an unregulated private
monopoly or cartel. In some cases, efforts to increase the efficiency of public
sector pharmaceutical entities can be justified as part of a program to prepare
parastatal bodies for sale to the private sector.

Finally, assuming that the willingness of donors to provide support cannot
always be foreseen, governments need to evaluate critically the availability of
foreign currency resources and the extent of their reliance on imported drugs. In
the absence of an open trade and exchange regime, a first step could be to establish interministerial agreements on reserving foreign exchange for drug purchases, a practice followed by Zimbabwe. A commitment to concentrate

Box 5-1, continued

Bulletins. Information can be promoted through television and other media, and governments can take steps to counter misleading information. International standards for ethical advertising have been established by the pharmaceuticals industry and by WHO.

Governments also have a critical role to play in *monitoring drug reforms*. Monitoring of reforms can be guided by:

■ Plans for drug reform, detailing anticipated improvements in efficiency, mobilization of the private sector, establishment of improved training and drug information for medical personnel, and provision of drug information to the public.

■ The proportion of drugs on an agreed national essential drug list that are accessible, without unreasonable constraints imposed by distance, irregular distribution, or financial barriers, to at least 80 percent of the population.

■ The efficiency with which resources are used in procurement, by determining (a) whether expensive specialty drugs are being imported in cases where a high-quality generic drug is much cheaper, and if so, why, and (b) the price paid for a standard mixed drug sample compared with that paid elsewhere.

■ Efficiency of prescribing. Sample drug use studies can be carried out using well-established methods, as in Zimbabwe (van der Geest and Whyte 1988). The African "Drug Utilization Research Group" sponsored by WHO provides guidance in this area.

■ Assessments of the ability and willingness of consumers to pay for drugs, analyzed for various socioeconomic groups.

use of foreign exchange on drugs used at health centers and district hospitals may help. Long-term agreements can sometimes be negotiated with donors. This is far more likely, however, if donors are satisfied that care at health centers is improving and waste is being reduced. This subject is revisited in the costing and financing of basic health services in Chapters 9 and 10.

A variety of new models for cooperation among interested parties is emerging, as in Benin and Cameroon. The essential characteristics are government leadership on policy, operational responsibility and program execution through a private voluntary association, and transparency of management of resources.

Conclusion

Drugs are essential to health improvement in Africa, but informational asymmetries, the separation of financiers from decisionmakers at the consumption

---

BOX 5-2. EVALUATION OF DRUG NEEDS IN AFRICA NEED NOT BE DIFFICULT

In Bobo-Dioulasso (Burkina Faso), officials used the WHO method to evaluate drug needs, based on morbidity figures at three dispensaries examined over a six-to-twelve-month period. It was assumed that standardized schemes of treatment would be used. Results were expressed per 1,000 inhabitants a year. Results proved to be reproducible. The method is so simple that after brief training it could easily be used by trained nurses. It resulted in important corrections of preconceived ideas about what was needed. For example, the need for injectable products proved to have been overestimated (Malkin, Carpenntier, and Lefaix 1987).

---

level, and poor management of drug supplies render pharmaceutical markets in most countries of Sub-Saharan Africa highly inefficient. Hence, there is great potential for increasing drug coverage while reducing costs. There is promising evidence that essential drugs can be provided for around $1.60 per capita annually for clients of well-functioning health centers and district hospitals and that community-managed drug revolving funds can help assure sustainability of supplies. Actions to reduce waste are required at all stages of the supply chain, from domestic distribution policies to the prescription practices of medical personnel and the use of drugs by patients. Monitoring of drug reform, and periodic assessments of progress, are essential.

The assignment of public policy responsibility for drug management to a national drug authority is needed. Consensus-building should be its style. Operational responsibilities for wholesale drug purchase and distribution need to be increasingly assigned to the nongovernment sector. To help facilitate this process, governments should foster the development of the private commercial and noncommercial drug sectors, reinvigorate public sector distribution efficiency, and promote cost-effective means of supplying essential drugs on a sustainable and affordable basis to the poorest groups in society.

CHAPTER SIX

Managing Human Resources for Health

TO PERFORM effectively, Sub-Saharan Africa's health systems need professionally trained and strongly motivated personnel who are paid fairly for what they do. Unless these conditions prevail, the quantity and quality of health services will be severely compromised. They can make or break otherwise cost-effective approaches to health care.

Personnel costs constitute the largest item in ministry of health budgets. On average, more than 60 percent of all public funds for health are allocated to wages and salaries. Since most of those who provide health services in Africa have been trained at public expense, those selected for such training must be carefully chosen, and government actions that affect their subsequent careers must be rational and wise. This chapter documents Africa's serious and widespread health personnel problems and assesses their causes and consequences. The rest of the chapter deals with what can be done to rectify the problems as part of countrywide health system reform programs.

The Contrasting Problems of Undersupply and Underuse

One of the chief problems that must be overcome if African health is to be improved to a satisfactory level is an *undersupply* of sufficiently trained personnel. High rates of attrition are often part of the cause. Attrition is especially damaging when public funds have been used to train personnel who later leave the public sector. In Zimbabwe, for example, it was projected that roughly 1,500 registered nurses would leave public service between 1991 and 1995, an annual attrition rate of 7.1 percent. Uganda lost about 40 percent of the nurses in public service and 50 percent of the medical assistants in public service in 1986. Another group with high attrition is female health workers, who leave their jobs to marry and raise children (Vaughan 1992).

Large numbers of health personnel have left African countries altogether in recent years. Those who emigrate are mainly highly trained staff, such as physicians, nurses, pharmacists, and senior laboratory technicians. The emigrés leave in hope of finding better salaries and working conditions in other countries while escaping from political and social problems in their home countries. Since senior personnel are those most likely to emigrate, medical training, health research, and management capabilities are weakened.

Emigration of health personnel whose training was financed by the government also means that the government suffers a direct financial loss. It has been estimated, for instance, that the average loss incurred when a doctor emigrated from Nigeria was $30,000 (Ojo 1990).

Table 6-1 shows that the population to doctor ratio in Africa is about six times higher than the ratio for all developing countries, although the situation has improved quite a bit over the last thirty years. In 1970 there were 19,000 persons per physician and 3,000 persons per nurse or midwife in Sub-Saharan Africa, but the most recent data show that the ratios had improved to 10,800 persons per physician and 2,100 persons per nurse or midwife. The supply of trained personnel remains woefully inadequate, however. Over the period 1988 to 1992, for example, fewer than 40 percent of African mothers had assistance from a doctor, nurse, or midwife during childbirth.

The averages shown in Table 6-1 conceal great variations from one country to the next. In 1987, for example, Gabon had one doctor per 3,000 inhabitants while Ethiopia had one per 29,000 inhabitants. In Botswana, there was one nurse or midwife for every 500 people but in Rwanda only one for every 20,000.

Although improvements in the supply of health personnel occurred in the 1960s and 1970s, the situation deteriorated in the 1980s. Between 1980 and

Table 6-1.   Supply of Human Resources In Health Services, 1985–90

Item	Sub-Saharan Africa	All developing countries	Industrial countries	World
Population per doctor	10,800	1,400	300	800
Population per nurse[a]	2,100	1,700	170	530
Nurses per doctor	5.0	1.0	2.0	1.5

Note: Doctors are MDs only; nurses are registered nurses and registered midwives only.
a. Includes midwives.
Source: WHO 1988e, 1992a.

1986, Sub-Saharan Africa was the only region of the world where the number of doctors for every 10,000 people fell.

A second problem, which might seem unlikely in Sub-Saharan Africa, is underuse of trained personnel. Underuse, as shown below, takes various forms:

■ High-level administrative positions in ministries of health are often filled by medical doctors rather than by professionals trained in management, planning, and budgeting. In Ghana, for example, the official view is that most of the top management positions in the Ministry of Health should be held by physicians. In Niger in 1984, nineteen out of the fifty-two doctors employed by the Ministry of Health also served as full-time or part-time administrators. But assigning physicians to managerial work means that their medical expertise is wasted. Their ability to deal with medical problems is underused, even though the country may lack the number of physicians it needs. The prestige of physicians, in short, leads to their being given tasks that they are seldom prepared to perform successfully.

■ In Uganda in 1990, doctors in Ministry of Health hospitals saw far fewer patients per day (1.3) than doctors in private voluntary hospitals (6.7). According to a government study, underuse was so prevalent that Uganda would be able to reduce the number of its health care personnel by 30 percent without affecting the quality of service (Republic of Uganda, Ministry of Health 1991). Similarly low productivity levels have been reported among public sector health personnel in Mali. Such low productivity, it should be noted, is frequently caused by lack of equipment and supplies.

■ If Rwanda's 500 midwives were fully used (meaning each urban midwife would attend around 300 births a year and each rural midwife about 200), about 36 percent of all deliveries would be assisted by trained staff. In fact, only 18 percent of all deliveries are attended by trained personnel. This suggests that around half of Rwanda's midwives are significantly underused (Figure 6-1).

In view of the above, it may seem ironic that a number of African countries are beginning to experience a surplus of health care providers. Even though the number of health personnel completing their education and training has risen, the demand in some countries for new staff in the public sector has fallen. In Tanzania, 1,500 doctors and other health school graduates used to be absorbed into public service annually, but this is no longer true. Mozambique also guaranteed public sector employment to graduates of health training institutions in the past but has had to cut back the number of trainees in recent years.

Benin, Madagascar, Mali, and Zaire now absorb only a fraction of their health school graduates through public employment. In Mali in 1987, the gov-

Figure 6-1. Undersupply and Underuse of Human Resources in Health Services: Percentage of Deliveries Attended and Not Attended by Trained Personnel, Rwanda, 1985

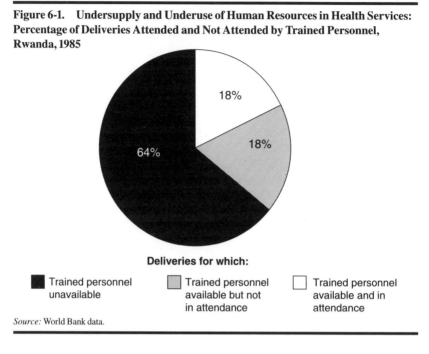

Deliveries for which:

| ■ Trained personnel unavailable | ▨ Trained personnel available but not in attendance | □ Trained personnel available and in attendance |

Source: World Bank data.

ernment recruited only four of the country's sixty new physicians, only one out of the thirty-five pharmacy graduates, and nineteen out of the eighty-five new nurses. Projections made in the late 1980s showed that at prevailing rates of absorption in the public sector, Madagascar might have a cumulative surplus of 2,600 to 3,200 physicians in ten years.

While there are sometimes too many physicians and other health care specialists, the supply of specialists in administrative posts is often perilously thin. Ministries of health and other public health institutions face serious shortages of planning and evaluation specialists, policy analysts, financial analysts and economists, maintenance and sanitary engineers, architects, statisticians, demographers, and legal and management professionals, including personnel specialists. A review of the situation in Zimbabwe, for instance, found a great need for equipment maintenance personnel, physiotherapists, dental therapists, pharmacists, and X-ray machine operators.

Causes and Consequences

The problems of underuse and undersupply can be traced in part to compensation problems, especially in the public sector. Wages and salaries tend to be so low that morale and motivation are affected adversely. A study of fifteen African countries showed that the index of civil service salaries for the lowest grades fell from 100 to an average of 53 between 1975 and 1985, and, for the highest grades, to an average of 41 (International Labour Office 1989, Table 4.1: 84). In Tanzania, salaries for workers in the lowest grades declined by 56 percent between 1981 and 1987 and by 75 percent for those at the highest levels. In Madagascar, entry level salaries in 1988 were only 20 to 25 percent of 1975 levels. That was too little to support even a small family. Health professionals in public service in Africa therefore often find themselves forced to find additional paid work of some kind.

Poor management, weak supervision, and unsatisfactory training are also to blame. Poor management is reflected in the creation of numerous categories of health personnel whose functions overlap or are ill defined. A 1991 study in Uganda found fifty-seven different job categories for personnel in the health sector, fifty of them clinically oriented (Republic of Uganda, Ministry of Health 1991). While Mozambique has reduced the number of categories, there were still around twenty in 1990. The large number of such categories interferes with effective personnel management and makes it hard to staff health centers and district hospitals because they need health care generalists rather than carefully classified medical specialists. The problem is compounded by the continuous addition of new categories, often created under new donor-funded projects.

Large numbers of low-level (and often superfluous) functionaries further demonstrate the weakness of managerial control. Prior to a restructuring in Ghana in 1987, the Ministry of Health had 38,000 employees. Twenty-two thousand of these were nontechnical workers who accounted for 53 percent of the budget. It was estimated that the nontechnical staff could be reduced by 8,000, producing a 19 percent savings in the budget. In 1991 Uganda's Ministry of Health found that around 4,000 of its 18,000 employees were "ghost workers"—people on the payroll who did no work. It concluded that up to 10 percent of total personnel expenditures might have been lost through poor management (Republic of Uganda, Ministry of Health 1991).

Undersupply and underuse problems are often compounded by the absence of standard managerial procedures. Clear and specific job descriptions, performance criteria, and supervisory guidelines are frequently nonexistent. Practical training in supervisory skills is lacking. In addition, budgetary restrictions in many countries have all but eliminated transportation and two-way radio and telephone communication between health officials in the cities and paraprofessionals in rural areas. In Niger, for example, nurses are supposed to visit a health center once every three months, but interviews revealed that eighteen of twenty-seven nurses had made only one visit in the previous six months. In Senegal, two-thirds of ninety-two supervisors had canceled planned supervision visits within the previous six months. And in Zaire, only 21 percent of fifty-seven village health workers reported a supervisory visit within the previous three months (Nicholas, Heiby, and Hatzell 1991).

Unsatisfactory training appears in several ways, not the least of which is a mismatch between the content of training and actual health needs. In Benin, Togo, and Zaire, to mention but three countries, medical training remains oriented to clinical work and hospital practice despite government policies that emphasize primary care. In Ethiopia, many training facilities were poorly designed and are badly maintained. The quality of health training in Guinea was found to be poor because of weaknesses in secondary education, inadequate teaching staff and facilities, inappropriate curricula, and excessively large enrollments. In Zaire, the overall quality of medical training declined throughout the 1980s and was accompanied by deterioration of training facilities and equipment.

A number of Sub-Saharan African countries are plagued as well by excessive medical specialization. In Côte d'Ivoire, for example, more than 40 percent of the physicians are specialists. Governments can address this issue by eliminating subsidies for specialist training and practice and by reviewing curricula.

Dependence on expatriates is yet another type of imbalance in the health sector work force of various African countries. Large numbers of foreign personnel work in the health sector in virtually every African country, many in vertical projects sponsored by donors. Foreigners in the public sector often act as district medical officers of health—for example, in Swaziland, Lesotho, Malawi, and Botswana. Other foreigners are found as technical assistance experts or advisors. In Rwanda in 1985, 60 of the 247 doctors and 130 of 337 high-ranking nurses were foreigners. In Zaire, one-third of the 2,500 physicians were non-nationals. It was estimated in late 1986 that more than half of the physicians in Mozambique were expatriates. In Burundi in the late 1980s an estimated 40 percent of the physicians serving in health facilities were expatriates. As qualified and committed as such individuals may be, their employment can be at odds with creating sustainable human resources for health when they are associated with vertical programs administered by donors, receive much higher salaries than their national counterparts, and contribute to high rates of turnover.

Achieving Effective Management of Health Care Personnel

Without suitably trained workers in appropriately located facilities, basic health services will remain unavailable to many millions of Africans. Resolving training and health facility problems will not be enough, however. Compensation for health workers must be increased, and competent supervision must be provided to ensure strong staff motivation. Ministries of health must engage themselves in the struggle for civil service reform, decentralization of personnel management, and especially career management decisions.

Since the Alma Ata Conference in 1978, only a handful of countries have formulated comprehensive health sector personnel policies. Tanzania has been among the most successful in this respect (Box 6-1), but others, including Botswana, Congo, Nigeria, and Zimbabwe, have also begun to address this issue seriously. While formulating a comprehensive national policy is the first step toward coming to grips with the kinds of problems reviewed here, it is equally important to consider how problems of morale, motivation, compensation, and supervision could be addressed through decentralization.

Opportunities at the Primary Care Level

A number of Sub-Saharan African countries have demonstrated that it is possible to improve local personnel management. A health decentralization program in Guinea, supported by the World Bank, UNICEF, and other agencies, has brought advances in the development of tools for community-level supervision, monitoring, and evaluation. Projects in Benin, Kenya, Nigeria, Lesotho, and

---

BOX 6-1. PLANNING HUMAN
RESOURCES FOR HEALTH IN TANZANIA

Tanzania is among the African countries that have been relatively successful in preparing and implementing plans for health personnel. The Arusha Declaration of 1967 resulted in preparation of a plan with explicit targets for various categories of health human resources for the period 1972 to 1980. Thirteen thousand new health workers were trained, with a heavy emphasis on the training and use of 10,900 health auxiliaries and 2,100 health professionals. These targets were met and even exceeded in some categories, especially rural medical aides, health assistants, medical assistants, and MCH aides. Tanzania's

work on the development of career streams and upgrading courses for health care personnel has been particularly important.

Despite past successes, however, personnel planning has been based on excessively simple assumptions concerning staffing standards for various types of health care facilities, without reference to variations in work load or disease patterns or to the resources available to finance associated salary costs or support complementary inputs to make health care personnel able to work effectively. Thus, the staffing standards of 1987, which doubled those previously in effect, are beyond the resource capacity of the health sector.

Ghana are improving district health information and supervision functions. An integrated system of in-service training is being introduced at the district level in Mali. In-service training in management at the district level is being provided to senior district health workers in Lesotho. Similar programs exist in Senegal (Unger 1991) and Ethiopia.

Successful health districts have information and management systems that allow providers and clients to identify performance problems, analyze them, and take immediate corrective action on their own authority. Providers using these systems have been able to acquire a sense of control and personal growth, which are powerful sources of motivation. Such a system was established in Kinshasa in the mid-1980s, covering sixty health centers and accounting for less than 2 percent of health care costs (Beza and others 1987). In Guinea and Benin, the entire management information system has been revised under the Bamako Initiative. Although health center staff spend considerable time registering patients, children, drugs, and receipts, most of them see this as an important part of their job (Knippenberg and others 1990, Ministère de la Santé Publique [MSP], Benin 1990; Ministère de la Santé Publique et des Affaires Sociales [MSPAS], Guinea 1990).

BOX 6-2. DEMONSTRATED LEADERSHIP AT THE DISTRICT LEVEL IN GHANA

African countries can provide an environment that encourages social entrepreneurship for health, as in this example from Tema, an industrial seaport city in Ghana. The Tema Health District is served by a network of health centers, health posts, and industrial clinics that are backed by Tema General Hospital, a district hospital. After an acute deterioration of services, with attendant low staff morale in the mid-1970s, a senior medical officer with demonstrated leadership skills was assigned. The district medical officer identified the following problems: (a) low staff morale and lack of discipline among hospital staff; (b) poor management in the various sections of the hospital; (c) absence of liaison between the hospital and the industrial community—one presumed beneficiary of hospital services; and (d) lack of supervision by the medical staff of health facilities (health centers, health posts, and clinics) in the urban/ industrial and rural parts of the district.

To address these problems, the district medical officer established the following agenda:

■ Visit all the factories in Tema to learn about their health problems
■ Familiarize institutions visited with the needs and problems of the hospital
■ Convene monthly meetings of an Ad-hoc Management Advisory Group of Tema residents with management expertise

By assigning the highest priority to giving health centers and first-referral hospitals adequate numbers of motivated personnel, African countries will at the same time discourage medical overspecialization and disproportionate concentration of health personnel in urban areas.

Good leadership is the most critical dimension if health centers and first-referral hospitals are to achieve the goals of decentralization. While much will depend on individual skills and personalities, district health management teams must be given greater autonomy, training, and support by national policymakers. Leadership skills should be an important criterion in selecting and evaluating the performance of district health team managers (Box 6-2).

The Role of Government

Human resource planning for health by geographic area, type of expertise, category of worker, gender, and various time horizons is an essential public sector activity (Box 6-3). Nearly every African country needs to strengthen its ability to perform such planning, particularly to determine staffing needs at health centers and district hospitals. This means that national governments must have employees with technical skills in preparing projections, setting norms, and

---

Box 6-2, continued

■ Visit all the health posts and health centers in the district to establish active working relationships of staff, especially of government clinics, with the hospital

■ Organize monthly meetings of senior clinical and management staff to discuss issues affecting the care of patients, concerns of staff, and efficient running of health services within the hospital and the district as a whole and to find solutions to them

■ Conduct daily administrative rounds of ancillary hospital departments, such as catering and maintenance, to learn about operational problems.

Within six months, a discernible im-provement was observed by staff of the hospital, the regional director of health services, the headquarters of the Ministry of Health, and generally by persons seeking care at health facilities in the district. Services offered free to the hospital, thanks to the initiative of the local health leader, included loan of a tractor for the hospital garden; sale of essential provisions to staff at concessionary prices on the hospital premises; and donation of material to make bedsheets, bedspreads, and pajamas for patients. By working directly with institutions in his area, the district medical officer was able to tap resources normally not available to the Ministry of Health for local use.

Source: Amonoo-Lartsen 1990.

designing and managing systems of performance planning and evaluation. Cost estimates and financing proposals are important parts of this work.

As health care systems become more diversified institutionally, it is important that public sector planning take into account all health personnel, including those working in the private sector and those who work for nonprofit or charitable institutions, such as religious missions. Particular attention should be paid to training senior cadres to provide better leadership on health matters, including research. Leadership in health requires not only a comprehensive knowledge of health matters as such but also some fundamental knowledge of such related subjects as pharmacology, economics, financial analysis, and public works construction and maintenance. Ministries of health should also encourage the establishment and work of voluntary associations of public health personnel.

It would be unrealistic, however, to expect public sector health care workers to increase their work load significantly without additional compensation and reliable payment of wages and salaries. Because civil service salaries are unlikely to undergo significant improvements in the near future, national authorities will need to give local health managers greater autonomy in salary decisions. Local retention of fees is one means of increasing compensation and ensuring regular payment of salaries at well-functioning health centers. Other salary possibilities include wage supplements for night duty and holiday work

---

BOX 6-3. STRENGTHENING HUMAN RESOURCES PLANNING AND MANAGEMENT IN LESOTHO'S MINISTRY OF HEALTH

Lesotho is undertaking a systematic program to strengthen its management of health personnel. Actions planned include:

■ Development, implementation, and maintenance of human resource management information systems for personnel administration, planning, and training

■ On-the-job training for development of the personnel planning process in the Ministry of Health to pro-vide senior managers with the information and planning framework necessary to make decisions on staffing and training priorities

■ Design and implementation of a system for selection, placement, and monitoring of training activities

■ Development and use of a personnel manual

■ Design and implementation of a computerized personnel management information system (PMIS), in coordination with the Ministry of Public Service

■ Training of Ministry of Health staff in using computers and in running the PMIS.

and supplying housing so that key staff members can live near the facilities where they work. The resources needed for such changes must in part be found by reducing the numbers of unskilled support personnel and by purging from the payroll the names of those no longer working. This is being done in Guinea.

Incentive payments in well-functioning health centers have become a feature of systems of community financing of health care in a number of African countries, including Congo, Kenya, Guinea, and Nigeria. With sixty-four health centers for more than 900,000 people, Guinea appears to have the most widespread practice of local incentive payments (UNICEF 1992c). Resources mobilized by the community to pay incentives have ranged from around 10 percent to nearly 50 percent of normal salary levels. Successful health districts have also applied a variety of techniques to recognize the best performers. In Ghana, the Ministry of Health established a prize fund to provide incentives for superior performance by individual health workers and health teams. In Mali, health districts are required to meet specific performance criteria to receive full government and donor support for their district health plans.

Training must be adapted to practical needs at the district and community levels, and health training should be given to others in the community, especially schoolteachers and agricultural extension workers. Much more attention should be paid to the study of society, demography, and the community, as well as to the principles and practices of health leadership. At the same time, training should be less oriented toward western models of medical practice. Governments trying to build up district-based systems also need to rationalize and consolidate health training schools, make them multidisciplinary, and show them how to foster the development of the district health team concept and better health leadership. Madagascar is taking action along these lines by decentralizing its training functions and putting them under field supervision.

Finally, as a part of long-term investment in capacity-building, male and female teachers in health care need to have periodic opportunities to improve their skills. They should also be able to obtain basic academic journals in their fields. Better compensation of teachers at health training institutions should be part of the improvement of salaries and incentives for all health workers.

African governments also need to take traditional healers into account in planning the use of human resources for health. There are approximately 10,000 traditional healers in Zaire and more than 3,000 traditional birth attendants who practice actively in the informal sector. The Ministry of Health has set up a unit to gain a better understanding of their roles and to weed out harmful practices. About 12,000 traditional healers are registered in Zimbabwe. A significant share of the rural population depends solely on them in Ghana, Benin, Nigeria, Senegal, and Zambia, among other countries. While some modern health care givers systematically reject traditional practices, Nigeria's health policy makes

BOX 6-4.   COOPERATION BETWEEN
TRADITIONAL HEALERS AND MODERN
HEALTH CARE PROVIDERS

The establishment of registered associations of traditional healers is a first
step toward collaboration between the
informal sector and modern health
care systems in Sub-Saharan Africa.
More than twenty African countries
have registered associations of traditional healers, including Nigeria,
Ghana, Senegal, Benin, Côte d'Ivoire,
Zimbabwe, and Zambia. The degree
of cooperation between traditional and
modern practices of care varies from
country to country. However, a number
of collaborative programs between
biomedicine and African indigenous
health practitioners exist, such as the
Araromi program in Nigeria, the Mam-
pong Center for Scientific Research
into plant medicine, the "Alkaloid Unit"
at the University of Science and Technology in Kumasi, and the Primary
Health Training for Indigenous Healers
(PRHETIH) at Techiman, all in Ghana.

Research in plant medicine and traditional healing is also taking placing in
Niger and Zimbabwe.
   Much more needs to be done to promote development of appropriate
training for traditional providers, especially traditional birth attendants. Research and dissemination of information on the strengths and limitations of
traditional medicine are also needed to
enable modern health workers to understand the social and psychological
rationale behind traditional practices,
to become sensitive to traditional be-
liefs concerning health and health
care, and to collaborate with these
practitioners. Studies have shown that
traditional healers are skilled in helping people to cope with the psychological and social stress that often accom-
panies rapid social and economic
change. Policies need to build on the
cultural norms and practices that facilitate this process, to promote greater
cooperation among practitioners in the
informal sector and those in the modern sector.

room for training traditional practitioners to increase their skills and effectiveness and promote their integration into the existing national health system. In
Ghana, Nigeria, and Zimbabwe, retraining programs have made it possible for
some traditional healers to use modern treatment modalities, such as oral rehydration (Box 6-4). Also, AIDS prevention programs are increasingly drawing
on the help of traditional healers.

Conclusion

Although the numbers of those who deal with health problems have grown
markedly since independence, there are still fewer on a per capita basis in Sub-
Saharan Africa than in other areas of the world. The numbers of those with
health skills in most countries remain imbalanced in relation to needs, and de-

BOX 6-5. DEVELOPING HUMAN
RESOURCES FOR HEALTH LEADERSHIP
AND RESEARCH IN SUB-SAHARAN
AFRICA

Despite the evident need, senior-level training institutions and opportunities for health leadership and research in Africa are scarce. Few universities or other institutions offer training to prepare people for these roles. In recognition of the unmet need, new and strengthened graduate programs are being established in some African countries, such as Zimbabwe and Nigeria, with an emphasis on field-oriented training, based on partnerships between universities and government departments responsible for public health programs. The development of such programs is responsive to the need to emphasize practically oriented disease prevention and development programs at the district level.

In anglophone countries, the increasing emphasis on public health has been nurtured by training in community medicine. This has existed for many years in Ghana, Nigeria, Kenya, and Uganda. New programs in public health have been created or are in development at the Universities of Ibadan, Accra, and Nairobi. New public health training programs have been developed at the University of the Western Cape in Capetown and through the University of Zimbabwe.

Among francophone countries, several training programs have evolved from a WHO-sponsored school of public health in Cotonou. The University of Kinshasa opened a school of public health in 1986, and the Universities of Abidjan and Dakar have developed training programs at the diploma or master's level. A school of public health—the Centre Inter-Etats d'Enseignement Superieur en Santé (CIESPAC)—has been initiated at the University of Brazzaville, and one is under consideration in Côte d'Ivoire.

Building on these and other initiatives, governments and donors need to collaborate at the national and intercountry levels to prepare and finance plans to strengthen health leadership and research capacity. Fortunately, new programs that have evolved over the last five years are being increasingly recognized by donors as suitable alternatives to training outside Africa.

Source: Bertrand 1992.

ployment, compensation, and motivation are weak. Many more trained people are needed to carry out the tasks of policy analysis, planning, and budgeting (Box 6-5).

The paramount need is for better supervision at the district level. The task at the national level will be to create an environment for effective management at the lower level. Personnel policies, including preparation of job descriptions and supervision norms, are central to this work and will require genuine collaboration within ministries of health, and with ministries of finance and planning, and civil service commissions.

CHAPTER SEVEN

Infrastructure and Equipment

THOUSANDS of vehicles and buildings and a wide range of sophisticated equipment (much of it imported) are used each day in Africa for health purposes. As populations grow, new buildings, vehicles, and equipment will be needed. If funds for this infrastructure and equipment are allocated inefficiently or inequitably or are poorly used, the delivery of health services will be severely impaired.

The challenge facing the public sector is particularly immense because most African governments are heavily involved in building, operating, and maintaining health facilities. Many Sub-Saharan countries, and especially poorer ones with low population densities, face high infrastructure costs. In the Sahel countries, for example, construction costs are estimated to be double or even more than those in other African countries.

The next section of this chapter discusses the status of Africa's health infrastructure and equipment. Three problems dominate: *insufficient maintenance, inappropriate and insufficient expansion,* and *poor planning.* This review of the current situation makes it possible to determine what is missing and what health system reforms are needed to improve the planning and management of physical facilities devoted to health purposes.

Infrastructure and Equipment Problems

Existing health facilities in many African countries have deteriorated in recent years. A study in Tanzania found that only 660 out of 1,800 rural government dispensaries were in good condition, while 810 were in fair and 330 were in bad condition. A 1990–91 survey of fifteen hospitals operated by the Kenya Ministry of Health found that 40 percent of the buildings were in poor or unsatisfactory condition (Porter 1992). Some hospitals, such as the Tres de Agosto Hospital in Guinea-Bissau, have crumbled beyond the point of repair. Equatorial Guinea has an extensive network of health facilities in most cities and small towns, but they will need major repairs to make them usable. And in countries such as Angola, Mozambique, Somalia, and Sudan, numerous health structures have been severely damaged by civil war.

Health equipment has also fallen into disrepair. In Nigeria, for example, one study (Erinosho 1991) found that close to one-third of the equipment in a series of health care institutions was not being used. In general, the more sophisticated the health care facility, the more equipment was out of use, and the longer it was out of service (Table 7-1). Studies of secondary hospitals in Nigeria carried out in 1992 suggest that equipment worth around $47 million (out of a total of $150 million) would require repairs, and that another $35 million is needed for reinvestment in essential items (Porter 1992). Studies of thirteen Ministry of Health hospitals in Kenya found 40 percent of all their equipment out of order and 40 percent of operating room equipment in need of repair (Porter 1992). A 1987 survey of seventeen hospitals in Uganda found that only 20 percent of inventoried equipment was in working order, while only about a third of the remaining 80 percent was worth repairing (Porter 1992).

The use of vehicles in the health sector has been greatly restricted by shortages of fuel, lack of maintenance, and repairs. A 1987 inventory of 660 Ministry of Health vehicles in Ghana found that 167 were roadworthy, 230 needed extensive repair, and 263 were worthless. In Guinea-Bissau, 42 percent of the Minis-

Table 7-1.   Health Care Equipment Not In Service in Nigeria, 1987

(percent)

Item	University teaching hospitals	State-owned hospitals	Non-government hospitals	Primary health centers	Total
Pieces in use	69	57	78	90	70
Pieces out of order	31	43	23	10	30
Share of equipment out of order for given duration					
<2 years	19	22	33	40	20
2–4 years	40	24	67	60	38
>4 years	41	54	—	—	42

— Not available.
Source: Erinosho 1991.

try of Health's vehicles were inoperable in 1990. This was not unexpected, since the ministry's vehicle maintenance program had ended in 1986.

Africa's tertiary hospitals have not escaped decline either. A report on Queen Elizabeth II Hospital in Lesotho found that its buildings were in poor physical condition and that it had other problems, including shortages of basic equipment, lack of maintenance capability, uneven distribution of work loads, weak planning, little staff development and supervision, and poor financial management.

Underfinancing of maintenance and repairs—virtually universal among African health facilities—is particularly apparent in public sector facilities. A study in one of Nigeria's states found that *public* hospitals and maternity clinics spent only 5 to 8 percent of their budgets on nonpersonnel items, such as maintenance, transport, and supplies, compared with private sector spending of 17 to 18 percent on such items. In Dar es Salaam, Tanzania, the budget for preventive maintenance of health facilities in the late 1980s was less than 1 percent of what should have been spent. In Guinea-Bissau, the total Ministry of Health budget allocation for preventive and routine maintenance in 1989 was a mere $5,000. A study of six district hospitals in Malawi found that an average of only 1.5 percent of recurrent expenditures was devoted to building maintenance and 0.2 percent to equipment maintenance in 1987–88 (Mills 1991). The maintenance problem is frequently complicated by division of responsibility because building maintenance is often the responsibility of other ministries.

The low priority given to training people in maintenance and repair further exacerbates the deterioration of physical infrastructure. In Senegal, civil service personnel assigned to maintenance do not perform adequately because suitable skills and appropriate supervision are lacking. In Zimbabwe, equipment maintenance personnel are in desperately short supply, and of all categories of workers employed by the Ministry of Health, the highest vacancy rate in 1990 was for medical equipment technicians.

The same factors that have caused poor maintenance have made it difficult for African countries to expand the health sector infrastructure. Assuming that one health center serves about 5,000 people, for example, Mali will need to increase the number of its health centers by 242 in the 1990s. This is nearly five times the actual increase of fifty-two during the 1980s (Table 7-2). Other countries face similar challenges. In Tanzania, population growth has led to a gradual decrease in health coverage.

Some countries, however, have strongly promoted expansion of health facilities at levels below the national level:

■ Botswana has given special attention to improving its infrastructure at the lowest levels. The number of clinics grew from 40 in

Table 7-2.   The Growth of Health Centers in Selected African Countries and the
Challenge Ahead
(number of centers)

	Actual number		Number needed in 2000	
	1980	1990	To maintain 1990 coverage	To reach 60 percent coverage
Burkina Faso	169	860	1,100	1,400
Mali	470	522	760	1,300
Niger	240	460	630	1,270
Senegal	470	690	900	1,200

Source: World Bank 1992a.

1974 to 150 in 1986, while health posts grew from 22 in 1974 to 227 in
1986. Over the same period in Botswana, the number of district hospitals increased by less than 10 percent.

■ In mainland Tanzania, the number of dispensaries rose from 1,847 in
1976 to 2,600 in 1980 and 2,935 in 1988.

■ In Mozambique, the number of "primary facilities" (the equivalent of
health centers) rose from 326 in 1975 to 1,195 in 1985. Similarly, the
number of district hospitals rose from 120 in 1975 to 221 in 1985.

For the most part, however, governments have made the funding of tertiary
and other inpatient facilities their leading infrastructural priority. In Ethiopia
the number of people per hospital bed fell from 3,500 in 1970 to 3,400 in 1980,
and in Rwanda from nearly 800 in 1970 to 650 in 1980. São Tomé and Principe
enjoys one of the highest ratios of hospital beds to population in the developing
world. In 1990 that small African country had roughly one hospital bed for
every 190 people, which was twice as high as in Nigeria and nearly three times
as high as in Colombia. These accomplishments have come at a high price, tend
to be concentrated in urban areas (Table 7-3), and provide disproportionate
benefits to relatively well-to-do households.

Poor infrastructure planning is evident in the location of health facilities, in
uncoordinated community initiatives for facility expansion and in weaknesses
in project design and execution. In Guinea-Bissau, for example, one region has
more than five times the number of hospital beds per person found in another,
more populated region. In Burundi, the population served by health centers
varies from 870 to more than 17,000, with a mean of around 2,500. Even in
Tanzania, where a special effort has been made to achieve equity in the health
sector, a sample of primary care facilities in 1984 revealed that some dispens-

Table 7-3.   Percentage of Population with Access to Health Care Facilities,
Selected African Countries, Late 1980s

Country	Urban	Rural
Botswana	90	85
Burkino Faso	51	48
Congo	97	70
Gabon	97	70
Ghana	92	45
Kenya	80	53
Liberia	50	30
Mauritius	99	99
Nigeria	87	62
Rwanda	60	25
Somalia	50	15
Tanzania	94	73
Togo	60	60
Zaire	40	17
Zimbabwe	90	80

Source: Statistical appendix in this volume.

aries served only about 1,500 people, compared with the target of 6,500, while
others were expected to serve populations many times larger than the target
figure.

Poor planning is particularly apparent in imbalances between urban and
rural areas. A study of rural health stations in Ethiopia in 1985–86 found that
they served only sixteen patients per day, many fewer than the ninety to 100
anticipated, and concluded that improper location of the facilities was responsible. Another study (Kloos 1990) found that more optimal location of maternal
and child health facilities in rural Nigeria would have increased coverage by 20
percent. In the fifteen African countries for which data on the matter are available, six are countries where less than 50 percent of the rural population has
access to health care facilities. In seven of the countries, however, 90 percent or
more of the urban population had access to health facilities in the same period
(Table 7-3).

Lack of coordination between the public sector and nongovernment providers has complicated matters because decisions on the location of public sector
facilities need to take into account the planning of the nongovernment providers.
In Uganda, church missions have built clinics to meet the needs of the population
in rural areas. Governments can build on, or complement, such networks.

Lack of coordination between government officials and community leaders is another manifestation of weak planning. In a number of African countries, health centers have been built by communities with the understanding that public authorities would operate them, but adequate resources have seldom been set aside for that purpose. In Mauritania, where community participation was encouraged by the government, health posts were built at random locations by local communities. In some regions, the proliferation of health posts has resulted in shortages of personnel and material resources. Financial and other constraints have frequently prevented the government from assuming responsibility for operations at health centers and have made local communities cynical about the national government.

Poor project design and execution are another manifestation of weak infrastructure planning. A wide range of construction standards and methodologies, combined with a lack of norms, has led to oversized facilities, substandard construction, and high unit costs. Unit construction costs for almost identical health centers in Mali in the late 1980s, for example, varied by a factor of four (World Bank 1992a). Construction costs in the Sahel countries range from $750 to $1,200 per square meter for primary care facilities, compared with $350 to $450 per square meter in other African countries (Porter 1992). In the absence of norms for designing catchment areas, national officials responsible for planning health sector construction have often been unable to identify the type and size of infrastructure needed to provide health services to local communities.

Renewing Health Sector Infrastructure and Equipment

Physical proximity to health care facilities is only the beginning of effective health care coverage. A facility that is near people's homes will have little value if it lacks basic equipment. In many African countries this problem has arisen partly because plans were made to construct new facilities before determining whether the money was available to operate them. Some of these problems can be resolved by charging fees and making improvements in the quality of care at lower level facilities. What remains critical, however, is to improve infrastructure planning, selection of equipment, and equipment maintenance.

Cost-effective allocations of financial resources for infrastructure and equipment tend to be those that give priority to rehabilitation over new investment, and to health centers and district hospitals instead of tertiary facilities, as discussed in Chapter 4.

Rehabilitation needs are widespread, but effective rehabilitation requires careful analysis of existing investments and a clear ranking of priorities compatible with a commitment to preventive and primary health care and to cost-effective interventions. Mali, for example, has begun to establish a foundation for this kind of analysis through the creation of a data bank on existing infra-structure, equipment, and associated health care services that will be available to local health administrators.

Norms, skills, and procedures for determining where to build health facili-ties and for the maintenance of buildings, equipment, and vehicles also need to be established and carefully monitored. The norms should cover actual mainte-nance work as well as its financing, and should apply to nongovernment as well as public sector facilities. As a general rule, African countries should expect to spend between 2 and 3 percent of the replacement cost of health centers and hospital buildings on maintenance annually. A detailed study of Kenya, for example, led to an estimate of 2.6 percent (Porter 1992).

Specific standards on spending for equipment maintenance, repair, and re-placement are also needed. It has been suggested as a rule of thumb that a sum equivalent to 20 percent of the value of existing stock should be allocated annu-ally to maintenance, repair, and replacement (Bloom and Temple-Bird 1988). Another way to look at the issue is in terms of the recurrent expenditures of operations. As a general rule, around 10 to 15 percent of recurrent costs will be required to maintain a first-referral hospital (Barnum and Kutzin 1993).

Standardized lists of the equipment used in the various types of health care facilities are also needed, along with norms for maintenance and repair. WHO has prepared such norms in a number of related areas, such as the estimated annual cost of maintaining specific types of medical equipment as a percentage of their capital cost (Kleczkowski and Pipbouleau 1983). Ghana is planning to set up a hospital equipment maintenance service with workshops, equipment and tools, vehicles, spare parts, and training programs. Mozambique is estab-lishing a national network of health facility and equipment maintenance cen-ters. The experience of nongovernment partners is often relevant (Box 7-1).

When health center facilities and equipment are well managed, local com-munities tend to be involved. The basic principle underlying this arrangement is that facilities planned without the active participation of beneficiaries will, at best, be viewed with indifference. If appropriately planned, partnerships consti-tute a powerful instrument for promoting local initiatives and strengthening man-agement through a sense of ownership. As part of a World Bank–financed health and population project in Mali, for example, a cost-sharing formula (50 percent government and 50 percent local communities) is supporting construction and planned maintenance of 120 community health centers during a five-year period.

The Special Problem of Tertiary Care Facilities

The management of tertiary-level health facilities (meaning mostly major urban hospitals) merits special attention. Improving efficiency at such facili-

---

BOX 7-1. MAINTENANCE IN HOSPITALS OF ZAMBIA'S MINING CORPORATION

The public sector in Zambia is facing great difficulties in providing and sustaining medical equipment services. In public hospitals, about 20 percent of medical equipment is working poorly and 40 percent is completely out of operation. Zambia Consolidated Copper Mines (ZCCM) has established a health care system of its own, separate from the public sector, that consists of eleven hospitals and fifty-eight health centers. It has developed a good maintenance system for its medical equipment, which is about the same age as that in the public sector. Its ability to do this has been due to the following factors:

■ It has established an autonomous body, the Medical and Educational Trust, to operate all health care facilities and train health care and operational personnel.

■ It has established work practices that encourage good staff performance, combined with strong supervision and incentives. It offers better service conditions than the public sector and has higher staff retention rates.

■ ZCCM has recognized the importance of maintenance in its operations and health care activities. Mine hospitals are financed significantly better than their public sector counterparts and therefore receive adequate maintenance budgets and foreign exchange.

■ It has separated medical equipment maintenance and safety policies from its operational activities and wisely applied technical and human resources, maintenance, and management expertise from industrial instrumentation to medical applications.

■ Initial training in management and maintenance for health care specialists has been conducted by mine operational staff. Some operational maintenance staff have been seconded to mine hospitals.

Source: Temple-Bird 1991.

---

ties without increasing their budget allocations in real, or even nominal, terms would be highly desirable. Management audits can lead to the establishment of specific targets for efficiency gains. At the Kenyatta National Hospital in Nairobi, for example, the performance targets include reducing the average length of an inpatient's period of hospitalization from 8.6 days in 1989–90 to 7.1 days in 1995–96, a reduction in staff from 5.4 to 4.0 per 1,000 patient days, and an increase in the ratio of maintenance to total recurrent expenditures from 2.2 percent to 6.0 percent. Malawi has prepared five-year efficiency plans for its three major hospitals that include reductions in funding for transport and utility systems, other items, and improved accounting and expenditure control.

Assessing Technology Choice

In many African countries, modern technology is often not used properly, even in leading hospitals and medical schools (Free 1992). It is complex technology that requires every component to interact at the right place and the right time, but the more complex the technology, the greater the risk that a link in the chain will break down. The introduction of any technology should therefore include the introduction of all the things needed to make the technology work: equipment, training, maintenance, quality control, and the capacity to translate the results of quality control analyses into corrective actions.

New technologies have expanded the potential scope of the health system; some examples follow.

■ Computerized systems make it possible to store and retrieve the large amounts of vital statistics and other data needed to assess risks and to plan, implement, and evaluate health programs. Pharmaceutical supplies can be managed more efficiently through computerized updating of inventories, thus preventing waste and reducing costs. Computers are only helpful, however, to the extent that they support a management information system with adequate software and maintenance.

■ Radio communication has proven essential in mobilizing the resources needed to deal with epidemics and natural disasters. Health activities in rural areas can be better integrated into district health care through the use of two-way radios, particularly if transport is available to evacuate patients when necessary. Supervisory consultation by radio improves the efficacy of services and reduces the cost of referral.

■ New diagnostic tests, such as "dipsticks" to diagnose HIV and other sexually transmitted diseases, or tests using saliva, may give community health centers diagnostic powers that were previously restricted to specialized urban laboratories.

■ Noninvasive diagnostic tools with high sensitivity and high specificity, such as ultrasound machines, may sharply improve diagnosis at the district level. Less invasive treatment—"keyhole" surgery, for example—can minimize patient trauma and reduce the length of hospital stays. A shift to one-day surgery with improved technologies and care practices, as is now being done in many industrial countries, could help to contain the growing demand for hospital beds and other health facilities (Porter 1992).

■ The development of powerful drugs that can be effective when administered in a single oral dose has drastically modified the therapeutic approach to such diseases as helminthiasis and amoebiasis. Similarly, thermostable vaccines that can be given in a single oral dose have increased the prospects for controlling common children's diseases, such as measles and polio. Drug kits and blister packs fall in the same category.

The greatest obstacle to improving medical technology in Africa may be "technology philanthropy"—the uncoordinated donation of equipment to African countries by foreign agencies and charities. Given their often precarious finances, developing countries find it hard to refuse such gifts, even when they are unsuited to the country's immediate needs. One solution would be to devise "donation protocols," whereby the kinds of equipment to be donated would follow a model—paralleling, for example, the selection of drugs by using essential drugs lists (Porter 1992).

BOX 7-2. ACQUIRING NEW TECHNOLOGIES

There is generally no established mechanism in African countries for planning the *acquisition* of new health technologies. Awareness of technologies is not a problem, because there is a sufficient pool of knowledge at universities, among staff returning from abroad, and among consultants and donors. It is the process of technology transfer that is problematic, since it is usually made on an ad hoc basis according to vested interests, pressures, and prejudices.

When there is some form of planning, the acquisition of new technologies is to a large extent controlled by physicians and, more likely than not, by clinicians trained abroad. They are generally not the best persons to perform this task. While the medical profession can readily pinpoint a problem, it generally has little idea of the complexity and extent of the engineering problems or the level of training associated with the technologies needed to solve them. Rather, a team is needed, including public and nongovernment health care providers, engineers, planners, and social scientists—to ensure that the broader cultural, social, and economic dimensions are considered. Public, private voluntary, and private commercial perspectives are all useful to this end.

Because the choice of health technologies determines the allocation of human and financial resources in health care, African governments need to support operationally oriented research that will facilitate decisions about whether to introduce new tests, treatments, and their associated technologies into their countries' health care systems. Factors to be considered include the appropriateness and cost-effectiveness of the intervention, its links to the basic package of health services, its impact on health equity, the ease of its use and maintenance, its training requirements, and its lifetime cost. A cautious attitude toward uncontrolled diffusion of medical technology is emerging in the industrial countries, and African policymakers would do well to exercise prudence in the face of quite understandable pressures for investment. Selection of appropriate equipment, and arrangements to ensure its maintenance, are appropriate ministry of health roles.

Much of the work of technology assessment will require intercountry co-operation, because the costs of undertaking assessments and preparing appropriate recommendations are likely to exceed the capacity of most individual African countries. Some support for such work exists at the international level, including a joint Technology Introduction Panel inaugurated by UNICEF in 1988 in cooperation with WHO and other international agencies (Box 7-2) (Free 1992).

Conclusion

Strengthening the management of infrastructure and equipment is one of the several health system reforms needed to achieve health goals in Africa. One concrete step would be for governments to assign responsibility for decisions about health facilities, equipment, and technology to a senior ministry of health official. Another would be to establish norms for health facilities at different levels in the system and to support operational research on the most cost-effective technologies available. Budgetary standards and provisions for maintenance and operating costs need to be established, particularly in public sector health facilities. Since the financial resources required to provide basic health services are frequently depleted by cost overruns and inefficiencies at the tertiary level, more efficient use of technologies, equipment, and facilities in large urban hospitals should be a priority. African ministries of health might take a look at the global action plan devised by WHO for the management, maintenance, and repair of health care equipment.

CHAPTER EIGHT

Management Capacity and Institutional Reform

PUBLIC administration in many African countries continues to remain weak despite changes made in the 1980s. Widely observed shortcomings are:

■ Government ministries and other agencies tend to wield authority and make spending decisions in a highly centralized fashion. As a result, local governments have little authority to make decisions and few methods of raising the tax revenues they need to be effective (Silverman 1992).

■ Public ministries and other agencies often employ far more employees than they need, and managers are ineffective in motivating and disciplining staff members. Overstaffing is often the result of a desire to provide stable and reasonably well-paid jobs, but the end result is waste of public funds and demoralization among employees who have no productive duties.

■ Public agency managers often have a poor understanding of the institutions they are supposed to manage or the broader context in which their agencies operate.

■ It is extremely difficult to determine the effectiveness of government spending because of inadequate transparency (how money was spent) and poor accountability (who decided to spend it).

For the most part, these systemic shortcomings need to be addressed as part of comprehensive public sector reform programs. It is difficult to reform one ministry on its own, but these constraints need not inhibit reform-minded health leaders. In any case, institutional reforms and greater decentralization require a systematic approach involving careful assessment of institution- and country-specific conditions and the establishment of a timetable for change. As the experience of many African countries shows, deeply entrenched problems in the health sector cannot be solved overnight. Nor is a single recipe likely to be appropriate for all.

This chapter summarizes lessons learned about reforms of the administrative and managerial functions shown in Figure 8-1. Recognizing the drawbacks of relying too heavily on centralized public bureaucracies, several African governments have considered various degrees of decentralization to the local and community level in the management and delivery of services including health, education, and public utilities. Success is particularly apparent when the planning and delivery of cost-effective health services are combined with community participation and public support at the district level. From the perspective of ministries of health, districts can also serve as effective administration units for communities to exert influence "upward."

Figure 8-1.   Some Dimensions of Capacity Building

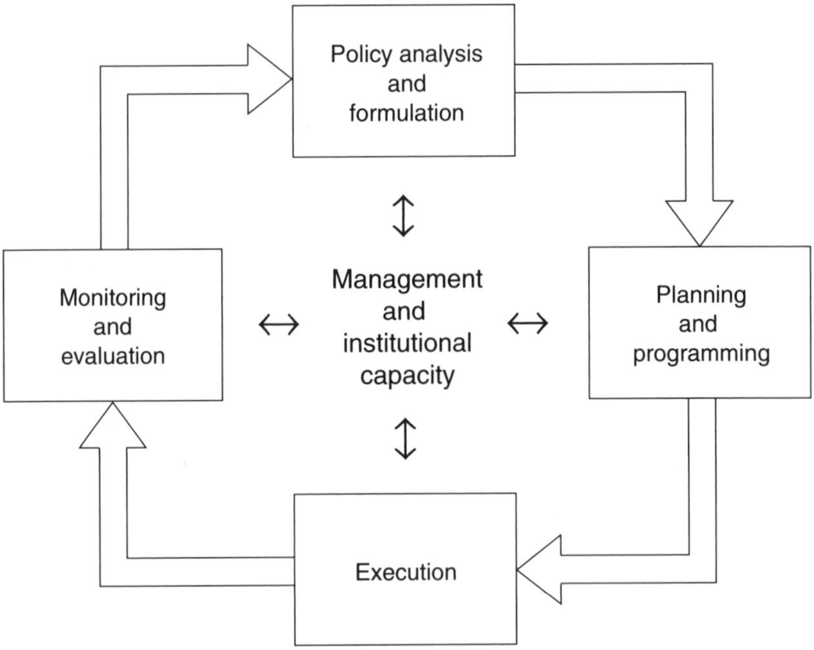

Several initiatives, discussed in this section, are needed to strengthen health sector institutional capacities and management practices at the central, regional, district, and community level (Vaillancourt, Nassim, and Brown 1992; North 1992).

Assessment of the Existing System

The processes of strengthening institutional capacity and improving managerial abilities need to start with a situational assessment of existing structures. Health system performance is often hampered by unforeseen bottlenecks. Weak links can be strengthened through internal reorganization, management changes, and, if need be, changes in legal status affecting decisionmaking and institutional coordination. The challenge is to replace piecemeal assessments of particular components of the system or of single institutions with more comprehensive assessments by those involved in the system's daily operations.

Situational assessments can be carried out through internally driven diagnoses of *current* versus *desired* structures, functions, and skills. This kind of assessment has been carried out in Guinea, Benin, and Togo (World Bank 1993b), where three groups of stakeholders (community representatives, health care personnel, and policymakers and planners who work at the regional and central levels) have been involved in identifying and resolving common problems. One group consists of community representatives, who speak in the interests of health services clients. A second group consists of health personnel, who often feel unable to modify the system at large yet seek to improve their credibility in the functions they perform by working together for change. A third group consists of policymakers and planners at the regional and central levels.

Workshops have been convened to assess how well the systems are perceived to be operating, gaps in their performance, and what is needed to fill the gaps. In the workshop for higher-level officials, for example, the process begins with an assessment of health needs as shown by current epidemiological data. That is followed by examination of the operations of sectoral programs and whether they need additional funding. Finally, the participants discuss potential strategies for closing the gaps. The procedure typically follows the five steps described in Table 8-1.

This approach has produced several benefits:

- The tendency to attribute long-standing problems to a shortage of financial resources is being supplanted by detailed diagnoses of what is required to resolve those problems.
- High-level officials in health, finance, and planning ministries have participated, resulting in a greater commonality of understanding across ministries of the problems involved.

Table 8-1. Diagnosing Health System Performance in Guinea, Benin, and Togo

Steps	*Situational analysis*
Step 1 Analyze current performance and major conditions affecting sector	→ Review of policies, strategies, and contents of actual programs; identification of strengths and weaknesses in the system; review of health services, their location and distribution; analysis of systems of financing and resource allocation; and assessment of formation and deployment of personnel.
Step 2 Identify and prioritize problems and constraints meriting attention	→ Inadequacies in current menu of policies and strategies; management, evaluation, coordination problems in programs; resource allocation and budget management problems; operational problems at various levels of service provision; and personnel management problems.
Step 3 Reflect on appropriate strategies and sectoral programs	→ Improved management and coordination systems; decentralization and mechanisms of community participation; resource mobilization through cost recovery; improving standards and norms in health care delivery; and training and redeployment schemes for personnel.
Step 4 Prioritize and define target groups	→ Women of reproductive ages; pregnant women; mothers and infants aged 0–5 years; young adults, the old and infirm; and groups susceptible to particular maladies.
Step 5 Determine indicators of performance for monitoring and evaluating progress	→ Total number of sick needing health care; disadvantaged groups; measures of reforms undertaken; management information systems used for project evaluation; health statistics and rates of coverage; and monitoring and evaluation of decentralization practices.

■ A corps of sector managers who speak the same language and share a conceptual framework is being created. The result should be a stronger consensus on how to break through major bottlenecks.

Equipping Managers with Needed Skills and Methodologies

Health systems cannot be run effectively unless managers are skilled in planning, programming, and budgeting. Such skills are required to translate policy into implementable projects and programs and to ensure the availability of human and financial resources. More managers with such skills are needed in Africa.

In Ghana, for example, a 1990 review of the Ministry of Health found an almost complete absence of planning capacity, few rational management procedures in place for day-to-day operations, and a lack of records on ministry decisions. The review concluded that no significant improvement could be expected in the delivery of health care services unless a core group of qualified managers was appointed to key positions. The Ministry of Health then decided to create new planning units with work programs and defined staffing and a management information system to monitor performance.

In Nigeria, Ministries of Health at the state and federal levels established departments of planning, following civil service reform, but qualified people were hard to find. To help meet this shortage, three Nigerian universities— Benin, Ilorin, and Maiduguri—began operating an accelerated three-month program in health planning and management, using a multidisciplinary curriculum and training manuals developed with the Universities of York, Leeds, and Keele in the United Kingdom and Johns Hopkins University in the United States. Close to 400 medical and nonmedical staff from Nigeria's local, state, and federal governments completed the program between 1990 and 1992.

Managerial skills and methodologies in public finance and information collection and management are especially important, to develop the following:

■ *Health expenditure data.* Expenditures on health need to be compiled by use and especially source—household and other private expenditures, public expenditures, and donor funds. Information on source of expenditures is particularly important to enable policymakers to assess the potential for private financing and cost recovery and the capacity of government to finance public health activities and provide subsidies. Time series data of this type were available for this report for only about one-third of Sub-Saharan African countries.

■ *Comprehensive health sector financial plans.* Such plans need to encompass public and nongovernment outlays. While such analyses are gradually becoming more widespread, such as in Senegal and Zimbabwe, they remain nonexistent in many African countries, thus rendering analysis of planned compared to realized expenditures piecemeal and incomplete. They need to encompass recurrent and capital expenditures, as well as cost estimates for future programs and targets. In this way, shortfalls can be anticipated and plans to fill gaps formulated. A particularly important area is information on present and future recurrent expenditure requirements of existing investments.

■ *Management information systems (MIS).* To facilitate health planning, information on the cost of services and health outcomes is required to determine the cost-effectiveness of basic health services. MIS should also cover revenue collection and monitor the cost of medical contacts by provider or institution. In Chad, for example, the Ministry of Health and Social Affairs has designed a health information system that has been operating successfully for several years. Annual reports are prepared with national-level information on health status, health services, and health facilities functioning. Information from the system is used in planning at the national and provincial levels, as well as in some districts (République du Tchad 1992).

Finally, institutional effectiveness cannot be assessed or investment allocations determined unless managers have the capacity to collect, compile, and analyze more up-to-date demographic and epidemiological information. In Ghana, as in many other African countries, the monitoring of primary care has been stalled partially because of poorly functioning statistical and data systems. Ghana's Center for Health Statistics is currently responsible for collecting only limited data from hospitals and health centers. Reporting is substantially incomplete; and institutions outside the public sector are only partly included. Most available data have not been analyzed, disseminated, or used systematically for policymaking (Box 8-1).

Promoting Decentralization

The pace at which countries pursue decentralization, and their understanding of its content, depend on the interaction of many factors. Some countries push hard for decentralization; others resist it. Among these factors are (North 1992):

- Changing attitudes toward governance and international trends favoring decentralization in support of primary care, countered by bureaucratic resistance to shifts in decisionmaking power by the political and medical establishment.
- Increased demands for control of budgetary resources at provincial and local levels in view of poor delivery of centrally financed and provided health services, with inertia and bureaucratic resistance from central governments that have traditionally controlled the purse strings for health.
- Motivation to attune health programs to local cultures and traditions in reaction to top-down programs that have sought to change behaviors with insufficient regard for sociocultural concerns.
- Desire to move away from investment programs associated with donor-driven agendas to nationally determined priorities with inputs from participants and beneficiaries down to the community level.

BOX 8-1. KNOWLEDGE-BASED MANAGEMENT AND PLANNING

All across Africa, health policymakers, planners, and researchers have been hampered by the lack of accurate, reliable, and timely data on households and communities. As a result, it is extremely difficult to profile the health status, needs, behaviors, and preferences of different demographic groups within countries, let alone the epidemiological characteristics of different socioeconomic groups.

Systems for registering births and deaths are very weak across Africa, thus depriving planners of a timely tally of births and deaths, by characteristic and by geographic area (African Population Advisory Committee, 1993a). Only relatively small islands have vital registration systems that have been classified as "complete" (meaning more than 90 percent complete). These include Cape Verde, Mauritius, Reunion, São Tomé and Principe, St. Helena, and the Seychelles. Several other African countries have vital registration systems but estimates

of completeness of death registration are only 10 to 25 percent. These include Botswana, Djibouti, Guinea-Bissau, Kenya, Rwanda, Sierra Leone, and Togo.

In the absence of needed information, health problems tend to be "invisible" or "moving targets" from a management and planning perspective. Moreover, household behaviors, including self-diagnosis, self-treatment, and willingness and ability to pay for help from traditional healers and modern practitioners, remain poorly understood. As a result the entire process of monitoring and evaluating progress is undermined.

Knowledge-based management of the health sector has been further undermined by failures to analyze data that have been collected and to use the resulting information effectively. In some cases, health information has been suppressed; in others, epidemiological and other information has been ignored in drawing up priorities for action. Suppression of information on the AIDS epidemic during the early 1980s is a case in point (Lucas 1992).

In Africa, district-based health care—as described in Chapter 4—is practiced widely in such countries as Botswana, Tanzania, and Zimbabwe; partially in such countries as Benin, Guinea, Mali, and Nigeria; and on an experimental basis in such countries as Burundi and Senegal. The decentralization of health responsibilities to the district level can be expected to bring major changes in institutional and managerial roles. Clear distinctions need to be made, however, among administrative supervision, technical supervision, and advisory roles. The functions typically performed at various levels in decentralized systems are summarized in Box 8-2.

The most important aspects of decentralization are to establish the level to which authority is to be decentralized, the precise authority being delegated, the policy instruments to be used to effect decentralization, and the types of activity to be decentralized (Conyers, Cassels, and Janovsky 1992). Even if discretionary authority is legally assigned to local authorities, the de facto structure of financial incentives and responsibilities for salaries and careers may continue to remain under the authority of central ministries. In Tanzania, for example, despite formal decisions to decentralize, vertical programs tend to establish national objectives before district health teams fix theirs, leading to distortions in resource allocation.

Experience strongly indicates that successful decentralization requires definition of specific objectives, clear delineation of functions and decision-making authority at each level, mechanisms for communication and coordination among the various levels, and sufficient training to enable full assumption of new responsibilities (Vaillancourt, Nassim, and Brown 1992). In district-based health systems, for example, central and regional staff will have to reorient their work to emphasize policy formulation and monitoring, strategy development, resource allocation, and technical and managerial backstopping. Such functions are in keeping with the mandates of ministries of health and are among the weakest links in district-based systems today.

Box 8-2, continued

employment of public sector health manpower
- Compilation of health expenditure budgets
- Approval of large-scale capital projects outside the public sector
- Supervision of district health teams
- Provision of logistical support to district health teams.

Districts tend to be responsible for:
- Management of all public sector health facilities with local responsibilities
- Monitoring and, often, implementation of community-based health programs
- Management and control over local health budgets

- Coordination and supervision of all government, NGO, and private health services
- Promotion of active links with local government departments
- Promotion of community participation in local health services planning, implementation, and monitoring
- Preparation of annual health plans and reports
- Raising additional local funds
- In-service training, especially on-the-job support, of health workers
- Supervision and control of community health workers
- Collecting and forwarding routine health information to regional and central offices
- Dialogue with beneficiaries of health services and their representatives.

Source: Adapted from WHO 1988a.

Day-to-day management of health services is carried out by district health teams (DHTS). In Zimbabwe, the DHTS are made up of a representative of each health center or hospital, the district administrator and his staff, district council representatives, a representative of village health workers, a resettlement officer, community and women's affairs representatives, nutrition coordinators, the family planning group leader, a psychiatric nurse, and a community nurse. Prior to the development of the district system in Zimbabwe, managerial functions were performed by provincial teams responsible for as many as seven districts. It is widely agreed that introduction of the new system has improved services and levels of coverage (World Bank 1993c).

DHTS have a particularly important role to play in ensuring the availability of the cost-effective package described in this report. Within a framework of national policies and norms, DHTS can be authorized to make decisions on the location of new public and private health care facilities, determine which services are to be provided by health centers and the district hospital, set standards for staffing local health care facilities, write financial management rules to ensure accountability, fix fee schedules and perhaps minimum salary levels, and establish management norms.

Experience suggests that the performance of district health teams will depend on whether (i) health services and programs have been integrated at the central level, (ii) the district has been given the authority to manage human and financial resources independently, and (iii) community control structures have been established. The last point is particularly important, especially to promote beneficiary confidence in the health care providers and equity in access of use of services. In Mali, for example, the introduction of democratic procedures made it possible to elect community representatives to district health teams, thus preventing domination by local elites (World Bank 1993c).

Effective district health teams cannot, of course, be created overnight. A number of Sub-Saharan African governments are involved in a process that begins by educating planners and policymakers at central, regional, and district levels about what is involved, then focuses on reaching consensus on roles and responsibilities, and then provides training in the skills required to carry out needed functions. This process is being assisted by international organizations and donors (Box 8-3).

District health teams also have an important role to play in coordinating the activities of public and nongovernment service providers at the district level. Experience in Zaire, Togo, Ghana, Zambia, and Kenya reveals significant vari-

---

BOX 8-3. TRAINING AND DEVELOPMENT OF DISTRICT HEALTH TEAMS IN GHANA

In Ghana, district health teams (DHTs) have existed for some time, but with increasing decentralization of the country's health system, skill requirements for planning and managing have expanded. To increase the capacity of DHTs to undertake problem analysis and strategic management, the government initiated a training program in 1988, with the assistance of the United Kingdom's Overseas Development Administration, the Finnish International Development Agency, the Ministry of Public Health of Austria, and the United Nations Development Programme.

Within a period of three years, 65 of 110 districts, covering over 75 percent of the country's population, were involved in the program. It consists essentially of three stages:

- A "start-up workshop," including sessions on problem identification, problem analysis, strategy development, and formulation of action plans. During the next three to four months these plans are actually implemented.

- A "review workshop" to assess the experience of participants in trying to implement their plans, analyzing achievements and constraints. Lessons learned for effective planning and implementation are reviewed, problem statements reformulated, and strategies reviewed and revised. The relationship between management strengthening and the implementation

ability in the performance of private voluntary organizations and private-for-profit providers. Different concepts of basic health services often result in patchy coverage, poor accountability to local communities, failure to mobilize community health endeavors, and weaknesses in management systems. To address such problems, DHTs in Swaziland include district-level officials and representatives of church missions within the district. Through planning workshops and regular meetings, the DHTs decide how to combine government and mission services, and identify budget needs. In the Kigoma region of Tanzania and the Bungoma district of Kenya, district planning workshops brought together DHTs and NGOs to jointly analyze health needs and the strengths and weaknesses of each type of provider. As a result, the NGOs reoriented their services to be more supportive of district priorities (World Bank 1992e).

Formal agreements can be used to help DHTs perform their coordinating functions by defining the public sector's obligations to private voluntary and private-for-profit providers (for example, if buildings, equipment, personnel, or training are to be provided, and according to what standards) and the obligations of private providers to the government (for example, maintaining of buildings, reporting, and ensuring continuation of public services). Contracts can also be used to define the obligations of public and private providers in imple-

---

Box 8-3, continued

of technical programs is also analyzed at this stage. Participants then draw up revised or new action plans to be implemented over the next six to seven months.

■ An "advanced review workshop" takes participants through another review and reformulation process and introduces them to a more comprehensive format for action planning. The new format requires that teams give greater emphasis to developing indicators for monitoring their achievements. A final review meeting is held at the end of the six- to seven-month implementation period.

Assessments of this program—now fully documented in a handbook for the

World Health Organization (Cassels and Janovsky 1991)—suggest it is having several positive effects. First, it builds a sense of ownership as participants analyze and tackle problems they themselves perceive to be important. Second, it fosters teamwork, as responsibilities for implementation are shared by different team members rather than just district medical officers. Third, it fosters incremental learning as the workshops are structured so that teams build on initial achievements and new ideas are introduced as they become relevant. And fourth, management and planning skills tend to be ingrained through repetition, practice with strategy development, and reviews of performance.

menting government programs, such as immunizations and TB control. A number of countries, such as Malawi, have long had such agreements, and Ghana recently concluded one.

Finally, through the process of decentralization and district-based services, intersectoral collaboration can have a real impact on the health of Africans. To make this a reality, comprehensive health policies need to be established at the national level, and interministerial committees formed to translate intersectoral aspects of these policies into countrywide strategies and targets. This sets the stage for intersectoral collaboration at the local government, district, and community levels. At this point, district development committees, made up of public sector representatives in health, education, nutrition, and public works (water, sanitation, and roads), can realistically assess the health implications of "nonhealth" investments and prepare district-level plans for complementary health, water, sanitation, nutrition, and other investments.

Enhancing Community Participation

There is overwhelming evidence that participation of local community groups in the design and implementation of health sector activities and the kinds of intersectoral interventions already described have a significant impact on success and sustainability (Vaillancourt, Nassim, and Brown 1992; Mburu and Boerma 1989). Moreover, community involvement in the *management* of health facilities is emerging as an important aspect of district-based health systems in many African countries. Giving appropriate legal status to community management structures within African health care systems can facilitate their operation, especially in the traditionally centralized systems of francophone countries where the accountability of public employees to local bodies is rarely recognized (Cosmas 1994).

Placing greater decisionmaking in the hands of community representatives tends to be associated with more rapid and comprehensive identification of health needs and expectations; more reliable identification of the poorest households in the community; easier adaptation to cultural and religious preferences; unbureaucratic employment of local or community staff; and greater flexibility in executing activities outside normal work hours (for example, nights, weekends); use of nonconventional and creative methods to promote education and information (for example, theater, animation, dances, and film production); and practical development of technologies that can be adapted to local conditions (for example, locally produced ceramic water-reservoir with simple tap to avoid secondary household contamination) (World Bank 1992e).

In a district-based system, with central, regional, and district-level responsibilities as described in Box 8-2, complementary community management functions commonly include the following (WHO 1988a):

- Recruitment, payment, and supervision of community health workers and trained traditional birth attendants
- Provision of community financial support toward the cost of health services
- Contribution of labor and materials to construct clinics and staff housing
- Participation in local health planning initiatives
- Organization and promotion of preventive health care, particularly activities concerned with maternal and child health, immunization, and oral rehydration
- Participation in health information and communication programs, particularly by translating suitable material into local languages and dialects.

Community management committees can improve the performance of health systems for four reasons. First, they can play a major role in holding health care providers accountable to their clients. Indeed, accountability and transparency, based on continuous dialogue and interaction between service providers and communities, characterize well-functioning health centers (Box 8-4).

Second, involvement of community management committees helps contribute to good governance at the subdistrict level in the sense that diverse kin, ethnic, social, and cultural groups have an opportunity to present their grievances and collaborate in overcoming them.

Third, participatory decisionmaking develops a sense of ownership. When community management committees participate in adopting a particular approach to resolving local-level problems, such as nutritional monitoring, they are more likely to become engaged in the activities involved, assessing results, and monitoring progress. And finally, when communities are involved in managing district health facilities, relationships of empathy and trust are more likely to evolve between health care providers and clients.

Building on community strengths is not only a matter of inviting communities to participate in management. Part of the challenge is to attune health care providers and the health professions to the advantages of involving community representatives. In some countries, this challenge is being met by reorienting formal medical training to include practice and research in community settings. For example, medical students are being exposed to community-based research at the University Centre for Health Sciences in Cameroon; the University of Nairobi, Kenya; the University of Dar es Salaam, Tanzania; the University of

BOX 8-4. ACCOUNTABILITY AND TRANSPARENCY IN THE USE OF COMMUNITY RESOURCES

When health centers use cost-sharing or drug revolving funds with community resources, transparency is vital for establishing accountability and trust between health providers and clients. Transparency can be facilitated by posting fee schedules and statements of receipts and expenditures for all to see. When persons are treated, the diagnosis can be entered in their individual treatment booklets, along with a receipt of the fee paid. Literate members of the household or community and supervisors can then verify whether what was paid corresponds to what is noted, as well as posted. Community participation in the management of funds generated through user fees also means that supervisors and community members can compare the balance in accounts with receipts registered at the health facility.

Recent studies of community financing of health centers in Rwanda, Zaire, Guinea, Benin, and Mali reveal that many collaborative management mechanisms are evolving. These include community control of money through accounts with double signa

tures, double locks on drug stocks with the community committee and the health staff each holding the keys to only one, and stamps or photos on registration cards to identify households that have paid local insurance fees. Efficiency indicators associated with these measures further show that, so far, there has been little "leakage" in these systems.

In Botswana, district councils, which are agencies of local government rather than of the Ministry of Health, ensure oversight over local health care providers. This prevents stakeholders from capturing the services, and ensures local accountability.

Arrangements such as those outlined above give beneficiaries a "voice" in management of care. The option of "exit" to nongovernment health care providers—an element of competition—contributes to transparency by making clear which providers are perceived most favorably by patients and their families.

Source of Country Studies: Galland 1990; Bitran and others 1986; Miller 1987; Knippenberg and others 1990; Gbedenou and others 1991; Ministère de la Santé Publique, Mali 1990; Shepard, Vian, and Kleinan 1990.

Zambia; and the University of Zimbabwe. To earn a Doctor of Medicine degree in Cameroon, students must serve as local interns and produce a report on "integrated community medicine" (Aleta 1992).

As caretakers of their own health, community members can be mobilized to participate in a wide range of basic health care and intersectoral activities for health, including needs identification, project design, and adaptation of project activities and technologies to local needs. To illustrate:

- In Ethiopia, community groups played an important role in mobilizing people for immunization, tracing defaulters, providing transport for immunization sessions, and educating people about the importance of immunization (District Health Development Study Core Group 1991).

- In Guinea and Lesotho, community representatives have formed health management committees to participate in the development of programs to strengthen nutrition and maternal and child health in health centers, and to define the role of cost recovery in meeting financing needs.

- In Benin, village management committees have made decisions about the ability of people to pay and have written off the costs of caring for indigents even though formal exoneration mechanisms did not exist.

Community groups can also participate in information collection, monitoring and evaluation, promotion and management of local-level services, and maintenance of infrastructure. In Iringa, Tanzania, communities have participated in monitoring and assessing their children's growth patterns, thus encouraging them to take action to reduce malnutrition. In Benin, communities took responsibility for preparing appropriate storage conditions for essential drugs supplied by the government. Within three Yoruba villages in western Nigeria, at least twenty-eight small and nonbureaucratic local organizations were available to mobilize community involvement in health center activities (Mebrahtu 1991). In Zaire, community management committees gradually assumed full responsibility for operating health centers (Lamboray and Laing 1984).

Finally, community groups can play a vital role in monitoring environmental problems and mobilizing resources in support of intersectoral interventions. Among the hundreds of thousands of communities in Africa that are not served by public works, such as piped water and sewer systems, community initiatives to install hand pumps and pit latrines could have a decisive effect on health and on the sustainability of health outcomes. In Ghana, community groups made viable recommendations for improving environmental sanitation, the most striking of which was to establish community-level environment tribunals to enforce public compliance. In Guinea and Benin, the role of local health management committees has already been extended beyond preventive health interventions to environmental health, water supply, and other matters (World Bank 1992b).

As district health teams and community management committees work together to improve the quantity and quality of health services, parallel processes need to be established to facilitate day-to-day problem identification. Even the best designed structures can fail because of unforeseen problems. Again, monitoring and evaluation are critical, especially at the local or health center level. Criteria may vary, but they usually include some combination of availability of services (for example, essential drugs and vaccines); access to care; actual use of services; and quality (Tanahashi 1978; and Knippenberg and others 1990) (Box 8-5). Indeed, the motivational benefits of such monitoring and evaluation cannot be overstated, especially when the identification and resolution of problems yield a sense that people at the local level have the power to change their lives.

Encouraging Institutional Pluralism

Improving management and institutional reform can hardly be undertaken by ministries of health alone. Cooperation with private voluntary and other non-government organizations is required, because they too manage health facilities

---

BOX 8-5. MONITORING THE PROVISION OF LOCAL HEALTH CARE SERVICES IN GUINEA

In Guinea, local monitoring of health care services has helped health care providers to identify specific problems and bottlenecks and to determine the actions required to address them.

As shown in the figure, health center staff monitored the following variables:

Availability: the percentage of time during which the resources required to implement an intervention are physically available at the health center

Accessibility: the percentage of the target population living sufficiently close to have easy access to service delivery points

Use: the percentage of the target population coming into contact with the service, as measured by use at least once

Adequate coverage: the percentage of the population receiving a complete intervention, such as the total number of vaccinations required

Effective coverage: the percentage of the population receiving services of standardized and verified quality, reflecting, in the case of vaccinations, adherence to the cold chain and use of unexpired vaccines.

The figure reveals that nearly 60 percent of pregnant women used some prenatal care in Seredou District, over the period covered, but that only one-quarter received adequate care, as measured in this case by the standard of three consultations. This suggests that active follow-up in the community on the quality of patient-provider interactions might merit examination. In contrast, in Sinko District, problems in ensuring effective coverage of pregnant women with tetanus toxoid vac-

at the district and community level. The same applies to private-for-profit providers. Of the 770 health clinics in Malawi, for example, 35 percent are operated by the Ministry of Health, 20 percent by private voluntary organizations (church missions), 13 percent by private companies and estates, 12 percent by the Ministry of Local Government, 13 percent by parastatals, NGOs, and other ministries, and 6 percent by private-for-profit providers.

The encouragement of institutional pluralism—and the willingness of governments to accept nongovernment bodies outside of direct state control—therefore needs to be seen in the wider context of broadening civil society. Governments can help to tap the enormous potential of NGOs by providing an enabling legal environment for their establishment and facilitating their registration. The health sector can make important contributions in this respect. A first step is simply to refrain from harassing professional and private voluntary associations by means of unnecessary regulations (Landell-Mills 1992).

Box 8-5, continued

cinations were principally attributable to low geographic accessibility to health care. As less than 40 percent of the population is within easy access of health care, there is a need to intensify outreach.

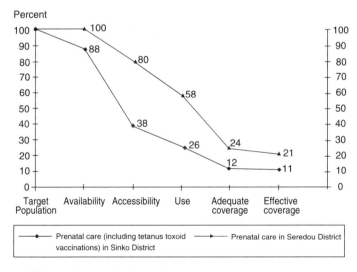

Source: Knippenberg and others 1990.

The benefits of institutional pluralism are apparent from the following examples:

■ Collaboration between governments and religious missions has been particularly important in Africa. At the district level in Zaire, for example, 50 percent of 306 health zones established by the Five-Year Health Plan of 1982–86 are managed by NGOs or closely collaborate with them. At the national level the SANRU (Santé Rurale) Basic Rural Health Project has combined the efforts of the Protestant Church of Zaire and USAID to develop 100 health zones throughout Zaire, 75 percent of which are being managed in collaboration with diverse local NGO groups. At the international level, upwards of 100 different international NGOs assist medical work in Zaire, largely by channeling assistance directly to hospitals or health zones. About half of the sixty-five member "denominations" of the Protestant Church are receiving assistance for their medical work from sister churches overseas (Sambe and Baer, n.d.).

■ Women's groups in Sub-Saharan Africa are striving to ensure that women's health issues receive adequate attention and support, and to encourage governments, international agencies, and religious organizations to take women's perspectives into account in designing health programs. In Uganda, for example, a group of women's NGOs formed a consortium in 1989 and are implementing a community-level program to reduce maternal mortality and morbidity, with funding from the World Bank and other agencies. Women's groups in Tanzania, Ethiopia, Uganda, Kenya, and other countries have taken the lead role in combating harmful traditional practices, such as female genital mutilation, through public information and advocacy targeted at national policymakers and local decisionmakers. In Ghana, the Ghana Registered Midwives Association provides a significant proportion of maternal health and family planning services and is a key member of a task force that is advising the government on ways to improve the quality of maternal health services.

■ A Coordinating Assembly of NGOs for primary health care has been established in collaboration with the Ministry of Health in Swaziland, and a Primary Health Care Forum has been established for collaboration between the government and local NGOs in Zimbabwe. These bodies include task forces on health education, water and sanitation, and health orientation and training. Partnerships of this nature help public and nongovernment bodies to share objectives and identify common targets. They can also facilitate the removal of barriers to establishing and operating private voluntary organizations.

■ National associations of public health professionals have been formed in Botswana, Kenya, Lesotho, Mozambique, Tanzania, Uganda, Zambia, Zaire, and Zimbabwe, in some cases in cooperation with the Canadian Public Health

Association. The formation of such bodies facilitates consensus-building among health care providers on future health policies and strategies. Their participation in the development, monitoring, and evaluation of health policies can go a long way toward improving health sector effectiveness, especially in view of the multidisciplinary nature of public health activities. These associations are members of the World Federation of Public Health Associations, an international NGO working to improve the health of people throughout the world. Regional public health associations are also evolving, including an East and Central African Association serving anglophone countries with headquarters in Arusha, and a francophone subregional association based in Kalimba.

Conclusion

Realizing the benefits of health investments in Sub-Saharan Africa requires more than improving the quantity and quality of pharmaceuticals, health care personnel, and so on. How those inputs are planned, allocated, organized, and managed can determine whether the services are cost-effective and can make the difference between sustainable and unsustainable outcomes. How institutions rationalize functions and devolve decisionmaking authority to various administrative levels can mean the difference between integrated, well-functioning systems and piecemeal approaches confounded by duplication, overlap, and lack of intersectoral coordination. How health and related personnel see their roles at central, regional, district, and community levels can make the difference between a structure featuring clear incentives and teamwork, and a structure immobilized by frustration, apathy, and pursuit of cross-purposes. And, how communities are involved in local management decisions can make the difference between health systems that treat people as objects and those built on community partnerships and ownership. The challenge now is to accelerate the process of institutional and management reforms, especially by clarifying managerial and decisionmaking roles, responsibilities, and authorities at the central, regional, district, and community levels.

Costing and Paying for
the Basic Package of
Health Services

ANY PLAN to expand preventive and primary care in Africa raises the questions of how much it will cost and where the money to pay for it will be found. It would be understandable if providers of health care estimated future needs on the basis of past expenditure levels, but that is clearly less desirable than determining the financing requirements for more cost-effective approaches. That is what this chapter does, because there is a strong interest among African countries in estimating the cost of the basic package of health services proposed in this study.

Two sets of costs are presented here. One set pertains to low-income countries in Sub-Saharan Africa (hereafter "low-income Africa") and presents the average costs of basic health care, supporting services, and intersectoral interventions in rural and periurban areas on the basis of experience in several African countries. The other set shows how costs are likely to rise with higher levels of income, wages, and prices. This set is based on Zimbabwe's experience.

The costing exercise for low-income Africa provides qualified grounds for optimism. It concludes that a basic package of health services can be made available to consumers at a cost of about $13 per capita. That figure should prompt reflection on what African households are getting now for the amount they pay, which in many cases exceeds $13 per capita. The next issues are how resources might be reallocated to produce more cost-effective results and where additional resources might be found to enable the poorest countries, and the poorest groups within countries, to pay for them.

The annual per capita cost of $13 for low-income Africa was derived from data on the costs of operating well-functioning health centers and district hospitals, and the costs of intersectoral interventions in several African countries. The overall cost was annualized by adding the yearly costs of recurrent items, such as salaries and essential drugs, to the amortized costs of capital investments, such as buildings and equipment. Amortization is required to translate initial outlays of capital into an annual amount, thus yielding information about the yearly cost of paying off the outlays over time (assuming a loan was used to finance the capital outlay). Capital costs were annualized on the basis of the economic life of the assets at a 4 percent discount rate (World Bank 1993a).

Pooled recurrent and capital costs were divided by the "catchment" population of district-based facilities to derive an average unit cost on a per capita basis. These per capita costs can then be reconstituted to produce total costs for the combined population of several communities: a network of districts that make up a region; or for all districts made up of rural or periurban populations.

Qualifications are in order. First, no pretense is made that the cost scenarios presented here are definitive or applicable to all Sub-Saharan African countries. The purpose here is to give a rough order of the magnitude of costs, to illustrate the process by which they can be determined, and to encourage African countries to prepare their own estimates. (The methodology employed and data used in this chapter are fully documented in World Bank 1993a.) Second, the indicative costs presented here are most relevant to people living in rural and periurban areas. Third, the costs of particular services can be expected to change as patterns of disease, income, and health expenditures change over time, implying that relatively static approaches to estimating costs should give way to more dynamic ones.

Low-Income Africa

Indicative costs for low-income Africa are presented in Table 9-1. These derive from an input approach—that is, what is needed to provide a package of basic services in terms of salaries, infrastructure, drugs, training, management, and related materials. (Health planners and budget officials find this approach useful because it provides cost estimates for line items that are similar to those found in traditional budget documents.) The total per capita cost of $13.22 has three components: health care and facilities (about 60 percent); intersectoral interventions (about 30 percent); and institutional support (about 10 percent).

Health care and facilities: Systems composed of well-functioning health centers and a first-referral hospital are capable of responding to and accommodating more than 90 percent of health demands in an average rural or periurban district at an annual per capita cost estimated at $7.74. It is assumed that these services are provided within administrative districts, each district having

Table 9-1. Annual Indicative Per Capita Costs for a District-based Health Care System: Input Approach

Type of service	Cost (U.S. dollars)		
	Low-income Africa	Higher-income African country	Difference (percent)
HEALTH CARE AND FACILITIES			
Level 1: Health center	4.60	6.72	46
Operating costs	3.78	4.84	28
Capital costs	0.73	1.75	140
In-service training	0.09	0.13	44
Level 2: District hospital	3.14	4.03	28
Operating costs	1.75	2.24	28
Capital costs	1.35	1.73	28
In-service training	0.04	0.06	50
Subtotal, health care and facilities	7.74	10.75	39
INTERSECTORAL INTERVENTIONS			
Water	2.56	2.19	−15
Sanitation	1.42	1.36	4
Subtotal, intersectoral interventions	3.98	3.55	−11
INSTITUTIONAL SUPPORT			
District health care management team	0.29	0.40	38
Operating costs	0.15	0.24	60
Capital costs	0.13	0.16	23
In-service training	0.01	0.01	0
National management structure (15 percent of total health care costs)	0.82	1.15	40
Initial training (5 percent of total health care costs)	0.27	0.38	41
Incremental salary bonus (15 percent of total salaries)	0.12	0.14	17
Subtotal, institutional support	1.50	2.07	39
GRAND TOTAL COSTS	**13.22**	**16.37**	**24**
Total operating cost	7.86	9.50	25
Total capital cost	5.36	6.87	23

Note: District profile: 150,000 inhabitants; 15 health centers (10,000 in each center).
Source: Adapted from World Bank 1993a.

one district (or referral) hospital, fifteen health centers, and an average population of 150,000. Within such districts household members typically make their first contact with modern health care, and this is where equity can be effectively promoted. Health centers and hospitals should collect information on their operating costs, capital costs, and in-service training costs. That will make it possible to determine the staff profile, infrastructure, and equipment, and to assign indicative costs to them.

Intersectoral interventions: The cost of intersectoral interventions is also presented on an annual per capita basis. This indicative cost was derived from actual costs in several African countries that were then averaged for a prototype district with a catchment population of 150,000. These actual costs were the recurrent and capital costs of safe drinking water and sanitation facilities. The overall cost amounted to $3.98 per capita. Several qualifications involved in making this calculation are noted below.

▪ The cost of a water system in a rural or periurban area will vary considerably, depending on water source, community size, housing density, hydrogeological conditions, local drilling costs, water consumption, and pumping system (manual, electrical, diesel, or solar). The least expensive pumping alternative (and the one used in this study) in communities of less than 1,000 people will generally be hand-operated pumps. It is assumed that 250 persons are served per handpump, and that the cost includes drilling a borehole and purchasing and maintaining borehole equipment with an annual life of about twenty years.

▪ The cost of providing adequate sanitation facilities in rural and periurban areas will also vary considerably, depending on the design of the facility, the type of construction materials used, labor costs, housing density, groundwater and soil conditions, and the size of the families to be served. It is assumed that for a population of 10,000, each family of ten people (on average) would have its own ventilated improved pit (VIP) latrine made from local building materials. Total construction costs would include labor and materials as well as planning and mobilization four years hence, when replacement latrines would have to be constructed.

Institutional support: The district health management team (DHT) would handle administrative and support functions. These would include monitoring and supervising the district health care system, in-service training of hospital and health center staff, logistical support for the hospital and health centers, and liaison with local, regional, and central authorities. The DHT would have a staff of seven consisting of a medical doctor, a pharmacist, a registered nurse, a financial manager/accountant, a water and sanitation specialist, a sociologist or communication specialist, and a driver. The infrastructure would include one building, the necessary equipment (including furniture), and two vehicles.

The district team would also need support at a higher level that would include health research, planning, program formulation, logistical support, administration, coordination between districts, and initial personnel training. A national management structure would be required to coordinate the activities of the DHTs and prepare national standards. It is assumed that these overhead costs would amount to 15 percent of total operating, capital, and in-service training costs at the district level. Initial training of personnel is considered to be a capital cost amounting to 5 percent of total district costs. Finally, in view of the importance of monetary incentives for staff, as well as the lag in salary structures in most countries, an incremental salary bonus of 15 percent has been provided. The total cost of institutional support would be $1.50.

The indicative costs of these inputs (Table 9-1). are equal to the indicative costs of "outputs" (services to be rendered to households and communities, as well as institutional support) shown in Table 9-2. Maternal services, including predelivery care, delivery care, postdelivery care, and nutrition for pregnant and lactating women, for example, would be provided as part of the package. These maternity services would cost, on average, about $0.47, or 3.5 percent of $13.22.

Although "outputs" are not very useful for budgeting purposes, assessing outputs is helpful in determining priorities and estimating the cost-effectiveness of various interventions. For example, it is easier to determine the relationship between the cost of providing well-baby services and quantified improvements in the health of babies than it is to relate the capital cost of a health center to the health status of babies.

Costs in a Country with Higher Income

Zimbabwe was selected for comparative purposes because its per capita GNP is more than double the average of low-income Africa. Health care in Zimbabwe shares some of the features of the cost-effective approach described here, and data are relatively abundant. Zimbabwe's unit costs illustrate how much low-income countries might expect to pay in the future. Indicative costs for Zimbabwe are also presented in Table 9-1. The total per capita cost is $16.37 and covers health care and facilities (66 percent), intersectoral interventions (22 percent), and institutional support (12 percent).

Zimbabwe's costs are only 24 percent higher than those estimated for low-income Africa, but they are 39 percent higher for the health care component and 11 percent lower for intersectoral interventions. The basic health care services offered at the health center and first-referral hospital remain essentially the same, as do the demographic composition and epidemiological profile of the

Table 9-2.   Annual Indicative Per Capita Costs for a District-based Health Care System: Output Approach
(U.S. dollars)

Type of service	Low-income Africa
INDIVIDUAL HEALTH CARE SERVICES	
Level 1: Health center	
Maternal services	0.47
Pre-delivery care	
Delivery care	
Post-delivery care	
Nutrition: pregnant and lactating women	
Well-baby services	1.52
Expanded Programme of Immunization (EPI)	
Micronutrient supplements	
Nutrition: ages 0–5	
Supplementary feeding: ages 0–2	
Schoolchildren health program	0.21
Antihelminthic services (ages 5–14)	
Vitamin A plus iodine, as needed	
Curative care (especially children ages 0–5)	0.46
Basic trauma	
Malaria	
Diarrhea	
Opportunistic infections (AIDS related)	
Other local infections	
Limited chronic care	0.11
Tuberculosis treatment	
STD services (testing and treatment)	0.13
Family planning	0.87
Provision of contraceptives	
Incremental family planning	
IEC (for nutrition, family planning, HIV/STD)	0.82
Subtotal, level 1	4.60

Table continued on next page

communities served. While Zimbabwe has begun to enter the demographic transition, its main priority still is to provide a basic package to all. What differs between Zimbabwe and low-income Africa is the intensity of demand for certain preventive services. This is influenced by higher levels of education among households, reinforced by higher income levels. Greater demand translates into a need for additional staff and equipment, expanded facilities, and higher drug costs.

Table 9-2., *continued*

Type of service	Low-income Africa
Level 2: District hospital	
In-patient care	2.20
Obstetrics and gynecology	
Pediatrics	
Medicine: Infectious diseases	
Basic surgery	
Out-patient care	0.94
Emergencies	
Referrals	
Subtotal, level 2	3.14
Subtotal, individual health care services	7.74
INTERSECTORAL INTERVENTIONS	
Water	2.56
Sanitation	1.42
Subtotal, intersectoral interventions	3.98
INSTITUTIONAL SUPPORT	
National management support	0.82
Surveillance, monitoring and evaluation	
National capacity building	
Initial training	0.27
District health team	0.29
District-level salary bonus (15 percent of total salaries)	0.12
Subtotal, institutional support	1.50
GRAND TOTAL COST OF BASIC PACKAGE	**13.22**

Note: District profile: 150,000 inhabitants; 15 health centers (10,000 in each center).
Source: World Bank data.

Judging from the Zimbabwe experience, the costs that change the most as income increases are salary levels, funds for additional staff, and provision of housing for staff (a standard expectation in Zimbabwe). Four staff members in a health center are paid a total of about $10,500 a year, compared with $5,700 for the same number in a low-income country. Annual salaries of doctors at a first-referral hospital are about $12,000 each, compared with about $4,300 per doctor in a low-income African country. Zimbabwean drug costs are about 30 percent higher. In Zimbabwe, two staff housing units are provided for the four staff at the health center, and eighteen units are available to the staff at a first-referral hospital.

The costs of intersectoral interventions are 11 percent lower in Zimbabwe than in low-income Africa because greater demand for safe water and sanitation systems has produced economies of scale in the production of boreholes and water pumps, and construction of pit latrines.

Who Should Pay for What?

The basic package of health services includes some that are public in nature (institutional support), others of a mixed public-private nature (preventive and curative services for communicable diseases), and still others private in nature (care for injuries and noncommunicable diseases). This raises the question: Who should pay for what?

Alternate methods can be used to shed light on this question, each with advantages and disadvantages. One method, the "intervention approach," seeks to identify the inherent public or private nature of an intervention. For example, educating the public about a communicable health problem (e.g., measles) might be assumed to be an inherent public good that should therefore be paid for by the public. From this perspective, treatment of a patient's broken leg might be assumed to be of a private nature and therefore to be paid for with private funds. But most interventions in health have public and private benefits. Hence, using this approach means that a large number of interventions of various kinds must be identified and both the public and private benefits of each determine who will pay for what.

A second method, the "targeting approach" to determining public and private financial responsibilities, concentrates on identifying target groups in need of some type of health intervention. Such target groups might consist, say, of those living in low-income neighborhoods or all children suffering from a particular illness. The disadvantage of this approach is that providing the package only to target groups is not always administratively feasible. Moreover, a public intervention that produces mainly private benefits is essentially a subsidy, and therefore a relatively uneconomic use of public funds. The "targeting approach" addresses the issue from an equity perspective.

Each of these approaches is drawn upon to suggest an *indicative* financing mix. The first step is to identify pure public goods, which would be financed by public funds. All remaining interventions are relegated to an "other" category and include most of the mixed goods whose public and private benefits, in proportional terms, are hard to distinguish. The second step is to examine all of the "other" goods from a targeting perspective. What proportion of their cost should be covered by public funds, bearing in mind private demand, so as to ensure coverage of target groups, especially the poor?

Table 9-3. Who Pays for What in the Basic Package: An Indicative Intervention and Targeting Approach

Type of service	Cost (U.S. dollars)	Public or other service	Public financing Share (percent)	Public financing Amount (U.S. dollars)	Private financing Share (percent)	Private financing Amount (U.S. dollars)
A. INDIVIDUAL HEALTH CARE SERVICES						
Level 1: Health center (15 centers)						
Maternal services	0.47	Other	80	0.38	20	0.09
Well-baby services	1.52	Other	80	1.22	20	0.30
Schoolchildren health program	0.21	Other	80	0.17	20	0.04
Curative care (especially children 0–5)	0.46	Other	60	0.28	40	0.18
Limited chronic care	0.11	Other	60	0.07	40	0.04
STD/HIV services	0.13	Other	60	0.08	40	0.05
Family planning	0.87	Other	70	0.61	30	0.26
IEC (for nutrition, FP, HIV/STD)	0.82	Public	100	0.82	0	0.00
Subtotal, level 1	4.60		79	3.69	21	0.96

Level 2: District hospital						
In-patient care	2.20	Other	50	1.10	50	1.10
Out-patient care	0.94	Other	40	0.38	60	0.56
Subtotal, level 2	3.14		47	1.48	53	1.66
Total, individual care services	7.74		66	5.12	34	2.62
B. INTERSECTORAL INTERVENTIONS						
Water	2.56	Other	30	0.77	70	1.79
Sanitation	1.42	Other	30	0.43	70	0.99
Total, intersectoral interventions	3.98		30	1.20	70	2.78
C. INSTITUTIONAL SUPPORT						
National management support	0.82	Public	100	0.82	0	0.00
Initial training	0.27	Public	100	0.27	0	0.00
District health management team	0.29	Public	100	0.29	0	0.00
District-level salary bonus	0.12	Public	100	0.12	0	0.00
Total, institutional support	1.50		100	1.50	0	0.00
TOTAL FINANCING OF BASIC PACKAGE	13.22		59	7.82	41	5.40

Source: World Bank data.

An indicative financing mix for the package of basic health services for low-income Africa is provided in Table 9-3. Most of the services in parts A and B yield a mixture of private goods and positive externalities. Under this arrangement, rough calculations suggest that about four-fifths of the health center package would be financed by the public sector and about one-fifth would be paid for by households. Services such as water and sanitation are estimated to have a 30 percent public component and a 70 percent private component. Services included in Part C are deemed to be purely public goods and as such would be financed exclusively by the public sector.

Table 9-3 is not intended to serve as a model that all countries or districts should follow. Its purpose, rather, is to illustrate a methodology that can help resolve the issue of financing. Each country and district would devise its own public and private financing configurations.

Affordability

The package costs less than what is now spent on health by countries representing about one-third of Sub-Saharan Africa's people. This statement is based on expenditure data in Table 9-4. Countries for which reliable data are available have been divided into three groups, according to their relative levels of per capita GNP and expenditures on health. Grouping countries in this way, though somewhat arbitrary, is conducive to analyzing differences in health expenditures and to making estimates of the affordability of the package of cost-effective interventions discussed in this report.

The "high" group of countries, representing only about one-twentieth of Africa's population, spends $68 per capita, on average, on health services. Reallocation is the key issue here. Are these countries receiving the same benefits that could be provided for around $16 per capita in a country like Zimbabwe? Private expenditures per capita in this group are about $19 and, on average, are clearly sufficient to pay for the package. A number of the countries in this group are now moving aggressively to institute or expand user fees at health care facilities and are exploring ways of expanding insurance to cover curative care. This should facilitate greater spending of government and donor funds on public health goods and services. Clearly, the basic package is affordable in these countries, assuming a reasonably equitable distribution of health expenditures. Indeed, these countries may soon be able to include services in the basic package that other African countries cannot afford.

The "medium" group of countries, representing nearly 30 percent of Sub-Saharan Africa's people, spends, on average, $16 per capita on health services. For this group, reallocation of sufficient funds from some of their current uses to ensure funding of the basic package is likely to be more difficult. Private

Table 9-4. Selected African Countries Grouped by Relative Level of Expenditure on Health, 1990

	Country grouping		
Item	*High expenditure*	*Medium expenditure*	*Low expenditure*
Country characteristics			
Population (millions)	14.1	95.5	340.3
Average GNP per capita (U.S. dollars)	757	395	225
Expenditure per capita (U.S. dollars)			
Private	19	7	4
Government	40	6	2
Donor	9	3	2
Total	68	16	8

Note: High-expenditure countries: Botswana, Lesotho, Swaziland, and Zimbabwe. Medium-expenditure countries: Burundi, Cameroon, The Gambia, Ghana, Kenya, Liberia, Malawi, Niger, Rwanda, Senegal, and Zambia. Low-expenditure countries: Burkina Faso, Ethiopia, Mali, Nigeria, Sierra Leone, Somalia, Uganda, and Zaire.
Source: United Nations Development Programme and World Bank 1992; World Bank 1993e.

expenditures per capita in this group are $7. Since per capita income in this group is almost double that of the "low" group, however, it seems reasonable to believe that households would be able and willing to spend more, especially if a cost-effective package of basic health services is offered to them (Chapter 10). If countries in this group followed Malawi's example and government expenditures on health were raised by a modest 0.5 to 1 percent per year, the $6 now available for health could be doubled within ten years. In that case, donors might also be expected to increase their participation if programs were well formulated with credible implementation plans. Overall, then, while a greater effort to reallocate and mobilize resources for health will be needed, the basic package is affordable in these countries.

Countries in the "low" group, representing about two-thirds of Sub-Saharan Africa's people, spend on average $8 per capita on health services. This does not include public and private expenditures on water and sanitation. Private expenditures on health in this group are about $4 per capita. Assuming a sufficient level of private *demand*, and that private expenditures could be mobilized and reallocated, a major part—though far from all—of the costs of the package could be met.

Governments and donors both spend another $2 in the "low" group, but much of this sum might not be available, given prior spending commitments to specific projects, central and teaching hospitals, and other obligations. Part of the shortfall could be covered if governments in the "low" group raised their financial commitment to health to a level comparable to the average for all less developed countries. On the basis of calculations in Chapter 10, this would result in an increase in health expenditures by those governments, from about $2 to $5 per capita, thus providing another $3 per capita. It is reasonable to think that another $2 per capita could be solicited from donors by governments that had sound health reform programs and a demonstrated commitment to implementation. That sum would probably suffice to cover shortfalls, especially when private expenditures on water and sanitation are factored in. It is clear, in any case, that a major resource mobilization effort will be needed in and for those African countries with the lowest per capita incomes and health expenditures.

Closing the Financing Gap

How much in additional resources needs to be raised for better health in Africa? Rough estimates in Table 9-5 suggest that about $1.6 billion more annually needs to be mobilized to help finance health services for the Africans in the low-income and low health expenditure countries. The donor share of about $650 million a year would raise external assistance by about 50 percent above the level of $1.2 billion attained in 1990.

Another means of assessing financial implications is to compare the per capita cost of the package as a percentage share of per capita GDP with what is being spent on health now as a share of per capita GNP. Among countries in the "low" group, the cost of the package represents about 5.2 percent of average per capita GDP ($248). This compares with actual per capita health expenditures, from all sources and for all purposes, of about 3.2 percent of per capita GDP in these countries. Closing the gap is not, however, simply a matter of boosting expenditures by another 2 percent of GDP per capita. A major challenge involves reallocating expenditures from current uses to more cost-effective ends, determining the share of public health goods and services, and apportioning responsibilities to the various stakeholders to fill gaps.

For countries in the "middle" group, the per capita cost of the package amounts to about 2.9 percent of average per capita GDP ($443). This compares with per capita expenditures on health from all sources of about 3.6 percent of per capita GDP. Here again, reallocating expenditures will be a major challenge.

Countries in the "high" group have far greater prospects of reallocating funds. Their current expenditures on health from all sources amount to nearly 9 percent of per capita GDP. The basic package would cost about 2 percent of per capita GDP.

Table 9-5.   Rough Estimates of Additional Revenue Effort For Health by Government and Donors in Low-Income Africa

Scenario	Additional funds (millions of U.S. dollars per year)
1. Governments more than double their expenditures on health as a percentage of total government expenditures, raising per capita expenditures from $2 to $5. Additional funds = $3 x 328 million people	984
2. Donors double their aid for low-income Africa from $2 to $4, thus nearly matching the government effort. Additional funds = $2 x 328 million people	656
Total **additional** funds **per year** over the next ten years	1,640

Assumption: Just as the "low" group represents 68 percent of the total population of all countries in Table 9-4, it is assumed to represent 68 percent of all people in Sub-Saharan Africa in 1992 (502 million, projected to increase to 634 million by 2000). This implies an average of 386 million people (68 percent multiplied by the average of 502 million and 634 million). The total rural and periurban population is assumed to be 85 percent times 386 million, or 328 million.
Source: World Bank data.

Conclusion

The pace at which cost-effective packages of basic health services could be made more widely available is a critical issue. There will undoubtedly be considerable variation among countries in their commitment to reform and capacity for implementation, and thus in the nature of the transition. In almost all cases, a phased-in approach makes the greatest sense. Some countries, such as Benin, Guinea, and Nigeria, are already experimenting with a district-based system of health care. Thus, part of the money needed to pay for the package is already on hand. As lessons are learned, groundwork can be carefully planned for expansion into new areas, involving information campaigns about basic services to be provided, the rationale behind charging fees, community involvement in mobilizing resources and making provision for the poor, and so on. Other countries are recovering from political upheaval and may wish to begin reconstructing their health sector by building health centers and first-referral hospitals. Still other countries may wish to take action to bring public providers of health care progressively together with private voluntary providers in the pursuit of cost-effective approaches.

Initially, expenditure requirements are likely to be most demanding when capital costs for new facilities require loans (and loan guarantees), or intersectoral services must be launched. In such contexts donor financial support will play a critical role. Equally important will be to map out the pace at which health expenditures might reasonably be reallocated toward more cost-effective basic services. Once a country has deliberated on a package of basic services to be offered through health centers and first-referral hospitals, a first step in determining financing might be to convene an expert or consultative group, made up of officials of the public and private sectors. This group would assess the willingness of households to pay for each component of the services, consider the extent to which external benefits extend beyond the immediate recipients, review the public goods aspects, and consider targeting and equity issues. Weighing benefits in this fashion could be used to determine the relative roles of government, donors, and households in financing the gaps discussed here.

CHAPTER TEN

Mobilizing Resources to Pay for Better Health

FINANCIAL resources for health are in jeopardy in many African countries. To combat shortfalls and mobilize resources for the basic package of care described in Chapters 4 and 9, action is required on several fronts simultaneously. More revenue for public health goods and services is clearly needed in most countries. This goal can partially be achieved by mobilizing resources from tax and nontax revenues and strengthening the political commitment to public spending on health. It is equally important to make more efficient use of public funds by reallocating them from expensive and relatively cost-ineffective tertiary care to cost-effective preventive and primary care services. The prevalent inefficiency in the use of public funds is partly to blame for insufficient health coverage and the declining quality of public sector health services, as well as the pressure to find more resources. Restructuring the financing and provision of health care to produce a shift from crisis management to more sustainable systems of cost-effective health care is crucial.

There is convincing evidence that African households are willing to expend substantial out-of-pocket sums for quality health services, and that strategies to mobilize these resources can help alleviate budgetary shortfalls among public providers, stimulate nongovernnment financing and provision of health care, and contribute to equity in the process. Cost-sharing strategies can help free public resources for public ends, especially by recouping public expenditures at tertiary-level hospitals. Private financing can also substitute for government involvement, as when large, urban-based employers sponsor private health insurance or finance private health facilities. In addition, public-private collaboration can help diversify the way that basic packages of care are financed, thus providing a stimulus to private-for-profit providers and, especially, private voluntary organizations. A wide variety of strategies is needed to mobilize resources to pay for better health.

The first part of this chapter describes expenditure levels and trends by governments, households (out-of-pocket), and donors. The second part suggests broad options for mobilizing resources. The chapter concludes by sketching out an incremental approach to resource mobilization and urges strong government leadership to bring it about.

Government Expenditures for Health

Because national governments are responsible for overall health policy and strategic planning for health, it might be assumed that governments are also the major sources of health financing and health expenditures. In reality, the government's share of total health expenditures varies widely throughout the world. Time series data on the government's share of health expenditures were available for this report for twenty-five African countries, and in only three—Burundi, Kenya, and Zimbabwe—did government expenditures account for more than half. Conversely, the private sector accounted for more than three-quarters of all health spending in Sudan, Uganda, and Zaire. Donors play an important financial role in many African countries, and accounted for around 20 percent of health expenditures in Africa in 1990.

Table 10-1, which covers the period from 1980 to 1990, summarizes central government expenditures for the twenty-five African countries for which data are available. It excludes foreign grants, foreign loans, and contributions from international NGOs. The countries were divided into three groups, according to relative level of per capita government expenditures on health and per capita GNP. Classifying the countries in this way helps to show differences in government health expenditures among countries with different income levels.

There was a fifteen- to twentyfold difference in central government health expenditures per capita between the "high" and "low" groups. This was far out of proportion to the fourfold difference in average per capita incomes between the two groups. Moreover, expenditures by the "high" group increased between the period 1980–85 and 1985–MR (most recent year for which data are available). Those of the middle group declined slightly, while those of the low group stayed nearly the same.

Table 10-1 also reveals that central government expenditures on health, as a percent of GDP, were smaller in the "low" and "medium" groups than in the "high" group, and showed little absolute change over time. Compared with all less developed countries worldwide, whose share of central government expenditures on health is about 1.5 percent of GDP, the "medium" group fell short by 0.2 percent and the "low" group trailed by 0.9 percent. This means that in

Table 10-1. Selected African Countries Grouped by Relative Level of Central Government Expenditure on Health, Population-Weighted Averages, 1980s

	Country grouping		
Item	High expenditure	Medium expenditure	Low expenditure
Country characteristics			
Population (millions)	21.4	94.7	218.3
Average GNP per capita (U.S. dollars)	818	395	225
Central government health expenditure per capita			
1980–85 (1987 constant dollars)	15.3	5.4	1.1
1986–MR (1987 constant dollars)	20.7	4.9	1.0
Percentage change	35.3	−9.3	−9.1
Central government health expenditure as a percentage of GDP			
1980–85	2.3	1.3	0.5
1986–MR	2.9	1.3	0.6
Percentage change	26.1	0.0	20.0
Central government health expenditure as a percentage of total central government expenditure			
1980–85	5.9	5.6	2.8
1980–MR	6.6	5.4	2.6
Percentage change	11.9	−3.7	−7.1

Note: MR, most recent available year. High-expenditure countries: Botswana, Lesotho, Mauritius, Swaziland, and Zimbabwe. Medium-expenditure countries: Burundi, Cameroon, The Gambia, Ghana, Kenya, Liberia, Malawi, Niger, Rwanda, Senegal, Togo, and Zambia. Low-expenditure countries: Burkina Faso, Ethiopia, Mali, Nigeria, Sierra Leone, Somalia, Uganda, and Zaire.

Because this table is designed to show change over time, data are in constant 1987 dollars. For this reason the data are not fully comparable with the current dollar estimates for 1990 in Table 9-4.
Source: United Nations Development Programme and World Bank 1992.

countries whose combined populations amounted to about two-thirds of the African total on which information is available, central government expenditures on health as a share of GDP were only one-third the average level of developing countries as a whole.

Table 10-1 also reveals that central government expenditures on health as a share of total central government expenditures were between 5.4 and 6.6 percent in the "medium" and "high" groups, but less than 3 percent in the "low" group. Since all developing countries worldwide spent an average of about 5 percent of their government budget on health, the performance of the "low" group was about one-half the norm. Furthermore, expenditures on health as a share of all central government spending fell in this group of countries in the 1980s.

Although part of the shortfall can be overcome by allocating a greater share of government funds to health, the crux of the challenge in the low-income countries is to raise absolute levels of spending. The first step for the "low" and even "medium" expenditure countries is to arrest the decline in real per capita health expenditures by the central government revealed in Table 10-1. Each country will need to examine its own individual performance in this respect. For the "high" countries in Table 10-1, and to some extent the "medium" countries, reallocation of some portion of current government expenditures is likely to be sufficient to satisfy the public sector's share of the cost of the package.

Explaining Shortfalls

It is not hard to say why some African governments have committed less to health than others. Three points are worth stressing. First, economic conditions matter, since government expenditures on health derive largely from general tax revenues, including duties on imports and exports. Analysis of the performance of countries in the "high" group in Table 10-1 reveals that all of them had positive rates of economic growth, the average being 3.7 percent per capita from 1965 to 1990. For the "medium" expenditure group, more than 60 percent of the countries experienced positive rates of per capita economic growth, the average being 0.5 percent. For the "low" group, however, 60 percent of the countries experienced negligible or negative per capita growth, the group average being minus 0.5 percent.

The second point concerns the possible effects of structural adjustment programs (SAPs). These programs have aroused considerable controversy. Some argue that SAPs have been indirectly responsible for cutbacks in government expenditures on social services. The chief counterargument is that structural adjustment programs, whose purpose is to help developing countries overcome long-term barriers to economic growth, give governments an opportunity to restructure their health sectors.

Several studies suggest that structural adjustment is not a principal cause of low or declining government expenditures on health in Africa (Box 10-1). Central government expenditures on health as a share of GDP in those countries engaged in adjustment programs remained almost the same in "adjustment" years as in "nonadjustment" years, although the mean value of health expenditures per capita was 5 to 6 percent lower in adjustment years than in nonadjustment years. Furthermore, central government expenditures on health as a share of total central government expenditures were 7 to 8 percent higher in the adjustment than in the nonadjustment years (Serageldin, Elmendorf, and El-Tigani, forthcoming).

That finding is particularly significant because it demonstrates that health expenditures were not reduced in association with adjustment lending to make room for increases in spending in other sectors. In Lesotho, for example, the government has shown a strong commitment to social services and has emphasized internal restructuring to improve efficiency. Health and welfare received about 6 percent of total government expenditures in 1982–83, and about 10 percent in the early 1990s. Over the same period, education's share increased from about 15 percent to 20 percent. In contrast, commitments to Lesotho's less productive sectors, such as military spending, were reduced from about 24 percent of total government expenditures in 1982–83 to about 10 to 12 percent during the early 1990s.

The health expenditure performance of the three groups of countries in Table 10-1 appears to have little correlation with structural adjustment programs. The average number of years that such programs were in place between 1980 and 1990 in countries in the "low" group was 2.6. Comparable figures for the "medium" and "high" groups were 4.3 and 1.0 years, respectively. Multivariate analysis revealed that structural adjustment was not significantly correlated with government expenditures on health as a share of total government expenditures, or with government expenditures as a share of GDP. This particular analysis not only controlled for levels of per capita GNP but also assessed the lagged effects of adjustment programs put into effect between 1980 and 1985 on health expenditures between 1985 and 1990. Again, no significant correlation was found.

Third, most African governments appear to be able to make substantial improvements in health expenditures. This is apparent from the priority they have given to public expenditures on defense. Six out of the eight countries in the "low" group in Table 10-1 devoted two to four times more money to defense than to health. In the "medium" group, eight out of twelve countries allocated more public funds to defense than to health, with three out of five countries in the "high" group doing so as well. Whether public health officials have much chance of changing this situation remains to be seen, notwithstanding the reductions in defense expenditures in the 1980s. But reciting these facts, as well as pointing out improvements (as in Lesotho and Ghana), casts a more realistic light on the "disabling" environment faced by many African ministries of health. Juxtaposed with the mass of evidence revealing that investments in health are an essential element of development strategy, there is little evidence to suggest that defense expenditures contribute positively to economic growth or sustainable development.

Combating Inefficiency and Inequity

Public expenditure surveys and World Bank health sector reports leave little doubt that large shares of the government resources allocated to the health sec-

BOX 10-1. MACROECONOMIC CHANGE,
STRUCTURAL ADJUSTMENT, AND
HEALTH

Following rapid deterioration in macroeconomic and sectoral performance in
Sub-Saharan Africa since the
mid-1970s, which reached crisis proportions in the early 1980s, many
countries started comprehensive economic reform programs with financial
support from the International Monetary Fund and the World Bank. Most of
these countries started the adjustment
process from a position of low and declining real income, sluggish or deteri-
orating growth rates, mounting external debt and debt service, very low
ratios of saving and investment to GDP
ratios, declining external competitive-
ness and growth in export volumes,
mounting current account deficits, and
rapidly declining agricultural output
per capita (Elbadawi, Ghura, and
Uwujaren 1992).

Between 1980 and 1990, 70 percent,
or thirty-two of forty-five, Sub-Saharan
African countries adopted structural
adjustment programs supported by
World Bank lending. Some countries,
such as Mauritius, Senegal, Côte
d'Ivoire, Kenya, and Nigeria, were
relatively more stable than others,
such as Burundi, Central African Republic, Congo, Mali, Niger, Somalia,
Zaire, Benin, Cameroon, and Ethiopia,
and started the adjustment process
earlier with strong adjustment measures. Others abandoned their efforts

toward adjustment after one or two initial loans, such as Burkina Faso,
Equatorial Guinea, Sierra Leone, and
Sudan. In sum, the adjustment process was rarely completed. For these
reasons, as well as gaps in data required for statistical analysis, it is difficult to assess the effects of adjustment
lending in African countries in the
1980s. Nonetheless, extensive reviews of available data and literature
suggest that the empirical basis is
weak for claims that adjustment policies have multiple negative effects on
health (Preston 1986; Behrman 1990;
Sahn 1992; World Bank 1992d).

In the health sector, consensus appears to be emerging on the following
points:

■ Analysis of public expenditure
data from African and Latin American
countries suggests that social expenditures, including health, have suffered
less than expenditures on economic
services, and that recurrent expenditures—the bulk of health outlays—
have suffered relatively less than capital expenditures for infrastructure
(Hicks 1991).

■ Analysis of ten African countries
undergoing adjustment suggests that
neither economic crisis nor resulting
adjustment policies has had a major
impact on critical health indicators. A
study using household survey data on
Côte d'Ivoire found no overall significant effect of either the pre- or postadjustment period on neonatal or postneonatal mortality. In contrast, an

Box 10-1, continued

adverse effect for the adjustment period on the postneonatal mortality of the urban nonpoor was observed (Diop 1991). A study of Ghana found no significant time period effects on mortality risks in the neonatal or child age ranges, whereas for postneonatal mortality, the protective effects of maternal education were reduced in the economic crisis and postadjustment periods (Saadah 1991).

■ Those most vulnerable to the negative, short-term effects of macroeconomic adjustment policies are not necessarily the poorest groups in society. Most people in Africa live in relatively scattered rural communities, which, unfortunately, have not benefited greatly from public expenditures and subsidies, and therefore have been relatively insulated from changes in government expenditures. Rather, the most vulnerable groups tend to reside in urban areas and tend to be those who have benefited disproportionately from public services and subsidies, often urban civil servants and other urban middle-income groups (Sirageldin, Wouters, and Diop 1992).

■ Adjustment appears to be related to the decline in the real value of civil servant salaries and may sometimes have squeezed nonpersonnel expenditures—especially for pharmaceuticals. While this is a cause for concern, it is also prompting a reassessment

and is providing grounds for restructuring health care systems to tackle the fundamental problems involved. Government surveys of civil service employment, for example, report overly heavy concentrations of employees at the center, redundancies, and the phenomenon of ghost workers, meaning salaries are collected by recipients not on the job. Inefficiencies in current procurement, prescription, and use of medicines appear to be far more significant than the effects of prices and incomes (Chapter 4). Ministry of health budgets are predominantly being eaten up by expensive curative care in hospitals, undermining government's capacity to finance recurrent expenditures in primary health services. And the preoccupation of donors in the past with financing capital development projects has not been accompanied by sustainable provisions to meet recurrent cost requirements.

■ Governments should restructure their health sectors as part of, not in response to, structural adjustment programs, taking measures to protect social priorities and putting into operation symbolic commitments to preventive and primary care with public health funds intended for such purposes. As the Minister of Health of Zimbabwe put it, "Recession [and] structural adjustment policies and plans have provided us with opportunities for creativity, innovation, and boldness" (Stamps 1993).

tor are eaten up by interventions that are not cost-effective, that the use of public funds for these ends impairs financing of public health services, and that this use of funds makes commitments to improve primary and preventive health care little more than symbolic.

Between 1985 and 1991, for example, almost 70 percent of the public health budget of Kenya was used for curative care, compared with only 4.5 percent for disease prevention and health promotion. Between 72 and 82 percent of the public health budget of Malawi was allocated to curative care between 1983 and 1988, compared with only 5 to 9 percent for preventive care. Other countries in which curative services account for 60 percent or more of government health expenditures include Tanzania and Uganda. In Nigeria, inadequate emphasis on preventive and primary care has been decried since the mid-1970s. Nonetheless, in eight of Nigeria's states for which data are available, curative care increased from 72 percent to 81 percent of the public sector health budget during 1981 to 1985. Only more recently has the government made a major effort to change the situation.

While it is true that the fiscal capacity of many African countries to finance health services has been undermined by poor economic performance, rapid population growth, and political upheaval, these factors do not constitute a valid explanation for low or declining percentages of government expenditures on public health. Structural adjustment programs may well be coupled with austerity measures, but they cannot be invoked as a root cause of low or declining government spending on health. Rather, adjustment lending has increasingly sought to protect social service expenditures. If health care expenditures are appropriately reallocated as part of structural adjustment programs—as has been done in Lesotho and Ghana, for example—these positive dimensions might be pushed a good deal further.

Private Expenditures

Surveys of household expenditures, including direct payments to private practitioners, traditional healers, private pharmacists, and others in the health sector, indicate that African households expend substantial out-of-pocket sums for health (Table 10-2), especially in relation to the $13 and $16 indicative per capita cost estimates in Chapter 8. In Côte d'Ivoire, where per capita GNP was about $900 in 1985, household expenditures on health averaged about $19 per capita, whereas central government expenditures averaged about $8.20 per capita. In Ghana, with a considerably lower per capita GNP of $240 in 1987–88, per capita household expenditures on health were also relatively high, at about $7.30 in 1986, particularly when compared with central government expenditures of about $4.20. In Nigeria, where per capita GNP was $400 in 1985–86,

Table 10-2.   Per Capita Household Expenditures on Health in Selected African Countries

(U.S. dollars)

Household quintile	Côte d'Ivoire 1985	Ghana 1987–88	Guinea-Bissau 1991	Nigeria 1985–86	Senegal 1991–92
Lowest	3.99	2.55	3.88	2.58	4.90
2nd quintile	6.59	4.25	4.63	5.88	10.27
3rd quintile	14.33	6.19	4.38	10.07	13.44
4th quintile	17.04	8.54	2.44	14.08	25.34
5th quintile	46.38	14.83	8.34	35.16	61.82
Average	18.88	7.27	4.74	15.05	23.14
Per capita income	911.31	239.00	196.00	400.00	393.00
Average as share of per capita income (percent)	2.1	3.0	2.4	3.8	5.9

Note: Household expenditures include traditional and modern health services and medicines.

Sources: For Côte d'Ivoire and Ghana, Serageldin, Elmendorf, and El-Tigani, forthcoming, except for per capita income, from Grootaert 1993 for Côte d'Ivoire and from IMF data for Ghana; for Guinea-Bissau, 1991 income and expenditure survey; for Nigeria, 1985–86 consumer expenditure survey; for Senegal, 1991–92 priority survey (Direction de la Prévision et de la Statistique).

average per capita household expenditures were about $15, whereas central government health expenditures were thought to lie between $1 and $2 per capita. At the very least, the public sector needs to provide households with the information they need to allocate, or reallocate, these expenditures to cost-effective packages of health services.

Out-of-pocket expenditures vary considerably between the poor and the non-poor. In Ghana, household expenditures varied fivefold across quintiles, ranging from about $15 per capita in the highest quintile to $2.60 in the lowest. In Côte d'Ivoire, household expenditures varied elevenfold across quintiles. In Senegal, household expenditures varied fifteenfold across quintiles, ranging from $62 in the highest quintile to $4.90 in the lowest. The data in Table 10-2 suggest that cost-sharing to pay for cost-effective packages of health services is feasible.

Because the more well-to-do groups spend significantly more on health, there would seem to be greater justification for cost recovery from them, especially since—at least in some countries—wealthier households tend to seek public care more often than those with less income. In Ogun state in Nigeria, for example, 53 percent of the highest income group who needed medical help went to public facilities first, including 27 percent who went to public hospitals first. A smaller share (21 percent) of the lowest income group sought care first in public hospitals.

International Aid

Donors are important financiers of health care in Africa, especially where the government has been unable to meet health needs due to revenue shortfalls. Between 1981 and 1986, external assistance for health from official and private voluntary sources averaged more than $1.50 per capita in Sub-Saharan Africa, equivalent to more than 20 percent of average central government expenditures on health (Tchicaya 1992). By 1990, total assistance had climbed to more than $1.2 billion, or almost $2.50 per capita, although wide variations were apparent—from $0.60 in Nigeria to $7 in Benin (Table 10-3). Furthermore, the limited information available suggests that more aid *per capita* went to countries in the high and medium groups than to the low group.

During the late 1980s, bilateral donors accounted for 62 percent of total health assistance in Sub-Saharan Africa, while multilateral agencies provided 32 percent and nongovernment agencies 6 percent. On average, 44 percent of donor funds were used for capital investment, 22 percent for technical assistance, 13 percent for operating costs, and 2.4 percent for training. Variations were large, however. In Lesotho, donor financing covered about 80 percent of the Ministry of Health capital budget between 1987 and 1992. In Uganda, donors financed 87 percent of total public development expenditures on health in 1988–89. In Mali, the share of donor funding for health development expenditures in 1990 was 63 percent. Since, on average, each $100 of capital investment in the health sector generates annual operating costs of $30, international funds not only determined how the government would invest in health but also shaped recurrent spending (Heller 1978).

Donor aid has also been paying for an increasing share of recurrent expenditures, especially for drugs and emergency and supervisory transport. Donors pay for virtually all drugs imported by Tanzania for dispensaries and health centers, for example. There are also a growing number of cases where donors are financing the salaries of health workers, particularly community outreach workers and nurses in rural health care centers. Funds for recurrent expenditures grew from about 13 percent of donor assistance for health in Africa in 1980 to 35 percent at the end of the 1980s, while capital expenditure support declined from about 55 percent to 35 percent (McGrory 1993).

At the same time that donor assistance has played an invaluable role in shoring up public initiatives for health, such assistance has had negative side effects that are at odds with the central messages of this report. Prominent among these are the following:

Table 10-3. External Assistance for the Health Sector, Selected African
Countries, 1990
(U.S. dollars)

Country	Level of expenditure (low, medium, or high)	Per capita aid
Benin	—	7.0
Burkina Faso	L	4.7
Burundi	M	2.8
Cameroon	M	3.3
Central African Republic	—	6.5
Chad	—	5.8
Côte d'Ivoire	—	0.9
Ethiopia	L	0.8
Ghana	M	1.9
Guinea	—	3.5
Kenya	M	3.5
Madagascar	—	1.5
Malawi	M	2.5
Mali	L	4.3
Mozambique	—	2.9
Niger	M	5.6
Nigeria	L	0.6
Rwanda	M	4.1
Senegal	M	4.9
Sierra Leone	L	1.7
Somalia	L	3.5
Sudan	—	1.5
Tanzania	—	2.1
Togo	M	3.9
Uganda	L	2.8
Zaire	L	1.3
Zambia	M	0.7
Zimbabwe	H	4.2
Population-weighted average		2.5

— Not available.
Note: For level of expenditure classifications, see note to Table 9-4. Estimates of development assistance for
health are expressed in official exchange rate U.S. dollars. Total aid flows represent the sum of all assistance for
health to each country by bilateral and multilateral agencies, international agencies, and international
nongovernmental organizations (NGOs).
Source: World Bank 1993e, Table A.9.

■ The Organization for Economic Cooperation and Development reports that "In spite of their stated commitment to primary health care, relatively large resources are devoted by donors . . . to sophisticated urban-based facilities including hospitals and specialist clinics" (OECD 1989). This suggests the need for closer scrutiny of the impact of health aid flows, as well as greater use of external finance to establish and run projects in remote or underserved areas. Examples include provision and distribution of essential drugs that are intended principally for consumption by less well served populations, as supplied, for example, by DANIDA in Tanzania and Médecins sans Frontières in Mali.

■ External financing has often worked against sustainability when it has been used for vertical programs or inappropriate capital or development expenditure. Although such funding may have the goal of expanding coverage and quality of services, the recurrent costs necessary to sustain the capital investments are often very high and beyond the country's ability to finance. Almost every African country has at least one big investment project, such as a large hospital, that is unlikely ever to function as originally planned because of a lack of ongoing funding. Underused facilities include, for example, the Maidugeri and Ibadan teaching hospitals in Nigeria.

■ While most donors have provided health assistance without conditions for explicit policy reform, the priorities implicitly embedded in donor funding have virtually driven the selection of health strategies in Africa. In some cases, heavy reliance on external assistance has led to virtual abdication of responsibility for health policy formulation. Furthermore, donor funding priorities are constantly shifting—tending to favor specific health themes at international conferences that detract attention from the need to strengthen basic health services. In Rwanda, for example, more than 20 percent of donor financing for health has recently been earmarked for AIDS alone, making it out of proportion to total health needs (Over and Piot 1991). The push between 1985 and 1990 for universal childhood immunization, which was "jump-started" in Africa largely by financing from UNICEF, Italy, WHO, and Rotary, vastly improved coverage throughout the continent. Declining rates of coverage in recent years indicate that many health systems were unable to maintain momentum without continued injections of outside funds. African governments are increasingly recognizing this problem, and some (such as Nigeria), are calling for African governments to assume responsibility for vaccine financing (WHO/AFRO 1993a).

■ Government information on external assistance programs is often spotty, resulting in ineffective coordination and monitoring. External evaluations are often conducted without involving the recipient country (Engelkes 1993b). Moreover, government and donor definitions of health programs and accounting requirements frequently differ, so that health planners and policymakers often do not know the overall purposes, locations, or amounts of external resources being used.

Governments can reduce dependency-related problems by taking the lead in donor coordination. In Ghana, for example, the Ministry of Health has organized a Local Assistance Group on Health, which functions as a quarterly forum with donor agencies to resolve health strategy issues. In Kinshasa, coordination led to standards for health center activities and user fee schedules respected by all participating health care providers.

To sum up, external assistance for health can help to bridge financial gaps in Africa in ways that are far more efficient, equitable, and sustainable than in the past. External funding sources need to reexamine their activities and emphasize a longer time horizon, broader programs of support to health sector reform and of intersectoral assistance, and national capacity-building rather than individual project-based support. Sub-Saharan African governments need to play a vital role in this process by developing comprehensive health policies, increasing their commitment to primary care, establishing overall health sector financial plans, and emphasizing cost-effective packages of basic services. This can help to persuade donors to make new financial commitments. In Guinea, Benin, Sierra Leone, and Zambia national action plans and comprehensive financing plans are already being drawn up by governments in collaboration with donors.

Raising Additional Domestic Resources

To ensure financing of the package of basic health services, a growing number of countries are increasing user charges for government health services (Lesotho, Zimbabwe) or establishing nationwide fee systems to replace free care (Uganda, Kenya). Other countries, such as Guinea, Benin, Nigeria, and Rwanda, are promoting the creation or strengthening of community-financing schemes. Alternative arrangements, such as community health insurance schemes, are filling gaps. These actions offer grounds for optimism that much more can be done to mobilize additional resources.

User Fees as a Cost-Recovery Method

Nontax sources of revenue, such as user fees, are becoming increasingly commonplace in African countries. This method of cost recovery directly addresses the problem of underfunding of government health facilities. By charging fees for services that primarily benefit the user, governments can reallocate tax revenues to public health activities whose benefits go beyond the individual client. User fees are also a tool for reinforcing the referral system. When the prices of all medical services are zero or are uniformly low, consumers have no reason to pay attention to costs. Their natural inclination, in fact, may be to use services whose cost to the government is high (Griffin 1992).

User fees make sense on purely economic grounds. Demand for health care tends to be income elastic, meaning that the more money people have, the more they are willing to pay for health. For any given level of prices, a disproportionate share of the demand for health care will be made by people with higher incomes. Charging wealthier people for services and then pooling those revenues to subsidize the costs of treating those least able to pay is also an important means of promoting equity. And when user fees are spent to expand and upgrade the quality of health services, they may actually reinforce demand.

Demand for health care, especially curative care, also tends to be price inelastic, meaning that any increase in user fees will result in a less than proportional drop in demand and thus an increase in revenues. Moreover, most of those dissuaded from seeking care at public sector facilities because of an increase in user fees will seek care from some other source, particularly if nongovernment providers are price-competitive.

When the user fees charged by public sector facilities are modest, they tend to be a very small proportion of the total cost of using health care. In two-thirds of the African countries for which data are available, the contribution of user fees to recurrent government expenditures on health was less than 5 percent in the years for which data are available (Table 10-4). This implies considerable scope for higher charges. In Ghana, for example, a large upward adjustment in prices in 1985 increased cost-recovery receipts as a share of Ministry of Health recurrent expenditures from 5.2 percent to 12.1 percent by 1987, and with needed quality improvements the government could reasonably expect even better performance.

User Fees in Hospitals

If systems of health care are to devote greater attention to preventive and primary care, the recovery of costs at public hospitals takes on monumental importance. If the high capital and recurrent costs of hospitals are financed by the government, the government's health budget will be skewed toward hospital services no matter what the government's stated priorities may be. Furthermore, if the typical residential and income characteristics of those receiving such care—predominantly urban, well-to-do families—are "superimposed" on this subsidy pattern, an equity problem is inevitable. Urban residents will capture a disproportionate share of the government's health subsidy because they live near the hospitals and use them. It is hard to see how African govern-

Table 10-4.   Revenue From User Charges as a Share of Recurrent Government Expenditure on Health, Selected African Countries

Country and year	Percentage of recurrent expenditure
Botswana, 1979	1.3
Burkina Faso, 1981	0.5
Burundi, 1982	4.0
Côte d'Ivoire, 1986	3.1
Ethiopia, 1982	12.0
Ghana, 1987	12.1
Kenya, 1984	2.0
Lesotho, 1984	5.7
Malawi, 1983	3.3
Mali, 1986	2.7
Mauritania, 1986	12.0
Mozambique, 1985	8.0
Rwanda, 1984	7.0
Senegal, 1986	4.7
Swaziland, 1984	2.1
Zimbabwe, 1986	2.2

Source: Vogel 1988, 1989.

ments can improve the health of all of their people until these problems are resolved.

Because it is exceptionally difficult to impose limits on hospital spending, the logical alternative is to increase user fees for those able to pay more. Because they offer many different services and have accountants, financial control procedures, and bank accounts, hospitals are better positioned than public clinics to recover their costs from patients.

The experience of private-for-profit and private voluntary hospitals also suggests greater possibilities for establishing user fees in public hospitals. Religious missions in Côte d'Ivoire, Ghana, Mali, and Senegal have been successful in covering a large percentage of their operating costs through user charges. A survey of nongovernment facilities in Tanzania revealed that 57 percent of the hospitals expected that from 50 to 80 percent of their recurrent costs for drugs, salaries, repairs, and maintenance would be financed by user fees (Mujinja and Mabala 1992). Even though public facilities provide free health care, those who visited private sector dispensaries and hospitals in the greatest numbers were peasants, people with jobs, and traditional healers. Nongovernment hospitals in Uganda have long relied on the willingness of households to pay for services and have recovered anywhere from 75 to 95 percent of their costs.

Even small fees can produce revenues for public hospitals that dwarf those generated by high fees at clinics. In Wad Medani, Sudan, a 0.25LS entrance fee at the main hospital generated gross revenues of 325,900LS in 1984, compared with 8,200LS generated by three evening clinics nearby that charged four to eight times the hospital entrance fee (Griffin 1988). In Senegal, the money recovered through fees in the hospital subsector was sufficient to pay for half of all hospital drug supplies.

The introduction or raising of user fees at hospitals can also make the referral system more efficient, stimulate greater use of private sector hospitals, and make public hospitals more available to the most needy (Box 10-2). In Zimbabwe, for example, fees increase according to the hierarchy of facilities, which induces consumers to seek care where the services can be provided at lowest

---

BOX 10-2. THREE STORIES OF COST RECOVERY IN HOSPITALS AND OTHER FACILITIES: GHANA, SENEGAL, AND MALAWI

Ghana: In 1983 the price structure for health services was judged to be too low in Ghana, resulting in a large upward adjustment in prices in 1985. By 1987, cost-recovery receipts as a percent of the Ministry of Health recurrent budget had climbed from 5.2 percent to 12.1 percent. A key to Ghana's progress appears to lie in the structure and application of prices, as well as in the administrative provisions of the cost-recovery law. Prices are hierarchical and directly related to the sophistication and expense of the health care delivered. The price of curative care at the hospital level is a large multiple of curative care at the health center. This feature of the pricing structure gives a strong price signal and reinforcement to use the referral system. Yet, facilities are obliged to differentiate the poor from the nonpoor and to give free care to the poor.

Another key to success in Ghana's cost-recovery experience has been the administrative provision that a portion of the proceeds should remain at the site of collection, improving service quality and stimulating incentives to collect fees. The general formula used is that 50 percent of user fee revenue goes to the Ministry of Finance, 25 percent to the Ministry of Health, and 25 percent is retained by the facility that collects the fee.

Senegal: In Senegal in the late 1980s, there was no cost recovery at large national hospitals. Cost recovery was being introduced at some regional hospitals, but was mostly practiced at the primarily level of the health care system. This policy gives the wrong signals from a systemic point of view. To illustrate, people may be inclined to not

cost. The basic outpatient charge for adults is Z$5 at a central hospital, Z$3 at a provincial general hospital, and Z$1.50 at a district hospital. In Cameroon, a desired by-product of introducing fees at public facilities was to encourage well-to-do patrons to obtain private care. This met the social objective of making public facilities more available to the poor. In Lesotho, the government explicitly sought to induce patients to switch from public to private care when it instituted a higher user fee policy in 1988.

Another option is to turn public hospitals into parastatals or autonomous bodies with reduced government funding, or to privatize selected services in national hospitals. In Burundi, for example, the Ministry of Health is pursuing an innovative approach to giving full autonomy to hospitals. The ministry first gave a 120-bed hospital a lump sum to cover the hospital's operating costs. Each year thereafter, the ministry reduced its contribution by 20 percent. Based on the positive outcome of this experiment, the ministry plans to apply the same

---

Box 10-2, continued

seek care at a health center in a suburb of Dakar, where they must pay for that care, when they can easily take a bus into Dakar and receive free care from the Dantec Hospital.

Given this asymmetry in user charge policy, hospitals such as Dantec have been operating at more than 100 percent of capacity, while local treatment facilities are underused. This, in turn, distorts public sector investment policy. Almost half of the project expenditures in Senegal's three-year investment plan in the mid-1980s were for renovations or additions to the Dantec Hospital.

Malawi: The government has determined that cost-sharing is an urgent, viable policy that can be used to acquire resources from users of medical services, then redeployed to extend and improve health care delivery to

rural-based families in the periphery. A phased approach is being implemented over three years, commencing April 1992, to introduce the cost-sharing system to central hospitals, then to general and district hospitals, and finally to health centers—all phases to be accompanied by improvements to strengthen quality.

Several concerns are behind the cost-sharing strategy. One is to increase the efficiency and use of the central/general hospitals and district hospitals by introducing a system to discourage the population from using hospitals as their entry point to the health system. Another is to improve the referral system by encouraging the population to enter the appropriate level of services—health centers. A related concern is to strengthen primary care with trained manpower and continuous availability of essential drugs.

procedure to its central hospital, which has 600 to 700 beds. Simultaneous action is being taken to stimulate the expansion of insurance schemes, under the assumption that hospitals would not be able to recover their costs otherwise. A similar approach was planned in Rwanda. In Rwanda and Burundi, a fundamental premise of the reductions in government funding for hospitals was that ministries of health are not created to manage hospitals and usually do so poorly.

Privatization of selected hospital services is underway in Tanzania, where some beds in government hospitals are private beds for which a fee must be paid. In Mozambique, government medical staff operate special hospital-based clinics outside normal working hours. The Kenyatta National Hospital in Kenya recently adopted a plan that requires a private wing in the hospital to generate a surplus and thus augment hospital revenues.

Cost-Sharing in Health Centers and Dispensaries

User fees or cost-sharing strategies take on immense importance at publicly operated health centers and dispensaries because at this level the need for preventive and primary care is most pressing, funds are relatively scarce, and quality improvements are essential. It is also at this level that the community can become actively involved in mobilizing and managing resources for health. At a meeting in Bamako in 1987, the World Health Organization adopted a resolution to introduce community cost-sharing mechanisms in support of primary care. Since that time, UNICEF has spearheaded a "Bamako Initiative" involving from one to fifty districts in thirteen countries, some 1,800 health facilities, and about 20 million people. In almost all cases, essential drugs have been priced to serve as a mechanism of cost recovery.

Experience from the Bamako Initiative and related endeavors suggests that cost-sharing in local health centers can pay significant dividends. In countries like Benin, Guinea, and Nigeria—where experience has been closely monitored—approximately 40 to 46 percent of local operating costs (including salaries) are being covered by fees in facilities participating in the Bamako Initiative. According to one study, up to 100 percent of local recurrent costs (excluding salaries) are being covered (Parker and Knippenberg 1991).

Cost-sharing at the local level has given rise to a number of principles:

■ *Clients' willingness to pay fees strongly depends on whether the fees are accompanied by improvements in quality.*

In Cameroon, use increased significantly among all income groups at health centers that simultaneously initiated fees and quality improvements (Box 10-3). Furthermore, use by poorer people rose proportionately more than

BOX 10-3. USE OF HEALTH CENTERS
BY THE POOR IN CAMEROON AFTER
INTRODUCING COST RECOVERY AND
QUALITY IMPROVEMENTS

A study at five public health facilities in
Cameroon demonstrated that the poor
may benefit more than the relatively
better-off population from concomitant
introduction of cost recovery and quality improvements.

In a "pretest-posttest" experiment,
three health centers introduced a user
fee and quality improvement (for example, reliable drug supply), and were
compared with two similar facilities
without such changes. Two rounds of
household surveys were conducted in
twenty-five villages, each with about
800 households, to measure the percentage of ill people seeking care before and after the changes. The experi-

ment was tightly controlled by conducting monthly observations at each
study site.

Results indicate that the probability
of using the health center increased
significantly for people in the "treatment" areas compared with those in
the "control" areas. Contrary to previous studies, which have found that
the poorest groups are most hurt by
user fees, this study found that the
probability of the poorest groups seeking care increased at a rate proportionately greater than the rest of the
population. Travel and time costs involved in seeking alternative sources
of care are too high for the poorest
people and thus they appear to benefit
from local availability of drugs more
than others.

Source: Litvack 1992.

use by the wealthier (Litvack 1992). A comprehensive survey of public sector
health facilities in Ogun state, Nigeria, produced similar results.

If, on the other hand, price increases are not matched by improvements in
service quality, there is likely to be a loss of demand. Introduction of user fees
caused a decline in user rates at health facilities in Swaziland, Mozambique,
and Lesotho, largely because the revenues were not immediately reinvested in
the facilities.

■ *Retention of a substantial portion of the revenues at the collection site is
an important incentive to collect fees and improve the quality of services, particularly where community representatives monitor collection and use of the
funds.*

Allowing facilities to retain all or most of the fees helps to remedy budget
cuts and allows the facilities to tailor their services to local needs. In contrast,
efforts at administrative decentralization in the collection of fees and monitoring of cost recovery appear to be hampered when little financial autonomy is
permitted. From the perspective of health care providers, the requirement to
remit funds to the Finance Ministry resembles a tax and thus discourages fee

collection (Vogel 1988). The user charge systems of Cameroon, Côte d'Ivoire, Mali, and Senegal used to require that fees be remitted to the Finance Ministry. In Cameroon, legislation adopted in 1993 granted a special waiver to health facilities, removing the requirement to remit the proceeds of the sales of drugs to the national treasury. Instead, the funds are retained and used to increase service quality by renewing stocks.

■ *Drug revolving funds are a good cost-recovery mechanism because they ensure customers a regular supply of drugs; meanwhile, drug sales generate a surplus for the facility.*

In Benin, a comparison of health facilities one year before and one year after a revolving drug fund was established showed an increase in use of 129 percent. Increases in use following the start-up of a cost-recovery program for drugs have also been seen in Niger, Liberia, Guinea, Nigeria, Senegal, and Zaire (World Bank 1992d). It is important to increase prices gradually, thus giving clients time to become aware of concomitant improvements in services (Blakney, Litvak, and Quick 1989).

■ *Good administrative and managerial practices are important to successful cost recovery.*

The conditions for successful collection of fees appear to include (a) well-defined entrance points to the health service, whether they be at the entry gate of the health facility itself, or at the entry point for each service at larger institutions, such as hospitals; (b) large public displays of the fee and service structure; (c) issuance of some paper instrument, such as a ticket, with duplicate copies, that serves as a proof of payment and as a management control device; (d) a tightly controlled mechanism for ascertaining who is truly poor, who is not, and the elimination of exemptions on any other basis; (e) careful training of staff to ensure that treatment is not rendered unless a ticket or certificate of indigence is produced by the patient; (f) spot-checks to ensure compliance; (g) periodic audits of financial transactions; and (h) a fairly high level of local retention of fees. One study concluded that total revenue raised appeared to be a function of the vigor with which cost recovery is pursued at the national and local levels, and of the competence and commitment of local health administrators (Vogel 1988).

Fee Structures and Provisions for the Poor

Which services should be charged for, and how much, are questions for public sector institutions and for private voluntary organizations and private-for-profit providers that receive government subsidies. Most private-for-profit providers, of course, are unsubsidized and have fees that are determined by supply and demand.

A rule of thumb can be applied to determine whether fee-for-service revenues in the public sector should cover costs: Is the service provided a private or public good? With the significant exception of highly contagious diseases, curative health care is generally private in nature and people are willing to pay for it, meaning that full cost recovery is a reasonable goal over the long run. In contrast, public health goods and services have strong positive externalities. Thus, they are often provided free or at reduced cost.

Improvements in social equity will also be contingent on differential charges based on income. Policies that exempt certain privileged groups, such as civil servants or the military, from paying fees can contribute to inequity. And if user fees deter low-income groups, the government may have to introduce subsidies, waivers, sliding-fee systems, or other appropriate means to rectify the situation.

A number of broad principles are applicable in determining fee structures:

- To the extent possible, the price should reflect the type of service provided and its cost. Private benefits, such as curative care, should be priced at or near cost. Services with major externalities (immunizations, family planning) and high cost-effectiveness should be free or provided at reduced cost.
- Groups with higher incomes, especially those covered by health insurance, should pay a much larger share of the actual costs of health services provided to them.
- Low-income households should be able to obtain basic health care at little or no cost.
- Prices at ministry of health facilities should be structured to encourage efficiency. They should reflect differences in the costs of providing service to encourage clients to seek care at the lowest-cost level (Hecht, Overholt, and Holmberg 1992).

The main practical issue in sliding-scale fee systems or exemptions for the poor is the administrative feasibility of ensuring that those who need subsidies receive them. Without strong political support, firm screening criteria, and retention of some portion of fees at the point of collection, health personnel will have little incentive to perform means tests, and exemption mechanisms may experience considerable slippage. Because there are no established rules to follow, a certain amount of "learning by doing" is inevitable.

Under the Bamako Initiative, the philosophy of user fees is that "everyone should pay something," no matter what his or her income. At the same time, however, the fee structure must reflect the fact that most clients are poor. For some primary care services, such as prenatal consultations, prices will be almost nil. Cost recovery for drugs is common, but charges vary according to drug cost and dosage.

The government of Malawi recognized the need for low-income exemptions when it began to phase in cost recovery, first at central hospitals, then at district hospitals, and finally at health centers. The government decided that the "core poor" would be exempt from its cost-sharing scheme and examined the structure of landholding to determine which households qualified for this status (Ferster and others 1991). These poor are families farming less than 0.5 hectares and have been estimated to account for about 500,000 households, or 18 to 20 percent of all households in Malawi. A fee schedule was devised in collaboration with the communities served.

NGO hospitals and dispensaries in Tanzania found that approximately 70 percent and 40 percent, respectively, of their patients were unable to pay their full fee (Mujinja and Mabala 1992). Only 10 percent of the hospitals and 5 percent of the other facilities said they offered no exemptions, while many facilities accepted alternative forms of payment. Some allowed deferred payment, payment in-kind with crops, temporary employment (without pay), or assigned tasks to the client. The proportions of hospitals and dispensaries exempting disabled people were 90 and 75 percent, respectively; people over 65 (9 and 20 percent, respectively); poor people (86 and 85 percent); children under five (36 and 30 percent); and retired workers (9 and 10 percent).

Health Insurance

User fees are an important part of cost recovery, but large parts of the population eventually must be covered by some form of health insurance if the full costs of inpatient care are to be recovered. In prepayment insurance plans, all participants pay a regular fixed amount. The money is pooled, allowing insurance providers to pay for all those needing care, especially the high costs of hospital-based curative care.

While health insurance is a mechanism for sharing risks and is not intended for resource mobilization or for achieving equity between high- and low-income groups, it has significant implications for resource mobilization and equity. Those Africans who are insurable are often better off than the rest of the population. Through insurance, they can self-finance the level of health care they desire. Schemes to promote insurance can therefore help relieve the government budget of the high costs of expensive curative care, thus releasing funds for preventive and primary care.

Health insurance is not intended to be a mechanism for purging inefficiency in the financing of health services, although it can contribute to that goal. With appropriate incentives, health insurers have a strong interest in containing reimbursement costs for health care, and then negotiating with suppliers to keep costs down.

Only a small proportion of the African population is currently covered by health insurance. Coverage ranges from virtually nil in Uganda to 13 percent in Senegal (Table 10-5). However, there is a potential to gradually increase the share of the population covered. In Kenya and Senegal, coverage has doubled since the mid-1980s.

One form of health insurance in low-income Africa is government-sponsored insurance financed by general tax revenues or special employment taxes. Enthusiasm over national insurance schemes is based on the assumption that they transfer wealth from the healthy to the sick and from the rich to the poor. This assumes that contributions are based on income and that benefits are provided according to need. In reality, however, universal government insurance systems in Africa have fallen far short of meeting the hopes of their advocates. One reason is that tax bases tend to be weak and unstable, undermining the predictability of public revenues. Improved performance in collecting taxes, especially direct taxes, which tend to be progressive, could help resolve this situation. In addition, government-sponsored social insurance schemes in Africa have tended to have substantial administrative expenses—for example, as much as 50 percent in Mali.

A more promising route is to impose mandatory insurance payments on employed workers as a percentage of their wages and to levy a similar or somewhat higher payroll tax on their employers, or to require employer coverage of care. Examples include compulsory social security for the formal labor market

Table 10-5.   Share of Population Covered by Health Insurance, Selected African Countries and Years

Country and year	Population (millions)	Percentage covered by insurance
Burkina Faso, 1981	6.7	0.9
Burundi, 1986	4.9	1.4
Kenya, 1985	21.2	11.4
Mali, 1986	7.6	3.3
Nigeria, 1986	103.1	0.04
Senegal, 1991	7.2	13.0
Uganda, 1991	16.8	0.0
Zambia, 1981	5.6	6.1
Zimbabwe, 1987	8.7	4.6

Source: Vogel 1990; World Bank sector reports.

in Senegal, compulsory programs for public employees in Sudan, and govern-
ment-mandated employer coverage of health care for employees in Zaire.
By making health insurance compulsory for employees in the formal sector, governments can encourage risk-sharing in a number of ways. The large number of
enrollees spreads risk more widely and makes the system more viable and more
fair. When insurance is compulsory, a large market is created that may encourage
entry by private suppliers. Under such a system, governments can collect premiums while allowing consumers to subscribe to any one of a number of public or
private plans. Finally, compulsory coverage eliminates the problem of adverse
selection—the tendency of the healthy to forgo purchasing insurance.

Employer-sponsored plans are a second form of insurance coverage. They
provide care directly through employer-owned, on-site health facilities or rely
on contracts with outside providers or health maintenance organizations. Examples include employer-provided medical care in Zambia and Nigeria, as well
as in the rubber forests of Liberia and Zaire. In Senegal, employees are covered
under one of two insurance programs: a system known as Institut Prevoyance
Maladie (IPM), for 53,000 wage earners and their families; and the Institut de
Prevoyance et Retraites du Senegal (IPRES) for 60,000 retirees. Approximately
445,000 family members are covered under the two schemes. In Nigeria, five
large parastatals offer comprehensive care for their employees and their families, either at their own health care facilities or by contracting with private hospitals and doctors.

A third category of risk-sharing is composed of prepayment plans with a
one-time annual collection fee. This avoids the need to adjust rates on the basis
of assessments of individual risk (Eklund and Stavem 1990). Examples include
personal prepayment plans, community sponsored plans (such as village funds
for purchasing medicines or a broader self-supporting network of local clinics),
and programs sponsored by cooperatives. In Kenya, an estimated 2.1 million
employees and their families earning more than K Sh 1000 per month pay a flat
rate of K Sh 20 per month to the National Hospital Insurance Fund (NHIF).
When employees are hospitalized, the NHIF will pay out K Sh 200 per day for
up to 180 days of care. In Guinea-Bissau a system of prepayment, limited to
prenatal care and treatment with a few essential drugs, has worked well. In
Zaire the Bwamanda health insurance system provides a model for the operation of community-based insurance (Box 10-4).

Fourth, there is private insurance to cover the fees of private providers.
Private insurance represents a means of earmarking family savings to self-
finance health care by selected groups. In countries like Côte d'Ivoire, Ghana,
and Senegal, private-for-profit insurance plans cater to groups with higher incomes that are willing to pay for a quality of care that their government cannot
finance. In Senegal, rapid development of private insurance over a three-year

period resulted in enrollment of 15,000 people in plans offered by eight companies. In other countries, such as Zimbabwe, private health insurance has also
grown (Vogel 1990).

The Role of Government in Health Insurance

Governments can and must play a critical role in encouraging risk-sharing. The
willingness to pay for health insurance is likely to be weak in countries where
publicly provided health services are "free" and no tradition of cost recovery
exists. When user fees become an established practice in the public sector,
households begin to take an interest in ways to spread the risk of substantial
health expenditures over time and across a wider population. With the subsequent evolution of risk-sharing financing mechanisms, a key obstacle to nongovernment financing and provision of health services—such as expensive
hospital care—can then be progressively removed.

The government can also encourage the use of deductibles and copayments
in compulsory and other types of insurance programs. If those covered by compulsory insurance can receive services at no out-of-pocket cost, they will probably overuse costly services. Deductibles (an amount that users must pay before
their insurance coverage begins) and copayments (a percentage of total costs
above the deductible paid by the user) can help prevent overuse of the system.
Even a small deductible, such as 1 percent of annual household income, or a
small copayment (such as 10 percent of the cost of services received) can go a
long way toward reducing unnecessary use of medical care.

To minimize the administrative costs of insurance programs and broaden
the range of coverage, governments can encourage competition among insurers. To this end, governments may decide to permit private firms to opt out of
the compulsory public health insurance plan if they provide a satisfactory alternative, or reduce the risks faced by private insurers through stop-loss provisions
and reinsurance.

Governments can also respond to the criticism that insurance schemes may
reinforce the maldistribution of health resources between rural and urban areas.
It has been argued—and the argument does have some justification—that the
extra funds generated by insurance programs in low-income countries typically
benefit urban, employed workers and their families, while doing little for large
rural populations. This problem can be aggravated by insurance plans, particularly if public insurance promotes hospital-based and doctor-centered care.
Thus, public funds that become available after insurance schemes are put into
place should be reallocated to cost-effective packages of primary care at facilities in periurban and rural areas (Mills and Gilson 1988). Another way to ensure
equity is to subsidize the cost of insurance premiums through vouchers for the

BOX 10-4. COMMUNITY-LEVEL
INSURANCE PLANS: LESSONS FROM
ZAIRE

Practice: Several features of the Bwamanda health insurance system in Zaire have contributed to its success. Offered by the health care provider, it avoids problems of setting prices for services and of transferring money from an insurance plan to the health care provider. The combination of simple fee structures and the requirement that patients be referred helps minimize overuse of the system. The scheme also benefits from a good marketing structure, as reflected in its high enrollment. Health center nurses, who enjoy high levels of access to the community, are given financial incentives in the form of a small percentage of premiums when they recruit new participants.

The insurance covers 80 percent of the standard charge for hospitalization or treatment of a chronic disease. Although associated with a hospital, the accounting of the insurance program is kept separately. The hospital bills the scheme for charges incurred by the beneficiaries. All hospital cases require referral through a health center, which serves as the site for verification of the need for treatment and enrollment in the insurance plan. Premiums are collected once a year following the harvest. To prevent inflationary losses in the value of funds collected, the money is invested with interest or used to buy drugs.

Community enrollment rose from an initial 30 percent in 1986 to 60 percent in 1989. Cost recovery through user fees at Bwamanda hospital went from 50 percent of recurrent expenditures in 1986 to 80 percent in 1988. Health insurance and interest income exceeded expenditures under the plan in 1987, 1988, and 1989: 89 percent of funds collected went to hospital

poor. The main practical problem with all such measures is to identify the poor. This is an administrative difficulty everywhere, since means tests are difficult to apply (World Bank 1987).

Conclusion: Resolving Crises

No single formula will solve the problem of financing health services for all of the people in African countries. Each country faces a different configuration of problems, prospects, and priorities. There is much to be said, however, for proceeding in incremental fashion. Governments can take a leadership role on several fronts.

First, each government controls the amount of public resources allocated to the health sector. It is therefore up to governments progressively to restore public funds for health in countries where they have diminished or to raise current commitments in recognition of the importance of health for sustainable development.

Box 10.4, continued

charges, 6 to 7 percent to health centers, and 5 percent to administrative costs. Although admission rates for insured patients are somewhat higher than for those who are uninsured, the high enrollment rate of the eligible population in the program allows absorption of this cost.

Lessons learned: Studies of a variety of entirely autonomous community insurance schemes in Zaire have identified a number of preconditions or correlates of success (Shepard, Vian, and Kleinau 1990):

■ Most successful plans have modest premiums. Where premiums are beyond the financial means of potential members, participation rates will be low.

■ A precondition for success is that health services be of acceptable quality.

■ Sensitization of potential benefici- aries can help reduce the tendency of any voluntary scheme to concentrate its members (unintentionally) among those predisposed or most likely to fall ill.

■ Committed, decentralized management provides flexibility and accountability.

■ Simple control methods, such as stamps for enrolled members and photo identification of beneficiaries, can help reduce error and fraud.

■ Enrollment of all family members, rather than individuals, increases the size of the pool of people among whom risks are to be spread.

■ Appropriate investment strategies are needed to preserve the value of premium income in periods of inflation.

■ Strong accounting systems are critical to effective functioning.

■ A financial guarantee can be an important catalyst to launching a successful start-up phase.

Second, symbolic commitments to preventive and primary care can be made into real commitments by reallocating public funds away from expensive and relatively ineffective urban-based curative care to cost-effective preventive and primary care services in rural and periurban areas. In Madagascar, between 1986 and 1991, public expenditures on secondary- and tertiary-level care fell from 51 percent to about 36 percent. In Nigeria the Fifth National Development Plan set out a strategy to begin moving federal funds away from expensive hospital programs, and the share of federal funds going to hospital programs was to be reduced by about a third by 1992 from levels established in the early 1980s.

Third, governments can progressively implement user fees and cost-recovery to help ensure financial sustainability of publicly provided health care. This study shows that there is considerable scope for expanding user fees and that households are willing to pay those fees, provided quality improvements accompany higher prices.

BOX 10-5. PUBLIC-PRIVATE COLLABORATION

Increasingly, African governments are deliberately fostering collaboration with the private sector in financing and providing health care because increased nongovernment health sector activity can ease pressure on the public budget. Despite the distortions that characterize the private market for health care, the private sector is generally more efficient than the public sector. A shift in the balance of health needs to more individual-level care among groups with higher incomes further signals an expanding role for private providers, with insurance mechanisms to protect against catastrophic financial losses.

In financing public support can take the form of public subsidies to private voluntary organizations, contracting out to nongovernment providers, and a variety of incentives (World Bank 1987). For example, in Rwanda, where missions provided 25 to 35 percent of health care services during the 1980s, the government reimbursed them for a large share of the salaries of Rwandese staff. These public subsidies accounted for about 5 percent of recurrent public health spending. In Zimbabwe, about 4 percent of central government health care spending went to subsidize missions, representing about 85 percent of their health service revenues in the early 1980s. This subsidy was provided in support of the missions' work in serving indigents. In Nigeria laboratory services have been contracted out, and in Zimbabwe equipment, maintenance, laundry services, and invoicing of insured patients have been contracted out.

Fourth, governments can create the conditions for expanding health insurance, thus generating increased revenues for the health sector in general and stimulating expansion in the numbers of nongovernment providers of health care.

Fifth, governments can promote public-private collaboration as a means of increasing efficiency and fostering the creation of new efforts in health care by private voluntary organizations and private-for-profit providers (Box 10-5). If private practice has been outlawed, it should once again be made legal.

Finally, governments can reap far greater sustainable benefits from better use of available external funds. Instead of molding national strategies around available donor funding, governments should develop national health policies and strategies, and then provide leadership to donors, to help put them into effect.

CHAPTER ELEVEN

Timetable for Change

ACHIEVING better health in Sub-Saharan Africa, as this report makes clear, will require a large number of interrelated actions, ranging from the formulation of comprehensive health policies to the identification of disadvantaged groups whose health needs must be clearly specified. Table 11-1 summarizes an action agenda under eight headings, and offers an informal timetable with actions classified as having short-term, intermediate, or long-term time horizons.

Like the rest of the report, this table is indicative rather than prescriptive. It is, in fact, indicative in two senses.

First, diversity among African countries means that the countries themselves will have to decide their own priorities for action. These will depend on differences in the conditions affecting health, the quality and quantity of public and personal health services, access to external assistance, and so on. In some countries, such as Mozambique, Somalia, and Uganda, civil war has taken an immense toll on health systems. In the immediate future these countries will be preoccupied with making basic assessments of the status of all the determinants of health outcomes and restoring and rehabilitating basic services. In other countries, such as Benin, Guinea, Mali, Malawi, and Nigeria, experimentation and positive experiences linked to well-functioning health systems can serve as a basis for broadening coverage. And in still other countries, like Botswana, Lesotho, and Zimbabwe, where per capita incomes and health expenditures are considerably greater, priority actions will include encouraging provision of health insurance to larger shares of the population, providing fuller health coverage for the poor, and privatizing selected hospital services.

Table 11-1 is also indicative rather than prescriptive in terms of the suggested time horizons. For example, a government can formulate an operationally relevant national health policy relatively quickly through collaborative

Table 11-1.   Action Agenda and Timetable

	Short term	Medium term	Long term
Policy formulation and data collection			
Formulate and review national health policy	✓		
Develop demographic and epidemiological data bases		✓	
Establish and review health targets	✓		
Identify the most disadvantaged groups	✓		
Establish a research agenda	✓		
Intersectoral interventions			
Provide more health information to the public and to health care providers	✓		
Produce behavioral changes by households and individuals through IEC methods		✓	
Carry out sustainable intersectoral interventions at the community level, particularly to improve water and sanitation			✓
Strengthen formal and informal education of girls and women		✓	
Health care delivery			
Identify cost-effective package of basic health services	✓		
Strengthen networks of health centers and first-referral hospitals			✓
Improve referral system through regulations, prices, and quality signals		✓	
Reduce concentration of financial resources at tertiary level and devolve Ministry of Health involvement in hospital management		✓	
Improve access to health services for the "core" poor			✓
Pharmaceuticals			
Establish national drug policies	✓		
Review legal basis and structure	✓		
Reserve foreign exchange for drug purchases	✓		
Adopt essential drug lists	✓		
Reduce inefficiency and waste through			
Use of cost-effectiveness criteria in purchasing drugs	✓		
Quantification of national drug needs	✓		
Competitive bidding for generic drugs	✓		
Improved storage and management	✓		
Better training and information for those who prescribe drugs		✓	
Measures to improve patient compliance with treatment regimens		✓	

Table 11-1. *continued*

	Short term	Medium term	Long term
Develop and support revolving funds for drugs		✓	
Personnel management and training			
Formulate human resource plans for health by geographic area, by expertise, and by gender and category of worker		✓	
Generate budgetary savings by reducing the number of ineffectual civil service workers while improving compensation for productive workers	✓		
Expand training in health management and administration		✓	
Adapt training curricula to district- and community-level services		✓	
Health infrastructure and equipment			
Establish rehabilitation plans for existing buildings and equipment		✓	
Establish norms and procedures for new health facilities, especially at the district level	✓		
Designate one hospital as a center of excellence for training	✓		
Institutional reform and management			
Conduct assessment of current system and its operation	✓		
Pursue decentralization and redefine roles and responsibilities at the central, regional, district and community levels		✓	
Develop management skills in planning and budgeting		✓	
Foster institutional pluralism		✓	
Stimulate and strengthen community organizations	✓		
Support training and other preparatory work for district health teams		✓	
Undertake training and preparatory work for community management committees		✓	
Strengthen management information systems through:			
Assessment of needs by component of health system	✓		
Training required		✓	
Implementation of systems and procurement of needed equipment		✓	
Develop capacity for essential health research			✓

Table continued on next page

Table 11-1. *continued*

	Short term	Medium term	Long term
Financing health care			
Increase per capita government health expenditures		✓	
Focus government expenditures on public health goods and services		✓	
Implement user fees and cost recovery in public facilities			
At tertiary hospitals	✓		
At first-referral hospitals		✓	
At health centers		✓	
Identify the poor and subsidize health services for them	✓		
Encourage expansion of insurance schemes, especially employer-based and community-level schemes			✓
Promote public-private collaboration		✓	
Donor collaboration			
Establish coordinating mechanisms headed by government	✓		
Assess profile and cost-effectiveness of donor activities	✓		
Establish donor role in cost-effective approach to better health	✓		
Progressively increase donor funding for primary and preventive care		✓	

efforts involving health sector experts, providers of health services, and community representatives. The demographic and epidemiological data used in formulating the plan need not be perfect, although they should be as accurate as possible under the given circumstances.

Over time, however, the initial national health plan will have to be revised as more complete demographic and epidemiological data are collected and the lessons that can be derived from country-specific experience become clearer. Moreover, some African countries might conclude that the formulation of policies and plans at this time would be premature because of serious flaws in the existing data.

Similarly, actions with a longer-term horizon tend, in general, to be more demanding of financial sources—for example, the construction of large numbers of health centers. Some countries, however, may find themselves able to complete longer-term actions within a medium-term time frame.

The next section of this chapter discusses the major actions listed in the table under the table's three time horizons. As will be evident, short-term actions fall largely within the public domain, given the government's critical leadership role in creating an enabling environment for better health as well as its substantial involvement in the financing and delivery of health services.

The second section provides a dynamic perspective on how key health priorities will change among the African countries as they move to higher levels of socioeconomic development.

The penultimate section of the chapter deals with the need to expand research and research capacity on Africa's health problems. The chapter's final section deals with the question of how international assistance might be used most effectively. While African governments must take the leading role in achieving better health in Africa, donor funding can play a vital role, particularly in those countries afflicted by widespread poverty.

Agenda for Action

Short-Term Actions

These are actions that are likely to demand immediate priority:

- Formulating comprehensive, operational health policies with explicit goals and methods of evaluating progress. These policies should include statements on how the enabling environment for health will be strengthened, prescriptions for the role of government in financing and providing public health activities, and preparation of a locally relevant research agenda to help fill critical gaps in knowledge. The policies should also include statements on how international initiatives will be integrated into national plans.

- Identifying the most disadvantaged groups and agreeing on indicators for monitoring and evaluating improvements in their health status. In particular, screening mechanisms should be developed to establish who should qualify for fee exemptions or subsidies. Community participation in this process is vital.

- Establishing national drug policies, including essential drug lists. Particular attention is needed to quantifying national drug needs over specific time periods, using cost-effectiveness criteria in selecting and purchasing them, using competitive bidding for generic drugs, and considering the desirability of interministerial agreements on reserving foreign exchange for drug purchases.

- Formulating human resource plans for health by geographic area, by expertise, and by category of worker. In particular, attention should be paid to drawing up a profile of the staff required to operate a district-based system of health centers and first-referral hospitals and reducing the number of job classifications.

■ Making a comprehensive assessment of existing health sector buildings and equipment and future needs. Particular attention should be paid to rehabilitating current buildings and establishing norms and procedures for locating new health facilities (especially at the district level).

■ Initiating institutional reform and assessments of management capacities and needs. These actions can be facilitated by participant/beneficiary assessments of current health systems, establishing management information systems (MIS) to monitor progress, and strengthening community involvement in the management of lower-level health facilities.

■ Establishing coordinating mechanisms, under the joint leadership of the ministry of health, ministry of planning, and ministry of finance, to assess the profile and cost-effectiveness of donor activities. Particular attention should be paid to developing a systematic approach for donor participation in the development of district health systems.

Medium-Term Actions

Most governments in Africa are deeply involved directly in the financing and provision of health care, so this selection of items for change over the medium term incorporates activities aimed at making public spending more efficient, equitable, and sustainable. Actions with a medium-term horizon include:

■ Supporting advanced training programs for senior public health managers and devising training curricula attuned to the specific needs of health services at the district and community level. In particular, emphasis should be placed on getting professionals trained in health management and administration into key policy, planning, and budgeting positions in ministries of health.

■ Progressively increasing government expenditures on health and earmarking larger shares of funds for public health goods and services, including cost-effective preventive and primary care. In many countries, real per capita expenditures on health need also to be increased.

■ Reallocating larger shares of public funds for health to well-functioning health centers and first-referral hospitals. This would mean progressive decreases in funding for relatively cost-ineffective services at urban hospitals.

■ Implementing cost-sharing, first at tertiary-level facilities, where those who bypass the referral system can be assessed full costs. This can be complemented with cost-sharing at health centers and first-referral hospitals, with a predetermined amount to be retained by the facility. There should be no compensatory reductions in overall ministry of health funding because of cost-sharing. The quality of services should improve at the same time as fees are being increased.

■ Launching training and information programs to reduce inefficiency and waste in the prescribing of drugs and to improve patient compliance with instructions on drug usage.

■ Using information, education, and communication (IEC) programs to improve the health-related practices of individuals, households, and communities.

■ Generating budgetary savings by reducing the number of ineffectual and unneeded workers while improving compensation by rewarding productive workers. Fees charged for health services can be used to supplement the incomes of health center staff.

■ Laying the groundwork for institutional reform and decentralization by redefining roles, responsibilities, and authority at the central, regional, district, and community levels. Emphasis should be placed on fostering institutional pluralism in support of decentralization. Training must be provided for health teams and community management committees.

■ Evolving sustainable forms of community health financing, including drug revolving funds and community insurance schemes.

■ Promoting public-private cooperation to enable private sector providers (especially private voluntary organizations) to play a more prominent role in health care.

■ Ensuring that donor funding is used to reinforce national strategies, and increasing the capacity of health care systems to absorb donor funding.

■ Devolving the management of tertiary-level hospitals from the ministry of health through various forms of decentralization and privatization, while gradually reducing public expenditures on tertiary-level care.

Long-Term Actions

Long-term actions include progressive expansion of health systems, and using financial commitments to make health systems more self-sustaining. They include:

■ Implementing sustainable intersectoral interventions at the community level. Particularly important are access to safe water, sanitation, nutrition, and family planning services.

■ Strengthening the quality and improving the quantity of primary care services by expanding systems of well-functioning health centers and first-referral hospitals. This implies the construction of new health centers and first-referral hospitals and increased public-private collaboration in their staffing, operation, and maintenance.

■ Strengthening the capacity for operationally relevant health research in ministries, universities, and private voluntary organizations.

The Dynamics of Change

The challenges implicit in Table 11-1 will differ across countries, depending on their socioeconomic conditions, political stability, epidemiological conditions, the effectiveness of health care services, and financial constraints. This can be illustrated by comparing the situations of three countries—Uganda, Mali, and Botswana.

Uganda: Uganda is typical of several African countries that have suffered political, social, and economic upheaval in recent years. Health indicators, such as infant mortality, have shown little improvement over the last ten to twenty years. Fertility rates have remained constant or have increased over the last decade, and economic setbacks have seriously impaired public funding for social services. Political turmoil and civil strife have reduced what once was one of Africa's most effective and efficient health services to near collapse. Health finance is in disarray, with individual government-owned facilities making unilateral decisions on fees to prevent outright collapse. Management problems abound in public sector health care delivery, where capacity utilization is 50 percent lower than in nongovernment health facilities. To make matters worse, Uganda's fledgling system of health care is burdened by an AIDS epidemic.

Uganda faces the challenge of taking action on virtually all of the items in Table 11-1. The government plays little role in ensuring the provision of public health goods and services. There is thus an urgent need for a sharp rise in the public financial commitment to health, and public expenditures need to be reallocated from tertiary-level hospital care to primary health care. This is the time to rethink the country's health strategies and health care system entirely and to emphasize the use of donor assistance in ways that contribute to an integrated system of health care.

Mali: The situation in Mali is typical of a handful of African countries that are progressively improving health outcomes despite tight financial constraints. Health indicators such as infant mortality and life expectancy are improving, though slowly. Low per capita incomes are gradually increasing, and the country enjoys somewhat greater social and political stability than many other African countries. Although the Ministry of Public Health has traditionally focused on providing health care through vertical programs and has neglected its role in policy formulation and planning, it is achieving a gradual expansion of district-based health care. The country's network of district-based health centers is expected to increase access to health care to 52 percent of the population by 1997. To promote public-private collaboration, the government lifted its ban on private medical practice in 1987.

Mali also needs to take action on most of the items in Table 11-1, but it has the distinct advantage that the groundwork is being laid for decentralizing services to the district level. Moreover, Mali's donors are actively supporting the expansion of district-level care. Perhaps the greatest challenges facing the country are rationalizing health sector expenditure patterns, increasing the government's financial commitment to health, promoting cost-sharing, improving the reliability of pharmaceutical supplies in public sector facilities, and encouraging nongovernment providers of health care.

Botswana: Health status in Botswana has been improving rapidly. Rising incomes and expenditures on public goods and services reflect increases in per capita GNP, illiteracy and fertility rates are on the decline, and the country enjoys a good measure of social and political stability. Access to health facilities is relatively good, and decentralization to the district and subdistrict levels has been in place for some time. Public expenditures on health are also relatively high—well over the $68 per capita annually discussed earlier for high-expenditure countries. Furthermore, health planning is given prominence in the organization and work program of the Ministry of Health, and the country has a solid tradition of cost-sharing for publicly provided services (though such revenues constitute only a small share of total government expenditures).

Predominant among the challenges facing Botswana are encouraging privatization or full-cost recovery at hospitals, encouraging the expansion of public and private insurance schemes, strengthening health research and research capacity, and reducing donor involvement in light of Botswana's growing financial and institutional capabilities. Botswana will also want to compare the profile of publicly provided health services now available to rural and periurban households with the cost-effective package of basic services costed in this study.

Developing Greater Research Capacities

Virtually all of the actions described thus far require additional research and policy analysis. To improve on the dismal state of health research and policy analysis in Africa (and other developing regions), an independent Commission on Health Research for Development recommended (Commission on Health Research for Development 1990):

- Investing in long-term development of the research capacity of individuals and institutions, especially in neglected fields such as epidemiology and management

- Setting national priorities for research, for using domestic and external resources
- Giving professional recognition to good research and building career paths to attract and retain able researchers
- Developing reliable links between researchers and the users of research at the national, district, and community levels
- Investing at least 2 percent of national health expenditures and 5 percent of externally funded programs in research activities.

Without such a commitment to research, the prospects are slim that African countries will be able to establish a policy agenda, identify cost-effective pack-

---

BOX 11-1. A HEALTH RESEARCH UNIT MAKES A DIFFERENCE IN GHANA

Ministries of health in Africa are often blamed for making decisions that are not scientifically informed. This is frequently because of a failure to use available information, especially research information that exists in academic institutions and scientific journals. Ministries of health often perceive themselves as service providers with little or no role in research, and research findings are often expressed in a way that is not intelligible to decisionmakers.

To address this problem, the Ministry of Health in Ghana created a health research unit. The unit is responsible for creating awareness of the need and usefulness of research information at all levels of the health system and articulating the research needs of the Ministry of Health to professional researchers. It is also involved in building capacity for operations research in the ministry, conducting health systems research, and ensuring that health research information is disseminated and used.

Within two years of its establishment, the research unit had determined a research agenda and circulated it to universities and research institutions. It had developed a research policy for the ministry. It also conducted workshops on research proposal writing and analysis for regional and district health teams.

To ensure use of research findings, the research unit has supported consultation meetings at the national level on topics such as safe motherhood, decentralization of health services, and community health worker programs, at which research findings are presented. Program guidelines have been prepared for implementors following such consultations.

The research unit works with an eighteen-member advisory committee made up of staff from the Ministry of Health, the Ghana statistical services, academic institutions, research bodies, local government authorities, nongovernment organizations, and the National Council of Women and Development.

Source: Adjei 1993.

ages of health services, target the households most in need, improve management of decentralized systems, mobilize the necessary financial resources for better health, and monitor and evaluate progress. Botswana can be cited as a country where health systems research on this type of issue has been encouraged. Like Ghana, it has set up a Health Research Unit in the Ministry of Health.

Numerous agencies and institutions are available to support the development of greater health research capacity in Africa. In fourteen countries in southern Africa, health workers at the national, provincial, and district levels have been trained in the development of research proposals with the help of the Dutch Government Technical Cooperation, the Royal Tropical Institute of Amsterdam, and WHO. More than fifty research proposals have been supported with small grants, and a technical advisory committee has been established on health systems research from each of the participating countries (Aleta 1992). Universities in Tanzania, Zambia, and Zimbabwe are engaged in developing and implementing research proposals through their faculties of medicine. The Rockefeller Foundation has provided grants for such activities for several decades and is currently supporting the establishment of a national epidemiological advisory board in Cameroon.

The International Health Policy Program (IHPP), supported by the Pew Charitable Trust and the Carnegie Corporation of New York in cooperation with WHO and the World Bank, is noteworthy for its support of a network of interested developing country researchers seeking ways to use resources more effectively to improve the health of the disadvantaged. The IHPP supports researchers in a number of African and Asian countries. World Bank and International Development Association commitments to population, health and, nutrition projects in Africa have almost always contained provisions for research, amounting to roughly 2 percent of total commitments of $1.3 billion through 1993.

The research agenda for better health will undoubtedly vary from country to country. In most African countries it is likely to include work to gain a better understanding of the lowest levels of the health care pyramid—self care, the intrahousehold dynamics of health, and community-based actions for health improvement. The endeavors of international, national, and local NGOs are particularly relevant to understanding health behavior at this level. As but one example, a project in South Africa is promoting women's participation in health policymaking. The project involves participative research, development of a national network of more than 600 individuals and organizations, production of a newsletter, and health information workshops (Tumwine 1993).

Links with the International Community

Virtually all African countries face the challenge of obtaining many more sustainable benefits from donor funding than they have in the past (Box 11-2).

Rather than molding national strategies around available donor funding, African governments need to develop national health policies and strategies on how to make the best use of external assistance.

Several African countries, under the leadership of the ministry of health, ministry of finance, or ministry of planning, are bringing together a diverse group of donor agencies to work with national health staff to build national capacities for health over the long term. In Benin, Guinea, Sierra Leone, and Zambia, for example, national action plans are being developed by governments that will be followed by identification of financial needs and the obligations that will be shared by donors. This is precisely the approach favored by this report, and promises to redress a major failing of donor assistance in the past—namely, the absence of sustainability in externally funded programs for health.

The donor community needs to extend its time horizon in supporting African efforts to develop integrated health systems. Once donors become involved

---

BOX 11-2. INTERNATIONAL INITIATIVES AND SUSTAINABLE OUTCOMES

In the 1980s, approximately half of external assistance for health in Africa was committed to internationally conceived and executed multicountry programs. The list of initiatives is long and impressive: the Expanded Programme of Immunization (EPI) of WHO, UNICEF, and USAID; the Diarrheal Diseases Control Program of WHO; WHO's program for control of acute respiratory infections; the Safe Motherhood Initiative; the Global Program on AIDS; the Child Survival programs of UNICEF and the United States; the Onchocerciasis Control Program; the International Drinking Water Supply and Sanitation Decade; and the Special Program of Research and Training in Tropical Diseases.

The 1990 World Summit for Children, sponsored by UNICEF, was an international initiative for overall improvements in the health and welfare of children at the highest political level. Its goals are fully consistent with the proposals in this report.

Valuable as these many initiatives have been on an individual basis, it is also widely believed that, collectively, they have had the unintentional effect of fragmenting systems of health care delivery; undermining national capacities in health policy, analysis, and planning; and discouraging the development of local health leadership within Africa.

At the country level, follow-up on the World Summit for Children through national plans of action, implementation of the Bamako Initiative, the WHO Three-Phase Scenario for development of district health systems, and other initiatives is merited. Follow-up should be pursued on an *integrated* basis, within a framework of local adaptation, leadership, and monitoring and evaluation of sustainable outcomes.

in funding health sector activities—particularly in countries with extremely low expenditure levels and institutional capacity—they should expect to remain partners for at least a decade. Although pressure to achieve measurable health gains over the short term is understandable, succumbing to such pressure is likely to be counterproductive in the long run. Donors also need to support broad-based health sector programs and concentrate efforts on those African countries that are firmly committed to and sustain the effort to achieve health improvement.

Future international assistance can make a significant contribution to better health in Africa in several areas:

- Support for *long-term capacity-building and institutional reform*, especially in the areas of policy analysis and formulation
- Support for identification, financing, and provision of *sustainable cost-effective packages of basic health care services* at the district level
- Support for *intercountry programs of public health training and practically oriented research*
- Support for *intersectoral actions* for health. These activities can reach beyond the health sector and its "international counterpart," the World Health Organization, to encompass other multilateral agencies, such as UNICEF and the World Food Program.

The priorities set out above are few, but their implications are complex. The push to expand Africa's health infrastructure is a case in point. Direct support for expansion should not be among the highest priorities for international assistance in most countries. Rehabilitation of *existing* infrastructure and equipment needs to be ensured first. Thereafter, donor support for facility expansion should be provided within a framework that considers not only proposed capital investments, but also their implications for recurrent expenditures in the future and the requirements of the sector as a whole. Under such arrangements, recurrent cost financing should be increasingly acceptable to the donor community.

Conclusion

African experts need to intensify the work of consensus-building and provide intellectual leadership in putting forward proposals for "compacts" for better health between African countries and the international community. Such compacts might envisage, in those African countries most in need, a doubling of government efforts to mobilize resources for health and comparable increases in. donor support. The specific items for inclusion in such compacts can be expected to vary considerably from country to country.

A forum might be established, extending beyond the country level, to ensure the coordination of international initiatives for training and operationally oriented research. Such a group could determine priorities and monitor the modest levels of financial support that are likely to be needed. The forum could also assume responsibility for reviewing health reforms at the country level and serve as a support group for ministries of health and other agents of change. To facilitate monitoring and evaluation, benchmarks would need to be established. A comprehensive independent evaluation of progress could be undertaken after, perhaps, five years.

A consultative group on health in Africa could be responsive to these needs for well-orchestrated actions for health improvement, perhaps following the lines of the so-called Donors to African Education—a group that has brought together Africans and donors for consultations on a wide range of education issues. Another example is the Global Coalition for Africa, a high-level group of Africans and donors that seeks to identify and monitor support for actions on issues that have previously received inadequate support.

A first step would be to build a consensus among African countries and their institutional partners on the mechanisms needed. Consensus-building of this nature, nationally and internationally, could amount to an unparalleled effort to assist Africa in overcoming intolerable levels of suffering, premature death, and waste stemming from ill health.

Statistical Appendix

Table A-1. Health and Development Indicators

Country	Midyear population (thousands) 1992	Annual rate of population growth (percent) 1992	Crude birth rate (per 1,000 pop.) 1992	Crude death rate (per 1,000 pop.) 1992	Total fertility rate (per woman 15–49) 1992	Life expectancy at birth (M/F) 1992	GNP per capita (US$) 1991	Adult literacy rate (percent) Female 1990	Adult literacy rate (percent) Total 1990
Angola	9,732	2.8	47	19	6.6	45/48	—	28	42
Benin	5,042	3.0	46	16	6.2	49/52	380	16	23
Botswana	1,360	3.0	36	6	4.7	66/70	2,530	65	74
Burkina Faso	9,537	2.9	47	17	6.5	47/50	290	9	18
Burundi	5,818	2.9	46	17	6.8	46/50	210	40	50
Cameroon	12,245	3.0	42	12	5.8	55/58	850	43	54
Cape Verde	389	2.3	36	7	4.3	67/69	750	—	—
Central African Rep.	3,166	2.5	42	18	5.8	45/49	390	25	38
Chad	5,977	2.5	44	18	5.9	46/49	210	18	30
Comoros	510	3.5	47	11	6.7	56/57	500	40	48
Congo	2,428	3.3	49	16	6.6	49/54	1,120	44	57
Côte d'Ivoire	12,841	3.6	45	12	6.6	53/59	690	40	54
Djibouti	465	3.2	46	16	6.6	47/51	—	—	—
Equatorial Guinea	437	2.3	41	18	5.5	46/50	330	37	50
Ethiopia	54,790	3.4	52	18	7.5	47/50	120	—	—
Gabon	1,201	2.8	43	15	5.9	52/56	3,780	48	61
Gambia	929	2.9	47	20	6.5	44/45	360	16	27
Ghana	15,824	3.2	44	12	6.1	53/57	400	51	60
Guinea	6,048	2.8	48	20	6.5	44/44	460	13	24
Guinea-Bissau	1,022	2.0	46	25	6.0	38/39	180	24	36

Kenya	25,838	3.3	45	10	6.4	57/61	340	58	69
Lesotho	1,860	2.5	36	10	5.1	58/63	580	84	73
Liberia	2,719	3.0	44	14	6.2	53/57	450a	29	39
Madagascar	12,384	2.8	42	14	6.1	50/53	210	73	80
Malawi	9,085	3.1	53	21	7.6	44/45	230	31	42
Mali	8,962	2.9	50	18	7.1	47/50	280	24	32
Mauritania	2,082	2.8	49	18	6.8	46/50	510	21	34
Mauritius	1,099	1.1	18	7	2.0	67/73	2,410	75	82
Mozambique	16,565	2.7	46	19	6.5	45/48	80	21	33
Niger	8,171	3.3	52	19	7.4	44/48	300	17	28
Nigeria	101,884	2.9	43	14	5.9	50/53	340	39	51
Rwanda	7,310	2.2	40	17	6.2	45/48	270	37	50
São Tomé and Principe	121	2.6	36	8	5.0	65/70	400	42	58
Senegal	7,845	2.7	43	16	6.1	46/49	720	25	38
Seychelles	69	0.9	23	7	2.7	68/75	5,110	95	88
Sierra Leone	4,354	2.6	48	22	6.5	40/45	210	11	21
Somalia	8,302	3.1	48	17	6.8	47/50	170a	14	24
Sudan	26,587	2.9	44	14	6.2	51/53	340a	12	27
Swaziland	860	3.6	49	12	6.6	55/59	1,050	65	100
Tanzania	25,965	3.0	45	15	6.3	49/52	100	88	90
Togo	3,899	3.2	45	13	6.5	53/56	410	31	43
Uganda	17,475	3.3	52	19	7.3	45/46	170	35	48
Zaïre	39,794	3.0	44	14	6.2	50/53	220a	61	72
Zambia	8,589	3.1	48	17	6.5	46/49	420a	65	73
Zimbabwe	10,352	2.6	34	8	4.6	58/61	650	60	67
Africa	**501,932**	**3.0**	**45**	**15**	**6.5**	**49/52**	**340**	**38**	**50**
World	5,441,205	1.6	26	9	3.2	64/68	4,000	55	65
Less developed counties	4,213,796	2.0	29	9	3.6	62/65	900	52	63
More developed countries	1,226,756	0.5	14	10	1.9	71/78	20,000	95	96

— Not available
a. 1990 GNP.

Table A-2. Population Projections (Standard/Medium)

Country	Midyear population (thousands) 2000	Midyear population (thousands) 2025	Annual rate of population growth (percent) 2000	Annual rate of population growth (percent) 2025	Total fertility rate 2000	Total fertility rate 2025	Population age structure (percent) 0-14 1990	65+ 1990	0-14 2025	65+ 2025	Urban population (percent) 1970	1990	2000
Angola	12,325	26,104	3.2	2.5	6.8	4.5	47	3	41	3	15	28	36
Benin	6,375	10,931	2.8	1.6	5.6	2.9	48	3	40	3	18	38	46
Botswana	1,694	2,699	2.6	1.3	3.9	2.1	46	3	31	5	8	29	37
Burkina Faso	12,047	22,745	2.9	2.0	6.4	3.5	45	3	39	4	6	15	24
Burundi	7,305	14,041	2.9	2.1	6.7	3.8	46	3	38	4	2	5	7
Cameroon	15,604	28,655	3.0	1.8	5.5	2.9	45	4	37	4	20	40	49
Cape Verde	470	726	2.2	1.4	3.7	2.1	44	4	27	4	20	29	36
Central African Rep.	3,867	7,330	2.7	2.2	6.2	4.0	42	3	39	3	30	47	55
Chad	7,353	13,622	2.7	2.0	6.1	3.8	42	4	37	4	12	32	42
Comoros	674	1,366	3.4	2.1	6.1	3.2	48	2	40	3	19	28	34
Congo	3,162	6,474	3.2	2.4	6.6	3.8	45	4	39	3	33	41	47
Côte d'Ivoire	16,878	33,140	3.3	2.0	6.2	3.3	48	3	43	3	27	40	47
Djibouti	606	1,175	3.2	2.1	6.5	3.6	45	3	40	4	62	81	84
Equatorial Guinea	525	839	2.3	1.5	5.4	2.9	40	4	37	4	27	29	33
Ethiopia	67,465	143,568	3.3	2.6	7.4	4.5	46	3	40	3	9	12	15
Gabon	1,515	2,986	3.0	2.3	6.4	3.7	36	5	37	4	26	46	54
Gambia	1,167	2,219	2.8	2.2	6.5	4.1	44	3	36	4	15	23	29
Ghana	20,334	36,221	3.0	1.7	5.5	2.0	47	3	36	4	29	34	39
Guinea	7,578	14,471	2.9	2.1	6.5	4.1	47	3	40	3	14	26	34
Guinea-Bissau	1,197	1,938	2.1	1.6	6.0	3.7	43	3	37	4	15	20	25
Kenya	34,091	72,853	3.4	2.6	5.9	4.0	49	3	35	4	10	24	32
Lesotho	2,282	3,647	2.5	1.3	4.5	2.2	43	4	32	6	9	19	27

Liberia	3,450	6,204	2.9	1.8	5.6	2.9	45	4	39	4	26	45	55
Madagascar	15,336	25,850	2.6	1.6	5.5	2.9	45	3	39	3	14	24	31
Malawi	11,555	24,409	3.0	2.7	7.6	5.2	47	3	41	3	6	12	16
Mali	11,430	23,760	3.2	2.5	7.0	4.2	47	3	40	3	14	24	30
Mauritania	2,628	5,415	3.0	2.5	6.8	4.4	45	3	38	4	14	47	59
Mauritius	1,192	1,450	1.0	0.6	2.0	2.0	30	5	20	13	42	41	42
Mozambique	20,768	43,063	3.0	2.5	6.9	4.5	44	3	39	4	6	27	41
Niger	10,737	24,286	3.5	2.9	7.5	5.2	48	2	41	3	9	20	27
Nigeria	127,806	216,900	2.7	1.6	5.0	2.8	47	2	38	4	20	35	43
Rwanda	8,762	16,701	2.7	2.0	6.2	3.8	49	2	42	2	3	6	8
São Tomé and Principe	150	239	2.6	1.3	4.4	2.2	39	5	28	7	—	42	—
Senegal	9,809	17,918	2.9	1.8	5.9	3.2	45	3	36	4	33	40	45
Seychelles	74	97	1.0	1.0	2.3	2.1	34	7	23	8	—	59	—
Sierra Leone	5,370	10,076	2.7	2.1	6.5	4.1	43	3	39	3	18	32	40
Somalia	10,648	21,004	3.1	2.2	6.6	3.8	46	3	40	3	20	24	28
Sudan	33,659	60,335	2.9	1.7	5.8	3.0	45	3	37	4	16	23	27
Swaziland	1,137	2,179	3.3	2.0	6.0	3.1	45	3	33	5	10	26	36
Tanzania	32,901	58,850	2.8	1.7	5.8	3.0	47	3	41	3	7	21	28
Togo	4,980	9,294	3.0	1.9	5.9	3.0	45	3	38	4	13	29	34
Uganda	22,551	48,223	3.2	2.7	7.3	4.9	49	3	40	2	8	11	14
Zaire	50,856	100,287	3.1	2.1	6.2	3.5	47	3	41	3	30	28	31
Zambia	10,867	20,739	2.9	2.1	6.7	3.9	48	2	40	2	30	42	45
Zimbabwe	12,360	17,613	1.8	1.1	3.5	2.2	45	2	32	4	17	29	36
Africa	**633,540**	**1,202,642**	**2.9**	**2.0**	**5.8**	**3.5**	**46**	**3**	**38**	**4**	**19**	**28**	**34**
World	6,160,486	8,319,501	1.4	1.0	3.0	2.4	32	9	25	10	37	43	48
Less developed countries	4,887,621	6,946,332	1.7	1.1	3.2	2.5	36	7	26	8	25	34	40
More developed countries	1,272,866	1,373,169	0.4	0.2	1.9	2.0	21	17	18	18	67	73	76

Table A-3. Population Projections (Rapid Decline in Fertility)

Country	Midyear population (thousands)		Annual rate of population growth (percent)		Total fertility rate		Contraceptive use (percentage of married women ages 15–49)			Population age structure (percent)	
							Esti-mated	Required for rapid decline		0–14	65+
	2000	2025	2000	2025	2000	2025	1990	2000	2025	2025	2025
Angola	12,128	17,752	2.4	1.2	5.4	2.4	3	33	69	29	4
Benin	6,240	7,073	2.3	1.2	5.0	2.4	6	40	71	29	4
Botswana	1,655	2,410	1.9	1.2	2.9	2.1	35	65	75	26	5
Burkina Faso	11,850	17,164	2.3	1.2	5.2	2.4	3	38	68	29	3
Burundi	7,189	10,264	2.2	1.2	5.5	2.4	9	40	72	29	4
Cameroon	15,380	22,907	2.5	1.3	4.8	2.2	2	29	72	28	4
Cape Verde	417	652	1.6	1.2	2.8	2.1	—	—	—	26	4
Central African Rep.	3,801	5,153	1.9	1.1	4.9	2.4	13	38	69	30	3
Chad	7,228	9,996	2.0	1.1	4.9	2.4	17	43	71	28	5
Comoros	669	1,057	2.9	1.5	5.3	2.2	—	—	—	28	4
Congo	3,088	4,937	2.9	1.4	6.0	2.3	11	30	74	30	3
Côte d'Ivoire	16,815	27,319	3.0	1.4	5.6	2.2	3	30	74	30	4
Djibouti	596	875	2.5	1.2	5.3	2.4	—	—	—	28	4
Equatorial Guinea	507	660	1.4	0.9	3.9	2.4	—	—	—	28	5
Ethiopia	66,450	104,549	2.8	1.3	6.3	2.4	4	34	73	30	3
Gabon	1,501	2,328	2.7	1.3	5.8	2.3	31	40	76	29	5
Gambia	1,148	1,598	2.2	1.1	5.3	2.5	0	33	65	29	5
Ghana	19,813	29,610	2.5	1.3	4.9	2.3	13	45	73	28	4
Guinea	7,452	10,593	2.2	1.1	5.3	2.6	0	32	64	30	4
Guinea-Bissau	1,196	1,571	1.7	1.0	5.4	2.7	19	36	68	31	3

Kenya	32,395	47,744	2.3	1.3	4.0	2.2	28	57	80	28	4
Lesotho	2,229	3,174	1.9	1.2	3.5	2.2	19	48	73	26	6
Liberia	3,420	5,167	2.5	1.3	5.0	2.3	7	41	72	27	5
Madagascar	15,206	21,982	2.3	1.2	4.9	2.4	0	37	68	28	4
Malawi	11,613	17,521	2.5	1.3	6.4	2.6	7	35	74	31	3
Mali	11,241	17,715	2.6	1.4	5.9	2.4	5	35	71	29	3
Mauritania	2,568	3,711	2.3	1.3	5.5	2.4	0	35	68	29	4
Mauritius	1,192	1,450	1.0	0.5	2.0	2.0	80	81	77	20	13
Mozambique	20,447	29,453	2.3	1.2	5.4	2.4	0	29	67	28	4
Niger	10,627	16,709	2.8	1.3	6.3	2.5	0	30	70	31	3
Nigeria	127,800	187,427	2.4	1.2	4.7	2.3	7	38	73	29	4
Rwanda	8,621	12,168	2.0	1.1	5.0	2.5	14	38	78	30	3
São Tomé and Principe	146	208	2.0	1.2	3.4	2.1	—	—	—	25	8
Senegal	9,634	13,802	2.3	1.2	4.9	2.3	15	46	73	29	3
Seychelles	74	95	0.9	0.9	2.2	2.1	—	—	—	22	8
Sierra Leone	5,277	7,296	2.0	1.1	5.3	2.5	4	39	67	29	4
Somalia	10,472	15,488	2.5	1.3	5.4	2.4	0	35	69	28	4
Sudan	33,368	49,352	2.5	1.3	5.1	2.3	3	36	69	28	4
Swaziland	1,127	1,743	2.9	1.4	5.2	2.2	—	—	—	27	5
Tanzania	32,639	47,951	2.4	1.3	5.1	2.4	3	34	70	29	3
Togo	4,939	7,444	2.6	1.3	5.2	2.2	34	57	81	28	4
Uganda	22,162	33,549	2.6	1.3	6.1	2.5	5	35	73	32	2
Zaire	50,426	80,287	2.8	1.3	5.6	2.3	14	34	73	30	3
Zambia	10,688	14,991	2.2	1.2	5.4	2.5	3	29	72	31	2
Zimbabwe	12,192	16,410	1.5	1.0	3.0	2.2	46	71	80	28	4
Africa	**626,000**	**933,000**	**2.5**	**1.3**	**5.2**	**2.3**	**11**	**45**	**75**	**29**	**4**
World	6,150,000	7,850,000	1.3	0.7	2.7	1.9	54	65	74	22	11
Less developed countries	4,880,000	6,560,000	1.6	0.8	3.0	2.0	51	64	75	23	9
More developed countries	1,270,000	1,290,000	0.3	-0.1	1.7	1.5	71	71	66	15	20

Table A-4. Mortality

Country	Infant mortality rate			Under-five mortality rate			Adult mortality rate (ages 15–59) 1990		Median age at death 1990
	1970	1992	% Reduction	1975	1990	% Reduction	Male	Female	
Angola	180	125	31	281	214	24	434	381	3
Benin	155	110	29	228	170	25	387	316	6
Botswana	101	35	65	111	48	57	—	—	—
Burkina Faso	178	132	26	254	159	37	429	352	4
Burundi	138	106	23	209	180	14	424	367	11
Cameroon	126	61	52	194	125	36	316	256	16
Cape Verde	87	40	54	133	52	61	—	—	—
Central African Rep.	139	105	24	209	132	37	346	288	15
Chad	171	122	29	271	212	22	445	358	7
Comoros	141	87	38	175	133	24	—	—	—
Congo	126	114	10	208	175	16	—	—	—
Côte d'Ivoire	135	94	30	194	150	23	332	277	10
Djibouti	160	111	31	—	194	—	—	—	—
Equatorial Guinea	165	116	30	259	203	22	—	—	—
Ethiopia	158	128	19	262	197	25	404	329	4
Gabon	140	92	34	224	159	29	—	—	—
Gambia	186	132	29	296	231	22	—	—	—
Ghana	111	81	27	169	170	−1	344	282	7
Guinea	181	133	27	291	236	19	452	395	2
Guinea-Bissau	185	147	21	297	268	10	—	—	—
Kenya	102	66	35	139	83	40	315	259	15
Lesotho	134	79	41	172	135	22	—	—	—

Liberia	178	131	26	244	185	24	—	—	—
Madagascar	181	93	49	200	170	15	389	333	11
Malawi	193	142	26	313	201	36	426	369	4
Mali	204	159	22	321	200	38	417	361	4
Mauritania	165	117	29	258	205	21	—	—	—
Mauritius	60	18	70	65	25	62	490	421	2
Mozambique	171	147	14	280	280	0	513	454	3
Niger	170	123	28	320	320	0	406	354	7
Nigeria	139	84	40	198	191	4	453	395	3
Rwanda	142	110	23	223	222	0	—	—	—
São Tomé and Príncipe	—	65	—	—	55	—	397	340	15
Senegal	138	80	42	265	156	41	—	—	—
Seychelles	—	16	—	—	21	—	503	436	2
Sierra Leone	197	143	27	375	360	4	443	390	4
Somalia	159	132	17	262	214	18	267	234	13
Sudan	149	99	34	152	104	32	422	354	11
Swaziland	140	108	23	188	148	21	379	335	5
Tanzania	132	115	13	202	165	18	325	268	7
Togo	134	85	37	193	143	26	424	367	4
Uganda	109	118	−8	173	185	−7	387	319	6
Zaire	125	91	27	223	190	15	—	—	—
Zambia	106	107	−1	167	190	−14	269	216	26
Zimbabwe	96	47	51	120	58	52	—	—	—
Africa	**145**	**104**	**28**	**212**	**175**	**17**	**381**	**322**	**5**
World	97	63	35	135	96	29	234	169	55
Less developed countries	111	70	37	152	106	30	250	199	39
More developed countries	24	14	42	25	15	40	188	86	74

Note: Rates are per 1,000 population.

Table A-5. Income and Poverty

Country	Average annual growth rate of GDP (percent)		Average annual rate of inflation (percent)		GNP capita (US$)		Percent share of income (1981–91)[a]		Population dependency ratio (percentage of working age)		Population below absolute poverty level, 1985 (percent)	
	1970–80	1980–91	1970–80	1980–91	1991	Annual growth rate 1980–91	Lowest 20%	Highest 20%	1970	1990	Urban	Rural
Angola	—	—	—	—	—	—	—	—	84	100	—	—
Benin	2.2	2.4	—	1.6	380	−0.9	—	—	92	98	—	65
Botswana	14.5	9.8	11.6	13.2	2,530	5.6	1.4	66.4	118	99	40	55
Burkina Faso	4.4	4.0	8.6	3.8	290	1.2	—	—	86	89	—	—
Burundi	4.2	4.0	10.7	4.3	210	1.3	—	—	92	95	55	85
Cameroon	7.2	1.4	9.8	4.5	850	−1.0	—	—	84	93	15	40
Cape Verde	—	2.3	9.4	9.4	750	2.3	—	—	111	93	—	—
Central African Rep.	2.4	1.4	12.1	5.1	390	−1.4	—	—	79	93	—	91
Chad	0.1	5.5	7.7	1.1	210	3.8	—	—	82	88	30	56
Comoros	—	−1.0	—	—	500	−1.0	—	—	96	103	—	—
Congo	5.8	3.3	8.4	0.4	1,120	−0.2	—	—	88	95	—	—
Côte d'Ivoire	6.6	−0.5	13.0	3.8	690	−4.6	7.3	42.2	93	104	30	26
Djibouti	—	—	—	—	—	—	—	—	81	92	—	—
Equatorial Guinea	—	2.8	—	−0.9	330	2.8	—	—	78	87	—	—
Ethiopia	1.9	1.6	4.3	2.4	120	−1.6	8.6	41.3	89	95	60	65
Gabon	9.0	0.2	17.5	1.5	3,780	−4.2	—	—	62	64	—	—
Gambia	—	−0.1	10.6	18.2	360	−0.1	—	—	81	89	—	—
Ghana	−0.1	3.2	35.2	40.0	400	−0.3	7.0	44.1	93	93	59	37
Guinea	—	—	—	—	460	—	—	—	91	97	—	—
Guinea-Bissau	2.4	3.7	5.7	56.2	180	1.1	—	—	69	82	—	—
Kenya	6.4	4.2	10.1	9.2	340	0.3	2.7	60.9	109	109	10	55
Lesotho	8.6	5.5	9.7	13.6	580	−0.5	4.5	61.3	82	84	50	55

Liberia	—	—	9.2	—	—	450	—	—	89	96	—	23
Madagascar	0.5	1.1	9.9	16.8	-2.5	210	—	—	86	93	50	50
Malawi	5.8	3.1	8.8	14.9	0.1	230	—	—	96	104	25	85
Mali	4.9	2.5	9.7	4.4	-0.1	280	—	—	93	98	27	48
Mauritania	1.3	1.4	9.9	8.7	-1.8	510	—	—	84	91	—	—
Mauritius	6.8	6.7	15.3	8.1	6.1	2,410	—	—	86	54	12	12
Mozambique	—	-0.1	—	37.6	-1.1	80	—	—	86	91	18	36
Niger	1.7	-1.0	9.7	2.3	-4.1	300	—	—	94	101	—	35
Nigeria	4.6	1.9	15.2	18.1	-2.3	340	—	—	95	100	—	—
Rwanda	4.7	0.6	15.1	4.1	-2.4	270	9.7	38.9	99	107	30	90
São Tomé and Principe	—	-3.3	4.0	21.5	-3.3	400	—	—	—	85	—	—
Senegal	2.3	3.1	8.5	6.0	0.1	720	—	—	90	94	—	—
Seychelles	—	3.2	16.9	3.5	3.2	5,110	—	—	—	73	—	65
Sierra Leone	1.6	1.1	12.5	59.3	-1.6	210	—	—	82	91	—	70
Somalia	—	—	15.2	49.7	—	170	—	—	92	99	40	—
Sudan	5.6	—	14.5	—	—	340	—	—	89	92	—	—
Swaziland	—	3.1	12.3	10.3	3.1	1,050	—	—	92	92	—	—
Tanzania	3.0	2.9	14.1	25.7	-0.8	100	2.4	62.7	97	99	42	—
Togo	4.0	1.8	8.9	4.4	-1.3	410	—	—	88	94	—	80
Uganda	—	—	—	—	—	170	8.5	41.9	98	103	—	—
Zaire	—	—	31.4	60.9	—	220	—	—	89	101	25	—
Zambia	1.4	0.8	7.6	—	—	420	—	—	94	103	—	—
Zimbabwe	1.6	3.1	9.4	12.5	-0.2	650	—	—	108	90	—	—
Africa	**4.0**	**2.1**	**13.9**	**18.4**	**-1.2**	**330**	—	—	**92**	**93**	**36**	**57**
World	3.5	3.0	11.2	15.4	1.2	4,000	—	—	75	63	—	—
Less developed countries	5.3	3.3	21.8	53.9	1.0	1,000	—	—	84	67	—	—
More developed countries	3.1	2.9	9.0	4.3	2.3	21,000	—	—	57	50	—	—

a. Latest available data for the specified period.

Table A-6. Education

Country	Adult literacy rate (percent of ages 15+) Total 1980	Total 1990	Female 1980	Female 1990	Percentage of age group enrolled — Primary Total 1970	Total 1990	Female 1970	Female 1990	Secondary Total 1970	Total 1990	Female 1970	Female 1990	Primary pupil/teacher ratio 1970	1990
Angola	—	42	—	28	—	—	—	—	—	—	—	—	—	—
Benin	28	23	17	16	36	61	22	44	5	11	3	6	41	35
Botswana	—	74	—	65	65	110	67	112	7	46	6	47	36	32
Burkina Faso	—	18	—	9	13	36	10	28	1	7	1	5	44	57
Burundi	27	50	15	40	30	72	20	64	2	5	1	4	37	67
Cameroon	—	54	—	43	89	101	75	93	7	26	4	21	48	51
Cape Verde	—	—	—	—	—	—	—	—	—	—	—	—	—	—
Central African Rep.	33	38	19	25	64	67	41	51	4	11	2	6	64	90
Chad	—	30	—	18	35	57	17	35	2	7	0	3	65	67
Comoros	—	48	—	40	—	—	—	—	—	—	—	—	—	—
Congo	35	57	24	44	—	—	—	—	—	—	—	—	62	66
Côte d'Ivoire	20	54	—	40	58	—	45	—	9	—	4	—	45	36
Djibouti	—	—	—	—	—	—	—	—	—	—	—	—	—	—
Equatorial Guinea	37	50	—	37	—	—	—	—	—	—	—	—	—	—
Ethiopia	—	—	—	—	16	38	10	30	4	15	2	12	48	36
Gabon	—	—	—	—	—	—	—	—	—	—	—	—	—	—
Gambia	20	27	12	16	—	—	—	—	—	—	—	—	—	—
Ghana	30	60	—	51	64	75	54	67	14	39	8	31	30	29
Guinea	—	24	—	13	33	37	21	24	13	10	5	5	44	40
Guinea-Bissau	19	36	13	24	39	59	23	42	8	7	6	4	45	—
Kenya	47	69	35	58	58	94	48	92	9	23	5	19	34	31
Lesotho	—	73	—	84	87	107	101	115	7	26	7	31	46	55

Liberia	—	39	—	29	—	—	—	—	—	—	—	—	—	—
Madagascar	—	80	—	73	90	92	82	90	12	19	9	18	65	40
Malawi	—	42	—	31	71	71	—	64	—	4	—	3	43	64
Mali	—	32	—	24	22	24	15	17	5	6	2	4	40	42
Mauritania	—	34	—	21	14	51	8	42	2	16	0	10	24	49
Mauritius	79	82	72	75	94	106	93	104	30	52	25	53	32	21
Mozambique	33	33	23	21	47	58	—	48	5	7	—	5	69	58
Niger	10	28	6	17	14	29	10	21	1	7	1	4	39	42
Nigeria	34	51	23	39	37	72	27	63	4	20	3	17	34	41
Rwanda	50	50	39	37	68	69	60	68	2	7	1	6	60	57
São Tomé and Principe	—	58	—	42	—	—	—	—	—	—	—	—	—	—
Senegal	—	38	—	25	41	58	32	49	10	16	6	11	45	58
Seychelles	—	88	—	95	—	—	—	—	—	—	—	—	—	—
Sierra Leone	—	21	—	11	34	48	27	39	8	16	5	12	32	34
Somalia	6	24	3	14	—	—	—	—	—	—	—	—	—	—
Sudan	—	27	—	12	38	49	29	—	7	20	4	—	47	34
Swaziland	—	—	—	65	—	—	—	—	—	—	—	—	—	—
Tanzania	—	43	—	31	34	63	27	63	3	4	2	4	47	35
Togo	52	48	—	35	71	103	44	80	7	22	3	10	58	59
Uganda	54	72	40	61	38	76	30	—	4	13	2	—	34	35
Zaire	—	73	37	65	—	—	—	—	—	—	—	—	—	—
Zambia	69	67	61	60	90	93	80	91	13	20	8	14	47	44
Zimbabwe	—	—	—	—	74	117	66	116	7	50	6	46	36	—
Africa	—	**50**	—	**38**	**46**	**68**	**36**	**61**	**6**	**17**	**4**	**16**	**43**	**41**
World	—	65	—	55	83	104	71	99	31	65	28	46	33	33
Less developed countries	—	63	—	52	79	104	64	98	24	61	18	39	35	35
More developed countries	—	96	—	95	106	104	106	104	74	93	73	96	26	17

Table A-7. The Health and Status of Women

Country	No. of women of child-bearing age, 15–49 (thousands) 1990	Maternal mortality (per 100,000 live births) 1988	Prenatal health care coverage rate (percent) 1985–90[a]	Births attended by trained health personnel (percent) 1985–90[a]	Pregnant women immunized for tetanus (percent) 1989–91[a]	Prevalence of anemia in pregnant women (percentage below norm)[b] 1970–80s	School enrollment (Female/100 Males) Primary 1990	School enrollment (Female/100 Males) Secondary 1990	African states parties to human rights convention Children's rights[c] Year	African states parties to human rights convention Women rights[d] Year
Angola	2,087	—	27	16	36	30	—	—	1991	1986
Benin	1,068	800	64	45	83	55	—	35	—	—
Botswana	299	250	74	79	62	—	105	110	—	—
Burkina Faso	2,065	800	49	33	26	25	60	50	1990	1987
Burundi	1,252	800	30	16	56	70	85	55	1990	—
Cameroon	2,480	450	56	25	35	10	85	65	—	—
Cape Verde	94	110	99	49	90	—	—	—	—	—
Central African Rep.	715	600	68	—	50	65	65	35	—	—
Chad	1,323	1,000	22	21	42	40	45	20	1990	—
Comoros	104	500	69	24	53	—	—	—	—	—
Congo	506	900	—	45	60	—	85	70	—	1982
Côte d'Ivoire	2,527	1,000	50	65	35	35	70	45	1991	—
Djibouti	95	750	75	80	10	—	—	—	1991	—
Equatorial Guinea	84	450	15	—	84	—	—	—	1984	1984
Ethiopia	10,174	500	14	9	6	10	65	65	—	1981
Gabon	269	200	77	—	86	—	—	—	1990	1983
Gambia	200	1,500	72	65	77	—	—	—	1990	—
Ghana	3,287	1,000	65	42	33	65	80	60	1990	1986
Guinea	1,315	1,000	36	25	25	—	45	30	1990	1982
Guinea-Bissau	233	700	29	39	44	—	55	50	1990	1985
Kenya	4,980	200	90	—	37	60	95	75	—	1984
Lesotho	410	370	50	40	—	—	120	150	1990	—
Liberia	553	—	85	50	20	—	—	—	1990	1984

Madagascar	2,542	400	76	71	17	—	97	99	1991	1989
Malawi	1,946	420	76	41	76	50	80	55	1991	1987
Mali	1,959	2,300	11	14	9	65	55	45	1990	1985
Mauritania	455	1,100	39	20	40	—	70	45	—	—
Mauritius	306	100	90	90	77	—	98	100	1990	1984
Mozambique	3,653	300	54	29	30	60	75	60	1990	—
Niger	1,704	700	33	21	44	50	55	40	1990	—
Nigeria	25,726	800	78	45	58	45	75	75	1991	1985
Rwanda	1,515	400	85	22	88	—	99	55	—	1981
São Tomé and Principe	27	—	76	63	48	—	—	—	—	—
Senegal	1,645	950	21	40	33	55	70	50	1990	1985
Seychelles	17	—	99	99	98	—	—	—	1990	—
Sierra Leone	945	—	30	25	77	45	70	55	1990	1988
Somalia	1,393	1,100	2	2	5	75	—	80	—	—
Sudan	5,562	660	40	—	10	35	75	—	1990	—
Swaziland	172	130	76	67	63	—	—	—	—	—
Tanzania	5,844	340	90	60	40	80	98	75	1991	—
Togo	823	720	83	56	81	45	65	35	1990	1983
Uganda	3,789	550	85	25	31	—	—	—	1990	1985
Zaire	8,092	800	85	—	29	45	90	—	1990	1986
Zambia	1,800	150	80	43	68	35	99	60	1990	1985
Zimbabwe	2,282	80	83	65	60	—	99	88	1990	—
Africa	**108,318**	**700**	**60**	**34**	**30**	**40**	**76**	**67**	—	—
World	1,312,949	400	67	55	33	42	84	76	—	—
Less developed countries	1,008,656	450	65	42	43	50	81	73	—	—
More developed countries	305,605	17	99	99	0	4	95	100	—	—

a. Latest available data for the specified period. b. Each value refers to one particular but not specified year within the time period denoted. c. Convention on the Rights of the Child. d. International Convention on the Elimination of Discrimination against Women.

Table A-8. Food and Nutrition

Country	Percentage of children affected by — Stunting (24–59 mos.) 1980–90a	Percentage of children affected by — Wasting (12–23 mos.) 1980–90a	Percent children fully breastfed (0–3 mos.) 1985–90a	Babies with low birth weight (percent) 1985–90a	Index of food production per capita (1987=100) 1975	1980	1985	1991	Food supply: calories per capita per day 1980	1989	Food supply: protein per capita per day (grams) 1980	1990
Angola	—	—	—	15	—	—	—	—	2,100	1,725	—	—
Benin	—	14	—	10	92	102	110	120	2,145	2,383	51	56
Botswana	37	6	39	8	196	139	129	104	2,155	2,260	71	69
Burkina Faso	28	11	—	12	89	79	96	107	1,815	2,219	58	68
Burundi	48	6	86	18	102	95	86	85	2,059	1,948	69	56
Cameroon	43	2	70	13	127	109	106	87	2,340	2,208	59	55
Cape Verde	26	3	—	—	60	88	54	62	2,587	2,778	68	5
Central African Rep.	—	—	—	18	120	110	93	99	2,136	1,846	43	46
Chad	13	—	—	11	104	112	96	104	1,762	1,852	—	38
Comoros	27	—	—	13	133	119	99	92	1,783	1,760	38	38
Congo	27	5	—	12	110	97	99	7	2,235	2,295	41	47
Côte d'Ivoire	20	17	—	15	99	101	100	94	2,844	2,568	60	54
Djibouti	—	—	—	9	—	—	—	—	—	—	—	—
Equatorial Guinea	—	—	—	10	—	—	—	—	—	—	—	—
Ethiopia	43	19	—	13	112	114	100	100	1,777	1,658	—	—
Gabon	18	—	—	10	116	17	99	96	2,243	2,396	—	—
Gambia	24	7	—	10	171	80	82	73	2,101	2,290	50	57
Ghana	30	8	81	5	132	100	98	96	1,973	2,144	44	46
Guinea	—	—	—	11	104	110	101	102	2,268	2,242	51	52
Guinea-Bissau	22	5	—	12	111	91	99	100	1,797	2,690	—	—
Kenya	32	5	48	18	103	99	97	105	2,148	2,064	57	56
Lesotho	32	3	—	10	123	115	103	89	2,354	2,121	69	60

Liberia	37	3	14	—	106	102	100	64	2,400	2,259	47	41
Madagascar	56	17	—	10	118	112	105	91	2,472	2,156	60	52
Malawi	61	8	82	11	118	119	101	93	2,273	2,049	66	59
Mali	24	11	—	10	107	109	100	109	1,898	2,259	57	64
Mauritania	34	17	—	10	102	118	104	99	2,081	2,447	71	74
Mauritius	22	16	—	8	81	79	92	88	2,701	2,897	62	70
Mozambique	—	—	—	11	153	131	106	89	1,951	1,805	33	31
Niger	38	23	61	20	25	168	101	125	2,224	2,239	64	62
Nigeria	43	9	—	17	123	103	104	120	2,129	2,200	46	45
Rwanda	37	5	—	16	109	112	118	98	2,064	1,913	52	48
São Tomé and Principe	26	5	77	7	173	135	113	94	2,060	2,153	45	43
Senegal	25	6	—	10	155	65	83	76	2,415	2,322	69	67
Seychelles	5	2	—	10	—	—	—	—	2,282	2,356	65	61
Sierra Leone	43	14	—	13	117	104	97	83	2,096	1,899	45	39
Somalia	30	40	—	—	119	110	102	52	1,942	1,874	64	61
Sudan	32	13	84	15	134	132	117	100	2,215	2,043	63	59
Swaziland	30	1	—	7	88	99	97	90	2,462	2,634	64	63
Tanzania	46	5	—	13	110	105	107	8	2,239	2,195	54	55
Togo	29	6	60	20	125	117	105	102	2,266	2,269	49	53
Uganda	45	2	76	10	151	105	103	105	2,114	2,178	50	51
Zaïre	27	3	64	13	109	03	102	96	2,133	2,130	35	34
Zambia	59	10	72	14	150	110	103	90	2,186	2,016	59	54
Zimbabwe	31	2	56	6	147	116	141	103	2,180	2,256	56	54
Africa	**39**	**10**	**63**	**14**	**120**	**108**	**101**	**94**	**2,123**	**2,100**	**54**	**53**
World	42	12	—	17	—	—	—	—	2,579	2,697	68	71
Less developed countries	46	13	47	19	—	—	—	—	2,324	2,473	56	61
More developed countries	4	3	—	7	—	—	—	—	3,287	3,404	99	104

a. Latest available data for the specified period.

Table A-9   Access to Water, Sanitation, and Health Care Services
(percent)

Country	Access to safe water (1985–1990)[a]			Access to sanitation facilities (1985–1990)[a]			Access to health care services (1988–1990)[a]		
	Total	Urban	Rural	Total	Urban	Rural	Total	Urban	Rural
Angola	38	75	19	22	25	20	24	—	—
Benin	50	79	35	41	60	31	32	—	—
Botswana	56	98	46	38	98	20	88	90	85
Burkina Faso	67	72	44	10	35	6	49	51	48
Burundi	38	92	34	57	80	15	45	—	—
Cameroon	34	47	27	—	25	16	41	44	39
Cape Verde	74	87	65	16	35	9	81	78	—
Central African Rep.	12	14	11	20	36	11	65	—	17
Chad	29	30	27	14	—	—	26	—	—
Comoros	70	75	52	83	90	80	82	—	—
Congo	20	42	7	40	—	—	83	97	70
Côte d'Ivoire	83	95	75	36	69	20	60	92	45
Djibouti	43	50	21	78	94	20	47	95	40
Equatorial Guinea	—	47	—	—	28	—	—	—	—
Ethiopia	18	70	11	17	97	7	55	—	—
Gabon	72	90	50	50	—	—	87	—	—
Gambia	77	92	73	77	—	—	30	50	30
Ghana	56	93	39	30	63	15	76	—	—
Guinea	33	56	25	24	65	9	32	—	—
Guinea-Bissau	25	27	18	21	30	18	80	—	—
Kenya	38	80	25	46	75	39	58	80	53
Lesotho	46	59	44	22	23	14	80	90	30

Liberia	50	93	22	15	24	8	34	50	30
Madagascar	31	81	17	—	12	—	41	90	30
Malawi	51	66	49	59	—	—	80	90	69
Mali	23	48	17	23	—	5	27	60	25
Mauritania	66	67	65	—	34	—	40	—	—
Mauritius	99	100	98	98	100	96	99	99	99
Mozambique	22	44	17	19	61	11	27	50	15
Niger	59	61	52	9	39	3	30	75	17
Nigeria	32	60	20	13	30	5	67	87	62
Rwanda	64	66	62	61	62	45	27	60	25
São Tomé and Principe	—	33	—	10	13	8	88	—	—
Senegal	53	79	38	32	87	2	40	—	85
Seychelles	98	100	97	65	96	19	89	99	11
Sierra Leone	43	83	22	43	59	35	30	61	15
Somalia	29	50	22	12	41	5	28	50	15
Sudan	34	90	20	12	40	5	51	90	40
Swaziland	30	—	7	36	62	25	55	—	—
Tanzania	52	75	46	76	77	75	80	94	73
Togo	70	—	60	23	42	16	30	60	20
Uganda	15	45	12	13	40	10	41	44	39
Zaire	34	59	17	14	15	13	—	—	—
Zambia	59	76	43	55	77	34	75	—	—
Zimbabwe	36	99	14	42	99	22	83	90	80
Africa	**37**	**68**	**26**	**26**	**51**	**16**	**54**	**71**	**45**
World	81	93	72	66	89	54	91	—	—
Less developed countries	75	88	68	56	72	48	89	—	—
More developed countries	100	100	100	100	100	100	100	—	—

a. Latest available for the specified period.

Table A-10. Immunization

Country	Immunization (per 100 children under one year old)							
	1980				1991			
	BCG	DPT3	POL3	Measles	BCG	DPT3	POL3	Measles
Angola	47	9	7	17	54	27	26	40
Benin	37	20	45	6	81	68	68	60
Botswana	76	70	71	68	92	86	82	78
Burkina Faso	16	2	2	23	60	38	38	36
Burundi	65	38	6	30	88	83	89	75
Cameroon	8	5	5	16	48	34	34	35
Cape Verde	64	31	39	54	99	87	88	76
Central African Rep.	22	13	13	14	79	46	45	46
Chad	—	—	—	—	59	20	20	32
Comoros	56	31	32	30	99	94	94	87
Congo	92	42	42	49	88	74	74	64
Côte d'Ivoire	—	42	34	28	47	37	37	47
Djibouti	5	6	6	15	95	85	85	85
Equatorial Guinea	28	3	4	11	97	80	80	79
Ethiopia	6	3	3	5	57	44	44	37
Gabon	50	14	44	58	96	78	78	76
Gambia	92	80	53	71	97	85	89	87
Ghana	9	7	7	15	55	39	39	39
Guinea	5	2	1	9	47	35	35	33
Guinea-Bissau	38	15	11	35	94	63	63	52
Kenya	—	—	—	—	50	41	45	38
Lesotho	81	56	54	49	76	75	74	76

Liberia	41	17	26	40	62	28	28	55
Madagascar	23	34	8	15	67	50	49	40
Malawi	86	58	28	49	96	81	78	78
Mali	19	18	0	10	68	34	34	39
Mauritania	57	18	18	45	60	26	26	29
Mauritius	88	87	87	34	87	91	91	88
Mozambique	46	56	32	32	63	42	42	50
Niger	28	6	6	19	26	17	17	23
Nigeria	23	24	24	55	57	44	44	46
Rwanda	51	17	15	42	94	85	85	81
São Tomé and Principe	95	42	48	25	96	78	77	68
Senegal	22	34	34	22	69	51	51	46
Seychelles	67	13	16	29	98	82	82	89
Sierra Leone	34	13	10	29	71	56	57	54
Somalia	5	5	5	5	31	18	18	30
Sudan	3	1	1	1	73	62	62	57
Swaziland	59	30	22	30	71	86	87	80
Tanzania	69	55	50	49	89	79	74	75
Togo	44	9	9	47	79	61	61	51
Uganda	18	9	8	22	99	76	76	73
Zaire	34	18	18	24	65	32	31	31
Zambia	71	44	50	21	96	65	70	69
Zimbabwe	64	39	38	56	87	83	81	83
Africa	**29**	**22**	**19**	**33**	**61**	**45**	**45**	**45**
World	—	—	20	—	88	82	84	80
Less developed countries	—	—	—	—	89	82	84	79
More developed countries	—	—	—	—	82	83	85	82

Table A-11   Health Care Personnel

Country	Doctors[b] 1985–90[a]	Para-medics 1980–88[a]	Nurses[b] 1985–90[a]	Tech-nicians 1980–88[a]	Assistant Nurses 1980–88[a]	Assistant Tech-nicians 1980–88[a]	Population per doctor 1970	Population per doctor 1985–90[a]	Population per nurse 1970	Population per nurse 1985–90[a]	Nurses to doctors ratio 1985–90[a]
Angola	480	—	1,200	—	—	—	8,500	15,000	4,500	6,000	3
Benin	280	—	1,700	50	1,000	300	29,000	13,000	4,000	2,500	6
Botswana	240	10	2,500	700	900	1,709	15,000	4,000	—	500	10
Burkina Faso	130	160	1,800	30	1,600	280	96,000	50,000	15,000	4,000	14
Burundi	280	130	1,200	50	450	90	59,000	15,000	14,000	4,000	4
Cameroon	940	2,000	6,000	300	5,000	300	30,000	11,000	4,000	2,000	6
Cape Verde	100	500	250	20	150	30	12,000	4,000	4,000	1,500	3
Central African Rep.	110	150	500	70	500	100	44,000	25,000	2,500	5,000	5
Chad	135	30	150	200	1,000	30	62,000	35,000	—	30,000	1
Comoros	70	2	300	50	550	—	15,000	6,000	9,000	1,500	4
Congo	500	30	2,000	250	3,800	300	10,000	4,000	1,500	1,000	4
Côte d'Ivoire	700	—	3,300	—	—	—	16,000	15,000	3,000	3,000	5
Djibouti	80	—	300	100	250	—	4,000	5,000	1,000	1,500	4
Equatorial Guinea	100	—	200	—	—	—	12,000	4,000	—	2,000	2
Ethiopia	1,500	220	3,500	850	7,000	—	92,000	29,000	21,000	12,000	2
Gabon	420	80	1,500	200	—	—	5,000	3,000	—	800	4
Gambia	60	—	700	200	700	—	25,000	13,000	2,000	1,500	12
Ghana	800	350	5,800	1,200	10,000	—	13,000	15,000	1,000	2,000	7
Guinea	130	—	550	180	1,300	400	51,000	40,000	—	10,000	4
Guinea-Bissau	120	20	300	150	1,800	800	18,000	6,000	5,000	2,000	3
Kenya	3,100	—	10,000	300	13,000	500	8,000	6,000	2,000	2,500	3
Lesotho	110	—	550	50	500	—	30,000	16,000	3,000	3,300	5
Liberia	220	150	1,200	—	—	—	13,000	10,000	2,000	2,000	5

Madagascar	1,400	1,700	5,000	450	8,000	550	10,000	8,000	9,000	2,000	4
Malawi	260	350	550	250	1,600	650	77,000	27,000	5,000	14,000	2
Mali	440	90	1,100	500	3,700	300	45,000	18,000	6,500	7,000	3
Mauritania	200	400	900	60	1,200	750	18,000	9,000	6,000	2,000	5
Mauritius	900	—	3,300	530	500	80	4,500	1,200	520	320	4
Mozambique	280	100	3,700	280	350	850	19,000	50,000	5,000	4,000	13
Niger	220	40	2,500	280	9,500	200	60,000	35,000	11,000	3,000	11
Nigeria	16,000	—	97,000	4,200	16,000	1,200	21,000	6,000	2,000	1,000	6
Rwanda	160	350	300	680	1,500	420	60,000	35,000	10,000	20,000	2
São Tomé and Principe	60	1	300	70	200	30	4,500	2,000	4,000	400	5
Senegal	410	250	1,100	400	7,000	—	16,000	16,000	1,500	7,000	3
Seychelles	30	—	350	—	—	—	4,500	2,500	170	200	12
Sierra Leone	260	150	1,300	160	250	—	18,000	13,000	3,500	3,000	5
Somalia	480	70	3,500	130	500	—	36,000	15,000	2,000	2,000	7
Sudan	2,100	2,700	5,600	1,300	18,000	—	14,000	10,000	4,500	4,500	3
Swaziland	80	—	1,300	—	100	—	8,000	9,000	500	600	16
Tanzania	770	950	5,700	200	1,400	—	23,000	29,000	3,000	4,000	7
Togo	260	150	1,700	730	1,300	200	29,000	10,000	2,500	2,000	7
Uganda	600	600	6,800	1,000	—	550	9,000	18,000	13,000	2,500	11
Zaire	2,500	150	5,100	1,100	13,000	200	28,000	14,000	4,600	7,000	2
Zambia	880	1,300	4,300	450	4,000	550	14,000	7,000	4,300	2,000	5
Zimbabwe	1,400	3,500	8,600	900	10,000	250	6,500	6,000	750	1,000	6
Africa	**40,000**	—	**205,000**	**18,000**	**148,000**	—	**19,000**	**9,000**	**3,000**	**2,000**	**5**
World	6,200,000	—	9,200,000	—	—	—	—	900	—	570	1.5
Less developed countries	2,800,000	—	2,300,000	—	—	—	—	1,500	—	1,700	0.8
More developed countries	3,400,000	—	6,900,000	—	—	—	—	350	—	180	2.0

a. Latest available data for the specified period.
b. Doctors are medical doctors only. Nurses are registered nurses and registered midwives only.

Table A-12. Health Care Facilities

Country	Number of health care facilities						Number of beds		Population per bed	
	Hospitals			Health centers and others			Hospital only	Total[a]	Hospital only	Total[b]
	Central/ Regional	District/ Rural	Total	Health centers	Others	Total				
Angola	53	—	—	226	1,231	1,457	—	—	—	850
Benin	12	9	21	364	392	756	—	—	—	—
Botswana	38	7	45	37	299	336	—	2,200	—	500
Burkina Faso	2	5	7	59	8,005	8,064	2,700	5,600	3,000	1,400
Burundi	34	21	55	218	114	332	3,100	5,800	1,600	900
Cameroon	—	—	—	528	1,006	1,534	—	29,000	—	400
Cape Verde	2	3	5	4	37	41	—	—	—	—
Central African Rep.	15	26	41	56	77	133	1,600	4,000	1,800	700
Chad	9	22	31	26	363	389	—	4,000	—	1,363
Comoros	5	—	—	7	72	79	—	—	—	—
Congo	45	—	—	92	515	607	5,700	7,300	350	300
Côte d'Ivoire	20	71	91	—	690	690	7,000	9,700	1,500	1,100
Djibouti	—	—	—	—	—	—	—	—	—	—
Equatorial Guinea	15	37	52	—	—	—	—	—	—	—
Ethiopia	86	42	128	140	1,820	1,960	—	—	—	3,500
Gabon	27	—	—	33	423	456	3,100	5,300	350	200
Gambia	2	4	6	19	67	86	—	—	—	—
Ghana	9	124	133	180	—	—	—	—	—	700
Guinea	29	—	—	62	551	613	1,200	—	4,500	1,700
Guinea-Bissau	7	10	17	126	181	307	—	—	—	—
Kenya	—	—	—	282	1,535	1,817	31,000	32,000	700	650
Lesotho	20	—	—	—	—	135	2,250	—	700	—
Liberia	15	15	30	26	275	301	—	—	—	—

Madagascar	7	72	79	99	581	680	—	—	—	1,100
Malawi	51	—	—	44	610	654	7,550	12,600	950	600
Mali	10	4	14	333	2,144	2,477	2,500	5,000	3,000	1,500
Mauritania	15	13	28	143	57	200	1,350	—	1,400	—
Mauritius	17	4	21	24	129	153	2,750	2,950	400	350
Mozambique	10	26	36	223	948	1,171	6,300	13,000	2,000	1,000
Niger	9	1	10	43	597	640	—	3,200	—	2,250
Nigeria	—	—	—	705	6,604	7,309	61,000	91,000	1,700	1,200
Rwanda	30	22	52	170	74	244	10,300	—	650	—
São Tomé and Principe	1	—	—	25	19	44	—	—	—	—
Senegal	—	10	—	47	1,117	1,164	3,450	5,500	2,000	1,250
Seychelles	—	—	—	—	—	—	—	—	—	—
Sierra Leone	51	37	88	57	163	220	3,200	3,900	1,100	950
Somalia	—	—	—	—	—	—	—	—	—	1,250
Sudan	—	—	—	—	—	—	—	—	—	1,100
Swaziland	9	—	—	8	113	121	—	—	—	—
Tanzania	26	104	130	300	10,453	10,753	—	—	—	900
Togo	23	—	—	317	402	719	5,300	—	650	—
Uganda	75	—	—	404	—	—	—	—	—	1,250
Zaire	—	153	—	1,095	3,983	5,078	60,000	—	500	—
Zambia	12	66	78	555	—	—	—	—	—	—
Zimbabwe	26	155	181	—	—	999	4,600	—	1,900	500
Africa	—	—	—	—	—	—	—	—	**1,100**	**900**
World	—	—	—	—	—	—	—	—	280	—
Less developed countries	—	—	—	—	—	—	—	—	500	—
More developed countries	—	—	—	—	—	—	—	—	110	—

a. Total beds include beds in hospitals, health centers, maternities, dispensaries.
b. Total includes health centers and others (maternities, dispensaries, clinics, health posts). Data are for most recent years.

Table A-13. Health Expenditures

Country	Health expenditures (1990) (millions of U.S. dollars) Public	Aid Flows	Private	Total	Per capita (U.S. dollars)	Health expenditure as a percentage of GDP (1990) Public	Aid Flows	Private	Total	Aid flow as a percentage of total health expenditure 1990
Angola	—	—	—	—	—	—	—	—	—	—
Benin	20.8	29.6	30.4	80.8	17	1.1	1.6	1.7	4.4	37
Botswana	120.0	32.0	42.0	194.0	155	3.8	1.0	1.3	6.2	17
Burkina Faso	21.3	158.0	43.6	222.9	25	0.8	6.1	1.7	8.6	71
Burundi	15.3	3.4	6.2	24.9	5	1.4	0.3	0.6	2.3	13
Cameroon	75.5	34.1	199.2	308.8	26	0.7	0.3	1.8	2.8	11
Cape Verde	3.6	9.3	5.1	18.0	48	1.3	3.4	1.9	6.6	52
Central African Rep.	14.5	19.7	21.4	55.6	18	1.1	1.5	1.6	4.2	35
Chad	20.9	36.0	18.9	75.8	13	1.7	3.0	1.6	6.2	47
Comoros	6.1	3.2	3.8	13.1	26	2.5	1.3	1.6	5.4	24
Congo	53.4	13.7	43.5	110.6	49	1.9	0.5	1.5	3.9	12
Côte d'Ivoire	161.9	11.3	161.0	334.1	28	1.6	0.1	1.6	3.4	3
Djibouti	—	—	—	19.1	45	—	—	—	—	—
Equatorial Guinea	4.2	4.9	2.2	11.3	27	2.8	3.3	1.4	7.5	43
Ethiopia	94.6	43.1	97.8	235.5	5	1.6	0.7	1.6	3.9	18
Gabon	108.9	13.3	73.1	195.3	172	2.2	0.3	1.5	3.9	7
Gambia	7.2	13.0	4.9	25.1	29	2.1	3.8	1.5	7.4	52
Ghana	71.5	26.9	105.6	204.0	14	1.2	0.5	1.8	3.5	13
Guinea	41.3	21.5	40.8	103.6	18	1.5	0.8	1.5	3.8	21
Guinea-Bissau	5.0	7.9	2.7	15.6	16	2.6	4.1	1.4	8.0	51
Kenya	150.1	83.1	142.1	375.2	16	1.7	1.0	1.6	4.3	22
Lesotho	18.5	17.0	12.8	48.4	27	3.2	2.9	2.2	8.3	35

Liberia	1.8	6.2	1.9	10.0	4	1.6	5.6	1.8	9.0	62
Madagascar	22.8	16.9	39.0	78.7	7	0.7	0.6	1.3	2.6	21
Malawi	32.4	21.5	38.6	92.5	11	1.7	1.2	2.1	5.0	23
Mali	32.5	37.0	60.8	130.3	15	1.3	1.5	2.4	5.2	28
Mauritania	11.4	12.0	16.7	40.1	20	1.1	1.1	1.6	3.8	30
Mauritius	—	—	—	—	—	—	—	—	—	—
Mozambique	17.7	45.1	24.0	86.8	6	1.2	3.1	1.7	6.0	52
Niger	43.5	43.0	38.2	124.6	16	1.7	1.7	1.5	4.9	34
Nigeria	330.9	55.2	573.7	959.8	10	1.0	0.2	1.7	2.9	6
Rwanda	11.0	29.2	38.2	78.4	11	0.5	1.4	1.8	3.7	37
São Tomé and Principe	1.4	2.5	0.9	4.8	41	2.7	5.0	1.7	9.4	53
Senegal	96.4	36.2	87.6	220.1	30	1.7	0.6	1.5	3.8	16
Seychelles	—	—	—	—	—	—	—	—	—	—
Sierra Leone	4.3	10.8	6.8	21.9	5	0.5	1.2	0.8	2.4	50
Somalia	—	—	—	—	—	—	—	—	—	—
Sudan	32.9	13.6	253.3	299.8	12	0.4	0.2	2.8	3.3	5
Swaziland	24.7	19.4	11.8	55.9	70	3.2	2.5	1.5	7.1	35
Tanzania	15.7	59.0	41.6	116.3	5	0.7	2.6	1.8	5.0	51
Togo	27.1	14.2	26.7	68.0	19	1.7	0.9	1.6	4.2	21
Uganda	12.6	32.0	50.2	94.8	6	0.5	1.2	1.8	3.4	34
Zaire	15.2	47.8	159.0	222.0	6	0.2	0.6	2.1	2.9	22
Zambia	76.5	4.8	35.8	117.1	14	2.1	0.1	1.0	3.2	4
Zimbabwe	167.7	45.8	202.9	416.4	42	2.5	0.7	3.0	6.2	11
Africa	**1,993**	**1,133**	**2,765**	**5,910**	**14**	**1.5**	**0.9**	**2.1**	**4.5**	**19**
World	1,018,221	3,252	680,982	1,702,455	323	4.8	0.0	3.2	8.0	0.2
Less developed countries	76,376	3,252	90,487	170,115	41	2.1	0.1	2.5	4.7	1.9
More developed countries	951,108	0	581,232	1,532,340	1,340	5.4	0.0	3.3	8.7	0.0

Technical Notes

In all tables, **Africa** is defined as Sub-Saharan Africa. It excludes Eritrea and Namibia (due to lack of data) and La Réunion and South Africa (due to differences from other Sub-Saharan countries). Africa-wide values are population-weighted, unless the context indicates otherwise.

"**More developed**" countries include Europe, the countries of the former U.S.S.R., North America (U.S. and Canada), Australia, New Zealand, and Japan. "**Less developed**" countries include the rest of the world.

Unavailable data are denoted by —.

The principal sources of the data are: World Bank and United Nations Development Programme, 1992; African Development Indicators (ADI92); the World Bank's Population, Health and Nutrition Department (PHN); World Development Report 1993 (WDR93); the World Health Organization—Geneva Headquarters (WHO) and African Regional Office (WHO/AFRO); the United Nations (UN); and the United Nations Children's Fund (UNICEF).

Table A-1. Health and Development Indicators

Population numbers for mid-1992 are World Bank estimates. These are normally projections from the most recent population censuses or surveys, which, in some cases, are very dated. Refugees not permanently settled in the country of asylum are generally considered to be part of the population of their country of origin.

Population growth rates are calculated from the midyear population by the exponential method. The rates are expressed in percents.

The **crude birth rate** and **crude death rate**, respectively, indicate the number of live births and deaths occurring per thousand population in a given year. They are World Bank estimates, based on various sources, including the United Nations.

The **total fertility rate** represents the number of children that would be born per woman, if she were to live to the end of her childbearing years and bear children at each age in accordance with currently prevailing age-specific fertility rates. Data are from the

UN (Population Division and Statistical Office) and the World Bank (PHN) based on demographic and health surveys and information from country statistical offices.

Life expectancy at birth is the number of years a newborn infant would live if subjected throughout life to the current age-specific mortality rates. Data are presented for males and females separately. The sources of data are the UN and the World Bank.

GNP per capita figures in U.S. dollars are calculated according to the World Bank Atlas method. Gross national product (GNP) measures the total domestic and foreign value added claimed by residents. It consists of gross domestic product (GDP, the total dollar value of all goods and services produced in the country), with adjustments for the value of goods and services produced by nationals abroad and by foreigners residing within the country. The atlas conversion factor for any year is the average of the exchange rate for that year and the exchange rates for the two preceding years, after adjusting them for differences in relative inflation between the country and the U.S. The resulting GNP in U.S. dollars is divided by the midyear population for the latest of the three years to derive GNP per capita. Data are from WDR93.

The **adult literacy rate** is the proportion of the population fifteen years old and over who can read and write a short, simple statement on their everyday life. The data are from WDR93.

Tables A-2 and A-3. Population Projections (standard/medium and rapid fertility decline)

Population estimates and projections are those made by the World Bank, with midyear 1990 as the base, from data provided by the UN, country statistical offices, and other reliable sources. The projections for 2000 and 2025 are made for each country separately by the component method, based on previous trends of fertility, mortality, and migration. Note that the data reflect the potentially significant impact of the human immunodeficiency virus (HIV) epidemic. A full description of the methods and assumptions used to calculate the estimates is contained in the World Bank's World Population Projections, 1992–93 Edition.

Annual rate of population growth. See note to Table A-1. The population projections for rapid fertility decline assume that each country will increase the use of contraceptives at the maximum possible rate.

Total fertility rate. See note to Table A-1.

Population age structure for under fifteen and sixty-five and over is expressed as the percentage of total population. Data are from the World Bank data files, 1993; and the UN (World Population Prospects, the 1992 Revision, UN 1993).

The data on **urban population as a percentage of total population** are from the UN's World Population Prospects, the 1992 Revision, supplemented by data from the World Bank. Because these estimates are based on different national definitions of what is urban, cross-country comparisons should be interpreted with caution.

Contraceptive use is the proportion of married women of childbearing age (15–49) in families using contraception. The data are from African Population Advisory Committee (APAC) 1993a.

Table A-4. Mortality

The **infant mortality rate** is the number of infants who die before reaching one year of age, per thousand live births in a given year. The data are from the UN as well as from the World Bank.

The **under-five mortality rate** is the probability of dying between birth and age five, expressed per thousand live births. The rates were obtained from a special background paper prepared for WDR93 and UNICEF. The methodology is described in the Hill and Yazbeck background paper cited in WDR93. The underlying information comes from the UN (Child Mortality since the 1960s, 1992), augmented by recently available census and survey data.

The **adult mortality rate ages 15–59** is the probability of an adult age fifteen dying before reaching age sixty. The figure here is per thousand. The rates were derived from the child mortality estimates for the same year, combined with assumptions about the relationship between child and adult mortality based on country-specific projections by the World Bank.

Median age at death is the age below which half of all deaths occur in a year. The indicator is affected by several factors, including the age structure of the population and the age pattern of mortality risks in the population. It does not represent the average age at which any group of individuals will die, and it is not directly related to life expectancy. Since African countries are characterized by very young populations (with nearly 50 percent of population under fifteen years old, due to high total fertility rates) and high infant and child mortality rates, the median age at death is very low (only five) compared with that of developing (thirty-nine) and industrial countries (seventy-four). The data are from WDR93.

Table A-5. Income and Poverty

Average annual growth rate of GDP. GDP measures the total output of goods and services for final use produced by residents and nonresidents, regardless of the allocation to domestic and foreign claims. The data are obtained from national sources, sometimes reaching the World Bank through other international organizations, but more often collected during World Bank staff missions. The data are from WDR93.

Average annual rate of inflation is measured by the growth rate of the GDP implicit deflator for each of the periods shown. The GDP deflator is first calculated by dividing, for each year of the period, the value of GDP at current values by the value of GDP at constant values, both in national currency. The least-squares method is then used to calculate the growth rate of the GDP deflator for the period. This measure of inflation, like any other, has limitations. It is used as an indicator of inflation, however, because it is the most broadly based measure, showing annual price movements for all goods and services produced in an economy. The data are from WDR93.

GNP per capita. See note to Table A-1. The data are from WDR93.

Percent share of income is the share of the lowest and highest population quintiles in total income or consumption expenditure. The data refer to different years between 1981 and 1991 and are drawn from nationally representative household surveys. The data have been compiled from two main sources: government statistical agencies and the

World Bank (mostly from the Living Standards Measurement Surveys). For further details, see Chen, Datt, and Ravallion, 1993.

Population dependency ratio is calculated as the number of persons under age 15 and at age 65 and over (dependent ages) for every 100 persons ages 15–64 (economically productive ages). It gives a rough indication of how many persons are economically supported by each 100 persons who are economically active. The sources of data are the same as for total population (Table A-1).

Absolute poverty level is defined as the country-specific income level below which adequate standards of nutrition, shelter, and personal amenities cannot be assured. The data are from ADI92.

Table A-6. Education

Data are from the World Bank data files (WDR93 and ADI92).

Adult literacy rate. See note to Table A-1.

Primary school enrollment data estimate the number of children of all ages enrolled in primary school. Figures are expressed as the ratio of pupils to the population of school-age children. Although many countries consider primary school age to be six to eleven years, others do not. For some countries with universal primary education, the gross enrollment ratios can exceed 100 percent because some pupils are younger or older than the country's standard primary school age.

The data on **secondary** school enrollment are calculated in the same manner, but again the definition of secondary school age differs among countries. It is most commonly considered to be twelve to seventeen years. Late entry of more mature students and repetition can influence these ratios.

The **primary pupil/teacher ratio** is the number of pupils enrolled in school in a country, divided by the number of teachers in the education system.

Table A-7. The Health and Status of Women

Women of childbearing age are those in the 15–49 age group.

The **maternal mortality rate** refers to the number of female deaths that occur during childbirth, per 100,000 live births. Because deaths during childbirth are defined more widely in some countries than in others, and many deaths are never recorded, the figures should be treated with extreme caution. The data are drawn from diverse sources: WHO/AFRO country reports; Maternal and Child Health, WHO/AFRO, 1990; UN Demographic Yearbooks; UNICEF; and mostly from Maternal Mortality, A Global Factbook, WHO 1991.

Prenatal health care coverage rate is the percentage of pregnant women who attended prenatal care clinics in a given year. The data suggest the service was used but do not imply that coverage was adequate or effective. The data are from the Health for All data base, WHO 6/92; Global Health Situation and Projections, WHO 1992; WHO/AFRO computer printout, 1990; and WHO/AFRO country reports.

Births attended by trained health personnel. Trained personnel include physicians, nurses, midwives, trained primary health care and other health workers, and trained traditional birth attendants. National coverage levels are drawn from official estimates and sample surveys. Where no direct figures were available, the percent of births in health care institutions has been substituted as a conservative estimate. The data are from the Health for All data base, WHO 6/92; Global Health Situation and Projections, WHO 1992; WHO/AFRO computer printout, 1990; and WHO/AFRO country reports.

Pregnant women immunized for tetanus is the percentage of women giving birth in a given year who received tetanus toxoid injections during pregnancy. The data are from the Health for All data base, WHO 6/92; Global Health Situation and Projections, WHO 1992; WHO/AFRO computer printout, 1990; and WHO/AFRO country reports.

Prevalence of anemia in pregnant women (percent below norm). Women are classified as anemic when the blood hemoglobin level is below the WHO norm of 110 grams per liter. The data are from WDR93.

School enrollment (females per 100 males) shows the extent to which females have equal access to schooling. The data are from WDR93.

African states parties to human rights conventions . The Convention on the Rights of the Child and the International Convention on the Elimination of Discrimination against Women contain provisions relevant to the status of women. The data indicate the years when the country ratified the convention(s). The data are as of February 1992, from the United Nations Center for Human Rights, Geneva.

Table A-8. Food and Nutrition

Nutrition status: wasting (low weight for height) and **stunting** (low height for age) refer to the percent of children with less than 77 percent (2 standard deviations) of the median weight-for-height or height-for-age of the U.S. National Center for Health Statistics (NCHS) reference population. Mild/moderate malnutrition is between 60 and 80 percent of the norm. Severe malnutrition is less than 60 percent of the norm. Chronic malnutrition is measured by stunting, and acute or short-term malnutrition is measured by wasting, whether the cause is inadequate food intake or infectious disease or both. Mild or moderate malnutrition is not considered disease, but all degrees of malnutrition increase the risk of death in children. The data are from WDR93.

Percentage of children fully breastfed is defined as those given breast milk with or without water, juice, or other liquids but no food or nonbreast milk before age four months. The data are from WDR93.

Babies with low birth weight is the proportion of children born weighing 2,500 grams (5.5 pounds) or less. The data are from WDR93.

The **index of food production per capita** relates food production from 1975 to 1991 to that of 1987. The value of the latter within each country is taken as 100. The data are from the World Bank data files, 1993 (STARS93).

Food supply: calories per capita per day were calculated by dividing the calorie equivalent of the food supplies in a country by the population. Supplies include domestic production, imports less exports, and changes in stocks. The data are from the Food and Agriculture Organization Yearbook (Production), 1991.

Food supply: protein per capita per day (grams) indicates one of the nutrient elements of food supply. Data are from the FAO Yearbook, 1991.

It is important to note that the quantities of food available relate to the quantities of food reaching households but not necessarily to the amounts of food actually consumed. The quantity consumed may be lower than the quantity shown, due to losses of edible food and nutrients in the household and to issues in the intrahousehold distribution of available food. The data represent only the average supply for the population as a whole.

Table A-9. Access to Water, Sanitation, and Health Care Facilities

The data are from the Health for All data base, WHO 6/92; Global Health Situation and Projections, WHO 1992; WHO/AFRO computer printout, 1990; and UNICEF data file 1993.

Access to safe water is the proportion of the population with reasonable access to safe water sources. Safe water commonly includes treated surface water or untreated but uncontaminated water such as that from protected boreholes, springs, and sanitary wells. Reasonable access in urban areas is defined as a public fountain or standpost located not more than 200 meters from a dwelling. In rural areas, reasonable access implies that members of the household do not have to spend a disproportionate part of the day fetching the household's water needs.

Access to sanitation facilities is the proportion of the population with adequate sanitary facilities in the home or immediate vicinity. The WHO indicators and definitions changed in the late 1980s, and caution is needed in interpreting the data.

Access to health care services is now defined in the WHO Health for All data base as the proportion of the population having treatment for common diseases and injuries and a regular supply of the essential drugs on the national list available within one hour's walk or travel. Caution is needed in interpreting the data.

Table A-10. Immunization

Data are from the Health for All data base, WHO 6/92; Global Health Situation and Projections, WHO 1992; WHO/AFRO computer printout, 1990; UNICEF data file 1993; and ADI92.

Immunization coverage is the percentage of children in a given year who were fully immunized against each disease or group of diseases by age one. The requirements for full immunization depend on the type of disease. The vaccination schedule recommended by WHO, which is used in this table to measure full immunization, is as follows:

- **Tuberculosis**: one injection of BCG vaccine (Bacterium Calmette-Guerin), which can be given at the time of birth.
- **Diphtheria, Pertussis, Tetanus**: three injections with DPT vaccine (DPT 3) before age one; the first is recommended six weeks after birth followed by two more at one-month intervals.
- **Polio**: at least three doses of oral polio vaccine (POL 3) before age one, given one month apart. In areas where polio is endemic, the first dose is recommended at the time of birth, followed by three more doses at the same time as the DPT injections.

■ **Measles**: one injection of measles vaccine, given after nine months of age.

Table A-11. Health Care Personnel

The data in this table are from WHO (Statistics Annual, 1988; Human Resources data base 1992; Global Health Situation and Projections, 1992); WHO/AFRO (computer printout, 1990) and WHO/AFRO country reports); and World Bank data files 1993 (PHN, WDR93). As explained in the WHO statistics annual, military personnel who do not provide assistance to the civil health services are not included in the data, but expatriate staff are included. Because definitions of various categories of health care personnel vary among countries and the definitions given below lack precision, cross-country comparisons of the data must be made with extreme caution.

Doctors are graduates of a medical school or faculty actually working in any medical field (practice, teaching, administration, research, laboratory, etc.). Practitioners of traditional medicine are not included in this category.

Paramedics are staff whose medical training is less than that of qualified physicians but who nevertheless dispense similar medical services, including simple operations.

Nurses (professional, high level) are graduates of a nursing school working in any nursing field (general nursing, specialized clinical nursing services in mental health, pediatrics, cardiovascular diseases, public health or occupational health, teaching, administration, research, and so on). These personnel are qualified and authorized to provide the most responsible and competent professional nursing service. Also included in this category are **midwives (professional, high level),** who are graduates of a midwifery school actually working in any field of midwifery (practice in institutions and community health services, teaching, administration, private practice, and so on).

Technicians are graduates of health technical school. They perform duties in laboratories, X-ray departments, dental departments, pharmacies, environmental health, and so on.

Assistant nurses (middle level) are personnel who provide general patient care of a less complex nature in hospitals and other health services, in principle under the supervision of a professional nurse. These personnel do not have the full education and training of a professional nurse. Also included in this category are **assistant midwives (middle level),** who are personnel carrying out the midwifery duties of normal obstetric care, in principle under the supervision of a professional midwife. Assistant midwives do not have the full education and training of professional midwives.

Assistant technicians (middle level) are health services personnel carrying out duties other than those of assistant nurses or assistant midwives. In principle, they work under the supervision of a technician. These personnel do not have the full education and training of a professional technician.

Population per doctor or per nurse represents the number of people served by one doctor or by one nurse. The data show only the average available for the population as a whole and must be interpreted with caution because of the concentration of highly qualified health staff in urban areas.

Tables A-12. Health Care Facilities

The data are from WHO/AFRO (computer printout, 1990); WHO/AFRO country reports; and World Bank data files (WDR93). Note that, in some respects, the definitions are not fully consistent with the usage in the text. Furthermore, terminology and definitions vary substantially from country to country; thus intercountry comparisons must be made with caution.

Hospitals are establishments permanently staffed by at least one physician that offer in-patient accommodation and provide medical and nursing care. Establishments providing principally custodial care are not included.

Central/regional hospitals are hospitals—other than local or rural hospitals—that provide medical and nursing care for several medical disciplines.

District/rural hospitals are, in principle, first-referral facilities, usually in rural areas, permanently staffed by one or more physicians, that provide medical and nursing care of a more limited range than that provided by central or regional hospitals.

Health centers are, in principle, the first point of contact of the population with the formal health care system. They are not permanently staffed by physicians but by medical assistants, nurses, midwives, and so on. Usually, they are small units (sometimes also known as rural health centers) that offer limited in-patient accommodation and provide a limited range of medical and nursing care.

Others include maternities, dispensaries, and health posts. They furnish a very limited range of medical and nursing care not provided by professional staff.

Beds. A **hospital bed** is situated in a ward or a part of the hospital where continuous medical care for in-patients is provided. The total of such beds constitutes the normally available bed complement of the hospital. Cribs and bassinets maintained for use by healthy newborn infants who do not require special care are not included.

Population per bed represents the number of people served by one hospital bed or other health care facility bed in the country. It is only an average and must be interpreted with caution because of the concentration of health care facilities with beds in urban areas.

Table A-13. Health Expenditures

Health expenditures include outlays for prevention of disease, health promotion, rehabilitation, and personal and public health care services; population programs; nutrition activities; program food aid; and emergency aid specifically for health. In this table, health expenditures do not include water and sanitation. **Per capita expenditures** are based on World Bank midyear population estimates. **Total health expenditure** is expressed in official exchange rate U.S. dollars.

Data on **public** and **private health expenditure** are from national sources, supplemented by Government Finance Statistics (published by the International Monetary Fund), World Bank sector studies, and other studies. Public expenditures include government health expenditures and parastatal expenditures. They do not include aid flows. **Private expenditures** are based on household surveys carried out by the ILO and other sources, supplemented by information from United Nations National Income Accounts, World Bank studies, and other studies published in the scientific literature.

Estimates for countries with incomplete data, including a number of African countries, were calculated, in a special exercise undertaken for WDR93, in three steps. First, where data on either private or public expenditures were lacking, the missing figures were imputed from data from countries for which information was available. The imputation followed regressions relating public or private expenditure to GDP per capita. Second, for a country with no health expenditure data, it was assumed that the share of GDP spent on health was the same as the average for the corresponding region. Third, if GDP was unknown but population was known, it was assumed that per capita health spending was the same as the regional average.

Aid flows represent the sum of all health assistance to each country by bilateral and multilateral agencies and by international nongovernment organizations (NGOs). National NGOs were not included because the available information was not separately available by recipient country. The estimates of aid in this table were prepared for WDR93 by the Harvard Center for Population and Development Studies.

Bibliographical Notes

Better Health in Africa is the product of the efforts of many people. Contributors to the study included B. Abeillé, I. Aleta, R. Amadi, R. Bail, A. Bhargava, G. Bloom, P. Brudon, A. Correia de Campos, J. L. Dubois, G. Dukes, A. E. Elmendorf, J. Hammer, R. Hecht, K. Hill, I. Z. Husain, M. Kirmani, R. Knippenberg. J. Kutzin, T. Lambo, J.-L. Lamboray, P. Landell-Mills, M. Lechat, M. Lioy, J. Litvack, T. McCarthy, J. McGuire, T. Marek, R. Ngong, R. Niimi, L. Obeng, S. Ofosu-Amaah, D. Peters, G. Pham-Kanter, D. Porter, W. Roseberry, R. P. Shaw, J. Silverman, D. Vaillancourt, W. Van Lerberghe, M. Venkatraman, and Z. Yusuf. S. Kim, A. Bohon, H. Dao, K. Dugbatey, G. McGrory, A. N'Diaye, and C. Stomberg assisted in the research; J. Shafer, A. Bohon, K. Goodwin, M. Thurston-Greenwalt, D. Jaekel, A. Kamau, D. McGreevy, M. Verbeeck, M.-C. Verlaeten, J. Watlington, and C. Yee provided administrative support; M. Vu and A. Sy prepared the statistical appendix; and P. Sawicki edited the manuscript for publication.

I. Ajayi, R. Bitran, K. Subbarao, and H. Wassef helped in the initial framing of the study. L. Boya, E. Brown, M. Dia, K. Dugbatey, M. Kirmani, M. Malonga, A. Nyamete, S. Ofosu-Amaah, M. Tall, D. Vaillancourt, and A. Williams assisted R. Amadi in reflections on culture and health. M. Blackden, P. Daly, M. Kirmani, E. Morris-Hughes, and A. Tinker helped on women and health; J. Doyen, D. Gray, J. Leitman, and L. Obeng, on the environment and health; D. Porter, on health equipment; M. Lechat, on technology and health; G. Dukes, on pharmaceuticals; S. Ofosu-Amaah, on human resources for health; G. Pham-Kanter, on health service outputs; A. Tchicaya and G. McGrory, on external assistance for health; J. Silverman, on management capacity and decentralization; and E. Heneveld and M. Zymelman, on education and health.

Commentators from outside the World Bank included S. Adjei, F.S. Antezana, F. Baer, R. Bail, K. Bezanson, G. Bloom, C. Cosmas, J. Davis, G. Dahlgren, J. Decaillet, J. Desmazieres, S. Duale, L. Erinosho, M. Fargier, R. Feacham, C. Forsberg, S. Foster, H. Gilles, H. Gorgen, J. P. Grant, A. Hamer, R. Heyward, D. Hopkins, R. Hore, M. Jancloes, R. King, R. Korte, M. Lechat, A. Lucas, C. Melvin, A. Mills, N. Mock, G.L. Monekosso, M. Moore, D. Nabarro, F. Nkrumah, H. Ntaba, S. Ofosu-Amaah, T. Park, E. Perry,

221

O. Ransome-Kuti, T. Rothermel, J. Roy, F. Sai, J. Seaman, D. Shepard, M. Skold, H. Sukin, A. Tchicaya, H. Van Balen, A. Vernon, G. Walt, J. Wolgin, and D. Yach. Commentators from inside the World Bank were M. Ainsworth, J. Armstrong, M. Azefor, J. Baudouy, D. Berk, J.-L. Bobadilla, E. Boostrom, E. Boohene, L. Boya, E. Brown, N. Burnett, A. Colliou, H. Denton, L. Domingo, M. Fardi, F. Golladay, R. Heaver, E. Heneveld, A. Hill, I. Z. Husain, D. Jamison, E. Johnson, S. Jorgenson, J. Kutzin, P. Landell-Mills, D. Mahar, W. McGreevey, A.R. Measham, P. Musgrove, O. Pannenborg, D. Peters, M. Pierre-Louis, M. Plessis-Fraissard, D. Radel, J. Salop, H. Saxenian, K. Subbarao, J.-P. Tan, and R. Vaurs.

The study benefited greatly from earlier work undertaken by F. Golladay with the assistance of T. Asefa; from workshops facilitated by P. Gittinger with the assistance of J. Dejong, held with African colleagues in Abidjan, Accra, Bujumbura, and Lilongwe; and from an internal World Bank staff workshop. Aside from the background papers and other sources mentioned below, the study also drew on World Bank population, health and nutrition sector and project appraisal reports.

Background Papers

Abosede, Olayinka, and Judith S. McGuire. 1991. "Improving Women's and Children's Nutrition in Sub-Saharan Africa." Working Paper 723. World Bank, Population and Human Resources Department, Washington, D.C.

Amadi, Regina. 1992. "Cultural Dimensions in Better Health in Africa." World Bank, Africa Technical Department, Population, Health and Nutrition Division, Washington, D.C.

Brunet-Jailly, J. 1991. "Health Financing in the Poor Countries: Cost Recovery or Cost Reduction?" PRE Working Paper 692. World Bank, Population and Human Resources Department, Washington, D.C.

Dejong, Jocelyn. 1991. "Nongovernmental Organizations and Health Delivery in Sub-Saharan Africa." PRE Working Paper 708. World Bank, Population and Human Resources Department, Washington, D.C.

———. 1991. "Traditional Medicine in Sub-Saharan Africa." Working Paper 735. World Bank, Population and Human Resources Department, Washington, D.C.

Diop, Francois, Kenneth Hill, and Ismail Sirageldin. 1991. "Economic Crisis, Structural Adjustment, and Health in Africa." Working Paper 766. World Bank, Population and Human Resources Department, Washington, D.C.

Eklund, Peter, and Knut Stavem. 1990. "Prepaid Financing of Primary Health Care in Guinea-Bissau." Working Paper 488. World Bank, Population and Human Resources Department, Washington, D.C.

Foster, S.D. 1990. "Improving the Supply and Use of Essential Drugs in Sub-Saharan Africa." Working Paper 456. World Bank, Population and Human Resources Department, Washington, D.C.

Liese, Bernard H., Bruce Benton, and Douglas Marr. 1991. "The Onchocerciasis Control Program in West Africa." Working Paper 740. World Bank, Population and Human Resources Department, Washington, D.C.

Mwabu, Germano. 1989. "Financing Health Services in Africa: An Assessment of Alternative Approaches." Working Paper 457. World Bank, Population and Human Resources Department, Washington, D.C.

Tchicaya, Anastase J.R. 1992. "L'Aide Extérieure à la Santé dans les Pays d'Afrique au Sud du Sahara." Africa Technical Department. World Bank, Population, Health and Nutrition Division, Washington, D.C.

Vaughan, Patrick. 1992. "Health Personnel Development in Sub-Saharan Africa." Working Paper 914. World Bank, Population and Human Resources Department, Washington, D.C.

Vogel, Ronald J. 1989. "Trends in Health Expenditures and Revenue Sources in Sub-Saharan Africa." World Bank, Population and Human Resources Department, Washington, D.C.

———. 1990. "Health Insurance in Sub-Saharan Africa." Working Paper 476. World Bank, Population and Human Resources Department, Washington, D.C.

World Bank. 1993. "A Framework and Indicative Cost Analysis for Better Health in Africa." Technical Working Paper 8. World Bank, Africa Technical Department, Human Resources and Poverty Division, Washington, D.C.

Yusuf, Zia. 1993. "A Framework and Indicative Cost Analysis for Better Health in Zimbabwe." Africa Technical Department, Human Resources and Poverty Division, Washington, D.C.

Bibliography

Abeillé, Bernard, and others. 1991. "Etude Sectorielle: Pratiques de Construction des Infrastructures Sociales dans les Pays du Sahel." Volume IV, Fiches d'Enquete. World Bank, Washington, D.C. Also in English as Abeillé, Bernard, and Jean-Marie Lantran. 1993. *Social Infrastructure Construction in the Sahel: Options for Improving Current Practices.* World Bank Discussion Paper 200. Washington, D.C.

Abosede, Olayinka, and Judith S. McGuire. 1991. "Improving Women's and Children's Nutrition in Sub-Saharan Africa." Working Paper 723. World Bank, Population and Human Resources Department, Washington, D.C.

Adjei, Samuel. 1993. Personal communication, July.

African Population Advisory Committee. 1993a. "Reliability of Population Estimates and Sources of Demographic Data for Africa." World Bank, APAC Secretariat, Washington, D.C.

———. 1993b. "African Population Programs: Status Report." World Bank, APAC Secretariat, Washington, D.C.

———. 1993. "Report on the African Population Agenda." World Bank, APAC Secretariat, Washington, D.C.

———. 1993c. "The Impact of HIV/AIDS on Population Growth in Africa." World Bank, APAC Secretariat, Washington, D.C.

Ageyi, William K. A., and Elsbeth J. Epema. 1992. "Sexual Behavior and Contraceptive Use Among 15–24 Year Olds in Uganda." *International Family Planning Perspectives* 18 (March):13–17.

Ainsworth, Martha, and Mead Over. 1992. "The Economic Impact of AIDS: Shocks, Responses, Outcomes." Technical Working Paper 1. World Bank, Africa Technical Department, Human Resources and Poverty Division, Washington, D.C.

Akoto, Eliwo, and Dominique Tabutin. 1989. "Les inégalités socioeconomiques et culturelles devant la mort." *Mortalité et Société en Afrique.* Institut National d'Etudes Demographique, et Presses Universitaires de France, Paris.

Aleta, I. R. 1992. "Health Research in the WHO African Region: Situational Analysis and Prospects for Development." WHO/AFRO, Brazzaville.

Alihonou, E., L. Miller, R. Knippenberg, and T. Gandaho. 1986. "L'Utilisation du Médicament Essentiel comme Base du Financement Communautaire." Paper presented at the International Symposium on Essential Drugs in Developing Countries. Paris.

Alihonou, E., and others. 1988. "L'interface des soins de santé de base et des soins primaires." Pahou, Health Development Project, Benin.

Amadi, Regina. 1992. "Cultural Dimensions in Better Health in Africa." World Bank, Africa Technical Department, Population, Health and Nutrition Division, Washington, D.C.

Amonoo-Lartsen, R. 1990. "Experiences of Cooperation for Health." Unpublished report. World Bank, Population and Human Resources Department, Washington, D.C.

Barnum, Howard, and Joseph Kutzin. 1993. *Public Hospitals in Developing Countries: Resource Use, Cost, Financing.* Baltimore, Md.: Johns Hopkins University Press for the World Bank.

Behrman, Jere R. 1990. "A Survey of Economic Development, Structural Adjustment and Child Health and Mortality in Developing Countries." *Child Survival Programs: Issues for the 1990s.* Baltimore, Md.: Johns Hopkins University Press.

Bentley, Chris. 1989. "Primary Health Care in Northwestern Somalia: A Case Study." *Social Science and Medicine* 28(10):1019–30.

Berman, P., C. Kendall, and K. Bhattacharyya. 1989. "The Household Production of Health: Putting People at the Center of Health Improvement." In I. Sirageldin and others, eds. *Towards More Efficacy in Child Survival Strategies.* Baltimore, Md.: Johns Hopkins University School of Hygiene and Public Health.

Bertrand, William E. 1992. Letter dated December 15, 1992, to Dr. Seth Berkley, Rockefeller Foundation. Tulane University.

Beza, B., and others. 1987. "Introduction of a Local Health Information System in Kinshasa Zaire." *Annales de la Société Belge de Médecine Tropicale* 66 (3). BP 4832. Kinshasa Gombe, Republique du Zaïre.

Bhargava, Alok, and Jian Yu. 1992. "A Longitudinal Analysis of Infant and Child Mortality Rates in African and Non-African Developing Countries." Unpublished technical paper. World Bank, Africa Technical Department, Human Resources and Poverty Division, Washington, D.C.

Bitran, R., M. Mpese, and others. 1986. "Zaire: Health Zones Financing Study." United States Agency for International Development, Washington, D.C.

Blakney, R. B., J. I. Litvack, and J. D. Quick. 1989. "Financing Primary Health Care: Experiences in Pharmaceutical Cost Recovery." Report by the Pritech Committee. Management Sciences for Health, Boston.

Bloom, G., M. Segall, and C. Thube. 1986. "Expenditure and Financing of the Health Sector in Kenya." World Bank, Department of Population, Health and Nutrition, Washington, D.C.

Bloom, Gerald, and Caroline Temple-Bird. 1988. "Medical Equipment in Sub-Saharan Africa: A Framework for Policy Formulation." Research Report 19. Institute for Development Studies, University of Sussex, Brighton, England.

Boateng, E. Oti, Kodwo Ewusi, Ravi Kanbur, and Andrew McCay. 1989. *A Poverty Profile for Ghana, 1987–88*. SDA Working Paper Series 5. World Bank. Washington, D.C.

Bocar, Dem. 1989. "Integration de l'hôpital de Labe dans le systeme sanitaire du district." Term paper for the International Course in Health Development. Institute of Tropical Medicine, Antwerp.

Boerma, J. Ties, A. Elisabeth Sommerfelt, and Shea O. Rutstein. 1991. *Childhood Morbidity and Treatment Patterns*. Demographic and Health Surveys, Comparative Studies no. 4. Columbia Md.: Institute for Resource Development/Macro International, Inc.

Bradley, A. K. 1976. "Effects of Onchocerciasis on Settlement in the Middle Hawal Valley, Nigeria." *Transactions of the Royal Society of Tropical Medicine and Hygiene* 70(3):225–29.

Bradley, David John, and others. 1992. *A Review of Environmental Health Impacts in Developing Country Cities*. Urban Management Program, Paper 6. World Bank, Washington, D.C.

Brieger, William, Jayashree Ramakrishna, and Joshua D. Adeniyi. 1986. "Self-Treatment in Rural Nigeria: A Community Education Diagnosis." *International Journal of Health Education (Hygie)*, 5:2 (June).

Brinkman, Uwe, and Brinkman, A. 1991. "Malaria and Health in Africa: The Present Situation and Epidemiological Trends." *Tropical Medicine and Parasitology* 42(3)204–13.

Brudon-Jakobowicz, P. 1987. "Evaluation et Monitoring dans le contexte du Programme d'action pour les Médicaments et Vaccins Essentiels." In: *Le Médicament Essential dans les Pays en Developpement*. Comptes Rendus du Symposium International, Paris, 19–20 Mai, 1987. Paris: Ministère de la Coopération.

Brunet-Jailly, J. 1991. "Health Financing in the Poor Countries: Cost Recovery or Cost Reduction?" PRE Working Paper Series 692. World Bank, Population and Human Resources Department, Washington, D.C.

Bulatao, R. A., and Patience W. Stephens. 1992. "Global Estimates and Projections of Mortality by Cause, 1970–2015." Working Paper Series 1007. World Bank, Population, Health, and Nutrition Department. Washington, D.C.

Caldwell, John, and others, eds. 1989. "What We Know about Health Transition: The Cultural, Social and Behavioural Determinants of Health." *Health Transition Series* No. 2, Vol. I. Proceedings of an International Workshop, Canberra, May 1989. Health Transition Centre, The Australian National University.

Cassels, Andrew, and Katja Janovsky. 1991. "Strengthening Health Management in Districts and Provinces: Handbook for Facilitators." World Health Organization Document. WHO/SHS/DHS/91.3. Geneva.

Castro, E. B., and K. M. Mokate. 1988. "Malaria and its Socioeconomic Meanings: The Study of Cunday in Colombia." In A. N. Herrin and P.L. Rosenfield, eds. *Economics, Health and Tropical Diseases*. Manila: School of Economics, University of the Philippines.

Chambers, R. 1982. "Health, Agriculture, and Rural Poverty: Why Seasons Matter." *Journal of Development Studies* 18(2):217–38.

Chen, Lincoln C., Arthur Kleinman, and Norma C. Ware, eds. 1992. *Advancing Health in Developing Countries: The Role of Social Research*. New York: Auburn House.

Chen, Shaohua, Gaurav Datt, and Martin Ravallion. 1993. "Is Poverty Increasing in the Developing World?" Policy Research Working Paper 1146. World Bank, Policy Research Department, Washington, D.C.

Chin, James. 1991. "The Epidemiology and Projected Mortality of AIDS." In Richard G. Feachem and Dean T. Jamison, eds., *Disease and Mortality in Sub-Saharan Africa*. New York: Oxford University Press.

Cleaver, Kevin, and Götz Schreiber. 1993. "The Population, Agriculture and Environment Nexus in Sub-Saharan Africa." Agricultural and Rural Development Series 9. World Bank, Africa Technical Department, Washington, D.C. Forthcoming as *Reversing the Spiral: The Population, Agriculture, and Environment Nexus in Sub-Saharan Africa*. World Bank, Washington, D.C.

Commission on Health Research for Development. 1990. *Health Research: Essential Link to Equity in Development*. New York: Oxford University Press.

Conly, G. N. 1975. "The Impact of Malaria on Economic Development: A Case Study." Scientific Publication 297. Pan American Health Organization, Washington, D.C.

Conyers, Diana, Andrew Cassels, and Katja Janovsky. 1992. "Decentralization and Health Systems Change." November. Unpublished manuscript.

Cook, Rebecca, and Deborah Maine. 1987. "Spousal Veto over Family Planning Services." *American Journal of Public Health* 77(3):L339–44.

Corbett, J. 1988. "Famine and Household Coping Strategies." *World Development* 16(9):1099–1122.

Cornea, A. G., Richard Jolly, and Frances Stewart. 1987. *Adjustment with a Human Face*. Oxford: Clarendon Press.

Cosmas, Cheka. 1994. Contribution to Report No. 12577–Afr:"Better Health in Africa." Personal communication.

Cross, P. N., M. A. Huff, J. D. Quick, and J. A. Bates. 1986. "Revolving Drug Funds: Conducting Business in the Public Sector." *Social Science and Medicine* 22(3):335–43.

Dabis F., A. Roisin, J. G. Breman, and others. 1988. "Improper Practices for Diarrhoea Treatment in Africa." *Transactions of the Royal Society of Medicine and Hygiene* 82:935–36.

Daniels, D. L., S. N. Cousens, L. N. Makoae, and R. G. Feachem. 1990. "A Case-Control Study of the Impact of Improved Sanitation on Diarrhoea Morbidity in Lesotho." *Bulletin of the WHO* 68(4):455–63.

Dejong, Jocelyn. 1991. "Nongovernmental Organizations and Health Delivery in Sub-Saharan Africa." Policy Research Working Paper 708. World Bank, Population and Human Resources Department, Washington, D.C.

———. 1991. "Traditional Medicine in Sub-Saharan Africa." Policy Research Working Paper 735. World Bank, Population and Human Resources Department, Washington, D.C.

Demery, Lionel, Marco Ferroni, and Christiaan Grootaert, with Jorge Wong-Valle, eds. 1993. *Understanding the Social Effects of Policy Reform*. Washington, D.C.: World Bank.

DeSweemer, C., and others. 1982. "Critical Factors in Obtaining Data Relevant to Health Programmes." In *Methodologies for Human Population Studies in Nutrition, Related to Health* 82–2462:59–81.

De Vries, T. 1992. "Experimental Application of the Groningen Prescribing Programme in 15 Universities." Unpublished status report. University of Groningen.

Diop, Francis. 1991. "Economic Determinants of Child Health and Utilization of Health Services in Sub-Saharan Africa: The Case of Ivory Coast." Ph.D. dissertation. Johns Hopkins University, Baltimore, Md.

Diop, Francois, Kenneth Hill, and Ismail Sirageldin. 1991. "Economic Crisis, Structural Adjustment, and Health in Africa." Policy Research Working Paper 766. World Bank, Population and Human Resources Department, Washington, D.C.

Dissevelt, Anthony Gerardus. 1978. *Integrated Maternal and Child Health Services: A Study at a Rural Health Centre in Kenya.* Meppel, Netherlands: Krips Repro.

District Health Development Study Core Group. 1991. "Review of District Health System Development in Ethiopia." August. Unpublished manuscript.

Dunlop, D. W., and A. Mead Over. 1988. *Determinants of Drug Imports to Poor Countries.* Greenwich, Conn.: JAI Press.

Edungbola, L., and others. 1988. "The Impact of a UNICEF-Assisted Rural Water Project on the Prevalence of Guinea Worm Disease in Asa Kwara State, Nigeria." *American Journal of Tropical Medicine and Hygiene* 39(1):79–85.

Eklund, Peter, and Knut Stavem. 1990. "Prepaid Financing of Primary Health Care in Guinea-Bissau." PRE Working Paper 488. World Bank, Population and Human Resources Department, Washington, D.C.

Elbadawi, Ibrahim A., Dhaneshwar Ghura, and Gilbert Uwujaren. 1992. "World Bank Adjustment Lending and Economic Performance." In "Sub-Saharan African in the 1980s." Policy Research Working Paper 1000. World Bank, Country Economics Department, Washington, D.C.

Elmendorf, A. Edward. 1993. "Structural Adjustment and Health in Africa in the 1980s." Paper prepared and presented at the American Public Health Association Conference, San Francisco, October.

Engelkes, Elly. 1993a. "Process Evaluation in Colombian Primary Health Care Programme." *Health Policy and Planning* 5 (December):327–35.

———. 1993b. "What Are the Lessons from Evaluating PHC Projects? A Personal View." *Health Policy and Planning* 8(1):72–77.

Erinosho, Olayiwola A. 1991. "Health Care and Medical Technology in Nigeria." *International Journal of Technology Assessment in Health Care* 7(4):545–52.

Esrey, S. A, J. B. Potash, L. Roberts, and C. Schiff. 1991. "Effects of Improved Water Supply and Sanitation (Excreta Disposal) on Ascaris, Diarrhoea, Dracunculosis, Hookworm, Schistosomiasis and Trachoma." *Bulletin of the World Health Organization* 69(5):602–21.

Evans, T. 1989. "The Impact of Permanent Disability on Small Households: Evidence from Endemic Areas of River Blindness in Guinea." *Institute for Development Studies Bulletin* 20:41–48.

FAO (Food and Agriculture Organization). 1991. *FAO Yearbook.* Rome.

Feachem, Richard G., and Dean T. Jamison, eds. 1991. *Disease and Mortality in Sub-Saharan Africa.* New York: Oxford University Press.

Feachem, Richard G., Tord Kjellstrom, and Christopher J. L. Murray, eds. 1992. *The Health of Adults in the Developing World.* New York: Oxford University Press.

Fendall, N. R. E. 1963. "Health Centers: A Basis for Rural Health Service." *Journal of Tropical Medicine and Hygiene* 66:219.

Ferster, G., P. H. van Kessel, Y. Abu-Bohene, and F. R. Mwambaghi. 1991. *Strategic Framework for the Cost Sharing System for the Malawi Government Health Services,* 1. Main Report, Government of Malawi, PHC Sector Credit Report Number 9036-MAI, May.

Foster, S. D. 1990. "Improving the Supply and Use of Essential Drugs in Sub-Saharan Africa." PRE Working Paper 456. World Bank, Population and Human Resources Department, Washington, D.C.

Free, Michael J. 1992. "Health Technologies for the Developing World." *International Journal of Technology Assessment in Health Care* 8(4):623–34.

Galland, B. 1990. "Systèmes d'autofinancement alternatifs au paiement à l'act-étude de cas au Rwanda." Unpublished report. World Bank, Central Africa and Indian Ocean Department, Washington, D.C.

Gbedonou, P., J. M. Ndiaye, D. Levy-Bruhl, R. Josse, and M. Yarou. 1991. "Enlarged program of vaccination and community participation in Benin." Bureau UNICEF, Cotonou. *Bulletin Soc. Pathol Exot.* France.

Gertler, Paul, and Jacques van der Gaag. 1990. *The Willingness to Pay for Medical Care: Evidence from Two Developing Countries.* Baltimore, Md.: Johns Hopkins University Press.

Global Coalition for Africa. 1993. *African Social and Economic Trends: First Annual Report.* Washington, D.C.

Golladay, Fredrick L. 1980. *Health.* World Bank Sector Policy Paper. 2d ed. Washington, D.C.

Govindasamy, Pavalavalli, and others. 1993. *High-risk Births and Maternity.* Demographic and Health Surveys, Comparative Studies no. 8. Columbia, Md.: Macro International.

Griffin, C. C. 1988. *User Charges for Health Care in Principle and Practice.* EDI Seminar Paper 37. World Bank, Washington, D.C.

———. 1992. "Cost Recovery." *Health Financing and Sustainability, Technical Theme Papers, Year Two.* Health Financing and Sustainability Project. Washington, D.C.: Agency for International Development.

Grimaud, Denise. 1992. *Evaluation de la Participation des Beneficiaries à la Gestion des Programmes de Santé.* Rapport Preliminaire sur l'Enquete. République du Benin: Banque Mondiale.

Grootaert, Christiaan. 1993. "The Evolution of Welfare and Poverty under Structural Change and Economic Recession in Côte d'Ivoire, 1985–88." Policy Research Working Paper 1078. World Bank, Washington, D.C.

Gwatkin, Davidson R. 1991. "The Distributional Implications of Alternative Strategic Responses to the Demographic-Epidemiological Transition." Paper Prepared for the National Academy of Sciences Workshop on the Policy and Planning Implications of the Epidemiological Transitions in LDCs. Washington, D.C.

Hall, Budd. 1978. "Man is Health: Mtu ny Afya." Clearinghouse on Development, Communication Academy for Educational Development, Washington, D.C.

Hall, David, and Gwen Malesha. 1991. *Health and Family Planning Services in Lesotho: The People's Choice.* Unpublished report. World Bank, Southern Africa Department, Washington, D.C.

Halstead, Scott B., Julia A. Walsh, and Kenneth S. Warren. 1985. *Good Health at Low Cost.* Conference Report. New York: The Rockefeller Foundation.

Hamel, L., and P. W. Janssen. 1988. "On the Average: The Rural Hospital in Sub-Saharan Africa." *Tropical Doctor* 18.

Harnmeijer, J. W. 1990. "The Issue of Recurrent Costs: Implementing PHC in Zambia." In Pieter Streefland and Jarl Chabot, eds., *Implementing Primary Health Care: Experiences since Alma-Ata.* Amsterdam: Royal Tropical Institute.

Hartnett, Teresa, and Ward Heneveld. 1993. "Statistical Indicators of Female Participation in Education in Sub-Saharan Africa." Technical Note 7. World Bank, Africa Technical Department, Human Resources and Poverty Division, Washington, D.C.

Haynes, R. B., and others. 1986. "Improvement of Medication Compliance in Uncontrolled Hypertension." *Lancet* 1(7972):1265–68.

Hecht, Robert, Catherine Overholt, and Hopkins Holmberg. 1992. "Improving the Implementation of Cost Recovery for Health: Lessons from Zimbabwe." Technical Working Paper 2. World Bank, Africa Technical Department, Population, Health and Nutrition Division, Washington, D.C.

Heller, Peter S. 1978. "Issues in the Allocation of Resources in the Medical Sector of Developing Countries: The Tunisian Case." *Economic Development and Cultural Change* 27(1):121–44.

Hicks, Norman. 1991. "Expenditure Reductions in Developing Countries Revisited." *Journal of International Development* 3 (January):29–37.

Hill, Kenneth, and Abdo Yazbeck. "Trends in Child Mortality, 1960–1990: Estimates for 84 Developing Countries." Background paper prepared for *World Development Report 1993.* World Bank, World Development Report office, Washington, D.C.

Ho, Teresa. 1985. "Managing Health and Family Planning Delivery through a Management Information System." World Bank, Population, Health and Nutrition Department, Washington, D.C.

Hodes, R. M., and H. Kloos. 1988. "Health and Medical Care in Ethiopia." *New England Journal of Medicine* 319:918–24.

Hogerzeil H. V., and P. J. N. Lamberts. 1984. "Supply of Essential Drugs for Church Hospitals in Ghana." *Tropical Doctor* 14:9–13.

Hogerzeil H. V., and G. D. Moore. 1987. "Essential Drugs for Church-Related Rural Health Care." *World Health Forum* 9:472–73.

Huff-Rousselle. 1990. "The Regional Pharmaceuticals Management Project and the Eastern Caribbean Drug Service." Paper prepared for the 17th National Council for International Health Conference. Washington, D.C.

Hunter, John M. 1966. "River Blindness in Nangodi, Northern Ghana: A Hypothesis of Cyclical Advance and Retreat." *Geographical Review* 56:409–10.

Imboden, N. 1980. *Managing Information for Rural Development Projects.* Paris: OECD.

International Labour Office. 1989. *World Labor Report 1989.* Brighton, England.

Isenalumhe, A. E. and, O. Ovbiawe. 1988. "Polypharmacy: Its Cost Burden and Barriers to Medical Care in a Drug-Orientated Health Care System." *International Journal of Health Services* 18(2):335–42.

Jacobson. 1989. "Tenwek Program in Kenya." *Social Science and Medicine.* Special issue on community-based health care in East Africa.

Jagdish, Vulimiri. 1985. "A Rapid Assessment Methodology for the Collection of Health Information in Developing Countries Using Existing Information." Doctoral thesis. Johns Hopkins School of Hygiene and Public Health, Baltimore, Md.

Jamison, Dean T., W. Henry Mosely, Anthony R. Measham, and José Luis Bobadilla. 1993. *Disease Control Priorities in Developing Countries.* New York: Oxford University Press for the World Bank.

Jancloes, M., and others. 1985. "Financing Urban Primary Health Care Services." *Tropical Doctor* 15:98–104.

Jarrett, Stephen W., and Samuel Ofosu-Amaah. 1992. "Strengthening Health Services for MCH in Africa: the First Four Years of the 'Bamako Initiative'." *Health Policy and Planning* 7(2):164–76.

Johnson, K. E., W. K. Kisubi, J. K. Mbugua, D. Lackey, P. Stanfield, and B. Osuga. 1989. "Community-Based Health Care in Kibwezi, Kenya: 10 Years in Retrospect." *Social Science and Medicine* 28(10):1039–51.

Johnston, Tony, and Aart de Zeeuw. 1990. *The Status of Development Support Communication in Eastern and Southern Africa.* Monograph Series 1. New York: United Nations Population Fund.

Joseph, Andre J., Peter N. Kessler, and Elizabeth S.M. Quamina. 1992. *Program Assessment and Future Development of the WHO Program on Strengthening District Health Systems Based on Primary Health Care.* New York: United Nations Development Programme.

Kamarck, Andrew M., and World Bank. 1976. *The Tropics and Economic Development: A Provocative Inquiry into the Poverty of Nations.* Baltimore, Md.: Johns Hopkins University Press.

Kaseje, Danny, and others. 1989. "Saradidi Project in Kenya." *Social Science and Medicine.* Special issue on community-based health care in East Africa.

Kasongo Project Team. 1982. "The Impact of Primary and Secondary Health Care Levels on Tuberculosis Control Activities in Kasongo (Zaire)." *Bulletin of International Union against Tuberculosis* 57(2).

———. 1984. "Primary Health Care for Less than a Dollar a Year." *World Health Forum* 5:211–15.

King, Elizabeth, and Yan Wang. 1993. "The Economic Burden of Illness: Evidence from Developing Countries." World Bank, Population, Health and Nutrition Department, Washington, D.C.

King, Cole S. 1984. *Information Systems, Monitoring, Evaluation, and Research.* New York: UNICEF.

King, M. 1966. *Medical Care in Developing Countries: A Primer on the Medicine of Poverty and a Symposium from Makerere.* Nairobi: Oxford University Press.

Kirby, Jon P. 1993. "The Islamic Dialogue with African Traditional Religion: Divination and Health Care." *Social Science and Medicine* 36(3):237–47.

Kleczkowski, B. M., and R. Pipbouleau, eds. 1983. *Approaches to Planning and Design of Health Care Facilities in Developing Areas,* 4. Geneva: World Health Organization.

Kloos, Helmut. 1990. "Utilization of Selected Hospitals, Health Centers, and Health Stations in Central, Southern and Western Ethiopia." *Social Science and Medicine* 31(2):101–14.

Knippenberg, R., and others. 1990. "The Bamako Initiative: Experiences in Primary Health Care from Benin and Guinea." *Children in the Tropics,* no. 184/185. International Children's Center, Paris.

————. and others. Forthcoming. "Strengthening African Health Systems through the Bamako Initiative: Operations Research Issues." UNICEF, WCARO.

Knippenberg, R., S. Ofosu-Amaah, and David Parker. 1990. "Strengthening PHC Services in Africa: An Operation Research Agenda." Draft. UNICEF, New York.

Korte, R., and others. 1992. "Financing Health Services in Sub-Saharan Africa: Options for Decision Makers during Adjustment." *Social Science and Medicine* 34(1):1–9.

Lamboray, J. L., and C. Laing. 1984. "Partners for Better Health." *World Health Forum* 5:30–34. World Health Organization, Geneva.

Landell-Mills, Pierre. 1992. "Governance, Civil Society and Empowerment in Sub-Saharan Africa." Presentation to the Society for the Advancement of Socio-Economics. May 5.

Leitmann, Josef. 1992. "Environmental Management and Urban Development in the Third World: A Tale of Health, Wealth and the Pursuit of Pollution from Four Cities in Africa, Asia, Eastern Europe, and Latin America." Ph.D. thesis. University of California, Berkeley.

Leneman, Leah, and G. Fowkes. 1986. *Health Centers in Developing Countries: An Annotated Bibliography, 1970–1985.* Geneva: WHO.

Leslie, Joanne. 1987. "Time Costs and Time Savings to Women of the Child Survival Revolution." Paper presented to the Rockefeller Foundation/IDRC Workshop on Issues Concerning Gender, Technology, and Development in the Third World. February 25–26. New York.

Liese, Bernard H., Bruce Benton, and Douglas Marr. 1991. "The Onchocerciasis Control Program in West Africa." Working Paper 740. World Bank, Population and Human Resources Department, Washington, D.C.

Litvack, Jennie I. 1992. "The Effects of User Fees and Improved Quality on Health Facility Utilization and Household Expenditure: A Field Experiment in the Adamaoua Province in Cameroon." Ph.D. dissertation. Fletcher School, Tufts University, Medford, Mass.

London School of Hygiene and Tropical Medicine. 1989. *An Evaluation of WHO's Action Programme on Essential Drugs.* London School of Hygiene and Tropical Medicine and Koninklijk Instituut voor de Tropen.

Lucas, Adetokunbo O. 1992. "Public Access to Health Information as a Human Right." In Centers for Disease Control,"Proceedings of the International Symposium on Public Health Surveillance." *Morbidity and Mortality Weekly Report* 41 (December, Supplement):77–78.

Malkin, J. E., D. Carppentier, and C. Lefaix. 1987. "Evaluation des besoins en médicaments en zone rurale africaine." In *Le Médicament Essential dans les Pays en Developpement,* Comptes Rendus du Symposium International, Paris, 19–20 Mai, 1987. Paris: Ministère de la Coopération.

Management Sciences for Health. 1984. *Improving the Availability of Pharmaceuticals in the Public Sector.* Boston, Mass.

Marzagao, C., and M. Segall. 1983. "Drug Selection: Mozambique." *World Development* 11(3):205–16.

Matomora, M. K. S. 1989. "Mvumi Project in Tanzania." *Social Science and Medicine.* Special issue on community-based health care in East Africa.

Mburu, F. M., and J. T. Boerma. 1989. "Community-Based Health Care 10 Years Post Alma-Ata." *Social Science and Medicine* 28(10).

Mburu F. M., H. C. Spencer, and D. C. O. Kaseje. 1987. "Changes in Sources of Treatment after Inception of a Community-Based Malaria Control Programme in Saraddidi, Kenya." *Ann. Trop. Med. Parasit.* 81(Supplement 1):105–10.

McGrory, Glenn. 1993. "External Assistance for Health in Africa." Unpublished report. World Bank, Africa Technical Department, Human Resources and Poverty Division, Washington, D.C.

McGuire, J. S., and J. E. Austin. 1986. *Beyond Survival: Children's Growth for National Development.* Cambridge, Mass.: James E. Austin Associates.

McNamara, Robert S. 1992. *A Global Population Policy to Advance Human Development in the Twenty-First Century, with Particular Reference to Sub-Saharan Africa.* Kampala, Uganda: Global Coalition for Africa.

McPake, Barbara, and others. 1992. *Experience to Date of Implementing the Bamako Initiative: A Review and Five Country Case Studies.* Health Economics and Financing Program, London School of Hygiene and Tropical Medicine.

Mebrahtu, Sabra. 1991. "Women, Work and Nutrition in Nigeria." In Meredeth Turshen, ed., *Women and Health in Africa.* Trenton, N.J.: Africa World Press.

Miller, L. 1987. *Les Possibilités d'Autonomie Financière de la Zone de Santé au Zaire.* Report of a UNICEF Mission, Kinshasa.

Mills, Ann, and Lucy Gilson. 1988. *Health Economics for Developing Countries.* Evaluation and Planning Centre for Health Care, London School of Hygiene and Tropical Medicine.

Mills, A. J. 1991. "The Cost of the District Hospital—A Case Study for Malawi." Working Paper Series 742. World Bank, Population and Human Resources Department, Washington, D.C.

Ministère de la Santé Publique et des Affaires Sociales, Guinea. 1990. "Evaluation des Systèmes de Gestion des Services de Santé en Ve Région." Direction Nationale de la Planification et de la Formation Sanitaire et Sociale, Conakry.

Ministère de la Santé Publique, République de Bénin. 1990. *Rapport de Supervision du Programme PEV/SSP.*

Ministère de la Santé Publique et des Affaires Sociales du Mali. 1990. *Evaluation des Systèmes de Gestion des Services de Santé.* Direction Nationale de la Planification et de la Formation Sanitaire et Sociale. Bamako.

Ministry of Health, Kenya. 1984. *Evaluation-Management of Drug Supplies to Rural Health Facilities in Kenya.* Nairobi.

Monekosso, G. L. 1989a. *Accelerating the Achievement of Health for All Africans: The Three-Phase Health Development Scenario.* WHO Regional Office for Africa, Brazzaville, Congo.

———. 1989b. *Implementation of the African Health Development Scenario.* WHO Regional Office for Africa, Brazzaville, Congo.

———. 1991. *Meeting the Challenge of Africa's Health Crisis in the Decade of the Nineties.* WHO Regional Office for Africa, Brazzaville, Congo.

———. 1992a. *Global Changes and Health for All: An Agenda for Action.* WHO/AFRO, Brazzaville, Congo.

———. 1992b. *Working for Better Health in Africa: Experiences in the Management of Change.* WHO/AFRO, Brazzaville, Congo.

———. 1993. "Statement at the WHO/AFRO Regional Committee Meeting." September 7. Gaborone, Botswana.

Mosley, W. Henry, and Peter Cowley. 1991. "The Challenge of World Health." *Population Bulletin* 46 (December).

Mujinja, P. G. M., and R. Mabala. 1992. *Charging for Services in Non-Governmental Health Facilities in Tanzania.* Technical Report Series no. 7. UNICEF, Bamako Initiative Unit, New York.

Mwabu, Germano. 1984. "A Model of Household Choice Among Medical Treatment Alternatives in Rural Kenya." Ph.D. dissertation. Boston University, Boston, Mass.

———. 1989. "Referral Systems and Health Care Seeking Behavior of Parents: An Economic Analysis." *World Development* 17(1):85–92.

———. 1990. "Financing Health Services in Africa: An Assessment of Alternative Approaches." PRE Working Paper 457. World Bank, Population and Human Resources Department, Washington, D.C.

Nicholas, David D., James R. Heiby, and Theresa A. Hatzell. 1991. "The Quality Assurance Project: Introducing Quality Improvement to Primary Health Care in Less Developed Countries." *Quality Assurance in Health Care* 3(3):147–65.

Niimi, Reiko. 1991. "Back-to-Office Report, Zaire." Office memorandum, World Bank mission. Washington, D.C.

North, W. Haven. 1992. "Addressing Management and Institutional Capacity Issues in the Health and Nutrition Sector." World Bank, Population and Human Resources Department, Washington, D.C.

Nur, El Takir M., and Hotim A. Mahram. 1986. "The Effects of Health on Agricultural Labor Supply: A Theoretical and Empirical Investigation. In Alandro N. Harrin and Patricia Rosenfield, eds., *Economics, Health, and Tropical Diseases.* Manila: University of the Philippines, School of Economics.

OECD. 1989. *Development Co-operation in the 1990s.* Paris.

Ofosu-Amaah, Samuel, and others. 1978. *Health Needs and Health Services in Rural Ghana,* 1. Institute of Development Studies, Sussex, England.

Ojo, K. O. 1990. "International Migration of Health Manpower in Sub-Saharan Africa". *Social Science and Medicine* 31(61):631–37.

Over, Mead, Randall P. Ellis, Joyce H. Huber, and Orville Solon. 1991. "The Consequences of Ill-Health." In Richard G. Feachem, Tord Kjellstrom, and

Christopher J. L. Murray, eds., *The Health of Adults in the Developing World*. World Bank, Population and Human Resources Department, Washington, D.C.

Over, Mead, and Peter Piot. 1991. "HIV Infection and Sexually Transmitted Diseases." In Dean T. Jamison, W. Henry Mosely, Anthony R. Measham, and José Luis Bobadilla. 1993. *Disease Control Priorities in Developing Countries*. New York: Oxford University Press for the World Bank.

Owuor-Omondi, L. 1988. "The Development of Health Systems Research as a Tool for District-Level Health Planning and Management: The Case of Botswana." In World Health Organization, *The Challenge of Implementation: District Health Systems for Primary Health Care*. WHO Document WHO/SHS/DHS/88.1/Rev.1. Geneva.

Pangu, K. A. 1988. "La santé pour tous d'ici l'an 2000: c'est possible. Experience de planification et d'implantation des centers de santé dans la zone de Kasongo au Zaire." Thesis dissertation. Universite Libre de Bruxelles, Brussels.

Pangu, K. A., and W. Van Lerberghe. 1988. "Financement et autofinancement des soins de santé en Afrique." In *Santé en Afrique, Perspectives et Strategies de Cooperation*. Sonderpublikation der GTZ N 218:63–88. Eschborn, Germany.

Parker, D., and R. Knippenberg. 1991. *Community Cost-Sharing and Participation: A Review of the Issues*. Technical Report Series no. 9. UNICEF, Bamako Initiative Unit.

Population Reference Bureau. 1992. *Adolescent Women in Sub-Saharan Africa*. Washington, D.C.

Porter, David. 1992. Personal communication, fax of November 20. Scottish Overseas Health Support.

Preston, Samuel H. 1980. "Causes and Consequences of Mortality Declines in Less Developed Countries during the Twentieth Century." In R. A. Easterlin, ed. *Population and Economic Change in Developing Countries*. Chicago: University of Chicago Press.

———. 1983. *Mortality and Development Revisited*. Philadelphia: University of Pennsylvania.

———. 1986. "Review of Richard Jolly and Giovanni Andrea Cornia, eds., *The Impact of World Recession on Children*." *Journal of Development Economics* 21 (May):374–76.

Raikes, Alanagh. 1990. *Pregnancy, Birthing and Family Planning in Kenya: Changing Patterns of Behavior: A Health Utilization Study in Kissi District*. Copenhagen: Center for Development Research.

Ransome-Kuti, O., and others. 1990. "Strengthening Primary Health Care at Local Government Level: The Nigeria Experience." Presentation at Abuja International Conference on PHC. Abuja, Nigeria.

Rasmuson, Mark. 1985. "Report on the 1982 'Happy Baby Lottery.' " Field Notes, Communication for Child Survival Project, Academy for Educational Development, Washington, D.C.

Republic of Uganda, Ministry of Health. 1991. *National Health Personnel Study*. Kampala.

République du Tchad. 1992. *Annuaire statistique*. Ministère de la Santé et des Affaires Sociales. Novembre 1992 supplement to 1991 version. N'Djamena.

Reynders, D., R. Tonglet, E. Mahangaiko Lambo, and others. 1992. "Les agents de santé sont capables de determiner avec précision la population-cible des programmes de santé." *Annales de Societé Belge de Médecine Tropicale* 72:145–54.

Roemer, M. I. 1972. *Evaluation of Community Health Centers.* Geneva: WHO.

Rogo, K. O. 1991. "Induced Abortion in Sub-Saharan Africa." Unpublished manuscript.

Saadah, F. 1991. "Socio-economic Determinants of Child Survival in Ghana: Evidence from the Living Standards Measurement Survey, 1987–88." Unpublished dissertation. Johns Hopkins University, Baltimore, Md.

Sahn, David E. 1992. "Public Expenditures in Sub-Saharan Africa During a Period of Economic Reforms." *World Development* 20 (May):673–93.

Sambe, Duale, and Franklin C. Baer. n.d. "Church-State Partnerships—Can They Really Work?" SANRU Basic Rural Health Project, Kinshasa, Zaire.

Sauerborn, R., A. Nougtara, and H. J. Diesfeld. 1989. "Low Utilization of Community Health Workers: Results from a Household Interview Survey in Burkina Faso." *Social Science and Medicine* 29(10):1163–74.

Schulz, T. Paul, 1989. *Returns to Women's Education.* PHRWD Background Paper 98/001. World Bank, Washington, D.C.

Senderowitz, Judith. 1993. *Adolescent Fertility, Health, and Nutrition: Issues and Strategies.* Prepared for the World Bank. Revised draft.

Serageldin, I., A. E. Elmendorf, and E. El-Tigani. Forthcoming. "Structural Adjustment and Health in Africa in the 1980s." World Bank, Washington, D.C.

Shaw, R. Paul, and Martha Ainsworth, eds. Forthcoming. *Financing Health Services through User Fees and Insurance: Lessons from Sub-Saharan Africa.* World Bank Discussion Paper. Washington, D.C.

Shepard, Donald S., Taryn Vian, and Eckhard F. Kleinau. 1990. "Health Insurance in Zaire." PRE Working Paper 489. World Bank, Population and Human Resources Department, Washington, D.C.

Shepard, Donald S., M. B. Ettling, U. Brinkman, and R. Sauerborn. 1991. "The Economic Cost of Malaria in Africa." *Tropical Medicine and Parasitology* 42(3):199–203.

Sheppard, James D. 1986. *Capacity Building for the Health Sector in Africa.* Washington, D.C.: U.S. Agency for International Development, Bureau for Africa.

Silverman, Jerry M. 1992. *Public Sector Decentralization: Economic Policy and Sector Investment Programs.* Technical Paper 188. World Bank, Africa Technical Department Series, Washington, D.C.

Simukonda, H. P. M. 1992. "Creating a National NGO Council for Strengthening Social Welfare Services in Africa: Some Organizational and Technical Problems Experienced in Malawi." *Public Administration and Development* 12:417–31.

Sirageldin, I., A. Wouters, and F. Diop. 1992. "The Role of Government Policy for Health: Equity versus Efficiency or Poverty versus Vulnerability." Unpublished manuscript. Johns Hopkins University, Baltimore, Md.

Slobin, Kathleen O. 1991. "Family Mediation of Health Care in an African Community (Mali)." Ph.D. dissertation, University of North Dakota. Available from UMI Dissertation Information Service, Ann Arbor, Mich.

Smith, T. D., and J. H. Bryant. 1988. "Building the Infrastructure for Primary Health Care: An Overview of Vertical and Integrated Approaches." *Social Science and Medicine* 26(9):909–17.

Soeters, Robert, and Wilbert Bannenberg. 1988. "Computerized Calculation of Essential Drugs Requirements." *Social Science and Medicine* 27(9):955–70.

South Commission and Julius K. Nyerere. 1987. *Statement by Julius K. Nyerere, Chairman of the South Commission.* 27th July. Dar es Salaam.

Stamps, Timothy. 1993. "Communication to the WHO Regional Committee for Africa." Gobarane, Botswana. September 2.

Steenstrup, J. E. 1984. "The Kenyan Management System of Drug Supplies to Rural Health Facilities." Unpublished manuscript. World Bank, Washington, D.C.

Stein, C. M., N. P. Gora, and B. M. Macheka. 1988. "Self-Medication with Chloroquine for Malaria Prophylaxis in Urban and Rural Zimbabweans." *Tropical and Geographical Medicine* 40:264–68.

Stinson, Wayne, and Marty Pipp. 1987. *Community Financing of Primary Health Care: the PRICOR Experience: A Comparative Analysis.* University Research Corp., Center for Human Services, Bethesda, Md.; U.S. Agency for International Development, Bureau for Science and Technology, Office of Health. Washington, D.C.

Stomberg, Claudia, and Christopher Stomberg. 1992. "Regression Results: Infant Mortality in Africa." Unpublished report. World Bank, Africa Technical Department, Population, Health and Nutrition Division, Washington, D.C.

Tanahashi, T. 1978. "Health Services Coverage and Its Evaluation." *Bulletin of WHO* 56(2):295–303.

Tchicaya, Anastase J.R. 1992. "L'Aide Extérieure à la Santé dans les Pays d'Afrique au Sud du Sahara." Africa Technical Department. World Bank, Population, Health and Nutrition Division, Washington, D.C.

Temple-Bird, C.L. 1991. "Training for Maintenance in Zambian Mine Hospitals." Unpublished paper prepared for the International Labour Office. Brighton, England.

Tumwine, James. 1993. *Issues in Health and Development from Oxfam's Grass Roots Experience.* Oxford: OXFAM.

Unger, J.-P. 1991. "Can Intensive Campaigns Dynamize Front Line Health Services?: The Evaluation of an Immunization Campaign in Thies Health District, Senegal." *Social Science and Medicine* 32(3):249–59.

UNICEF. 1987. *Guinea Worm Control as a Major Contributor to Self-Sufficiency in Rice Production in Nigeria.* UNICEF-Nigeria.

———. 1990a. "Country Program Recommendation, Botswana and Cape Verde."

———. 1990b. *The World Summit for Children.* New York.

———. 1990c. *The State of the World's Children 1990.* New York.

———. 1991. *The State of the World's Children 1991.* New York.

———. 1992a. "Achieving the Health Goals in Africa." Paper prepared for the International Conference on Assistance to African Children, Dakar, Senegal, November.

———. 1992b. *Africa's Children, Africa's Future.* New York.

————. 1992c. *The Bamako Initiative: Progress Report.* UNICEF Executive Board 1992 Session. New York.

————. 1992d. *The State of the World's Children 1992.* New York.

————. 1993. *The State of the World's Children 1993.* New York.

————. 1994. *The State of the World's Children 1994.* New York.

United Nations. 1991. *Demographic Yearbook.* New York.

————. 1992. *Demographic Yearbook.* New York.

————. 1992. *Child Mortality since the 1960s.* New York.

————. 1993. *World Population Prospects.* 1992 revision. New York.

United Nations Development Programme and World Bank. 1992. *African Development Indicators.* Washington, D.C.

Upanda, G., J. Yudkin, and G. V. Brown. 1983. *Guidelines to Drug Usage.* London: Macmillan Press.

U.S. Agency for International Development. 1993. *Nutrition of Infants and Young Children in Nigeria.* Africa Nutrition Chartbooks, Macro International, Inc., for the IMPACT Project of the U.S. Agency for International Development, Washington, D.C.

Vaillancourt, Denise, Janet Nassim, and Stacye Brown. 1992. "Population, Health and Nutrition: Fiscal 1991 Sector Review." PRE Working Paper 890. World Bank, Population and Human Resources Department, Washington, D.C.

van der Geest, Sjaak. 1982. "The Efficiency of Inefficiency: Medicine Distribution in South Cameroon." *Social Science and Medicine* 25 (3):293–305.

————, and Susan Reynolds Whyte. 1988. *The Context of Medicines in Developing Countries: Studies in Pharmaceutical Anthropology.* Dordrecht, Netherlands, and Boston, Mass.: Kluwer Academic Publishers.

Van Lerberghe, W., and Y. Lafort. 1990. *The Role of the Hospital in the District: Delivering or Supporting Primary Health Care?* Institute for Tropical Medicine. WHO/SHS/CC/90.2.

Van Lerberghe, W, and K. A. Pangu. 1988. "Comprehensive Can Be Effective: The Influence of Coverage with a Health Center Network on the Hospitalization Patterns in the Rural Area of Kasongo, Zaire." *Social Science and Medicine* 26(9):949–55.

Van Lerberghe, W., K. A. Pangu, and N. Vandenbroek. 1988. "Obstetrical Interventions and Health Center Coverage: Spatial Analysis as a Routine Evaluation Tool." *Health Policy and Planning 3:4.*

Van Lerberghe, W., H. Van Balen, and G. Kegels. 1989. *District and First Referral Hospitals in Sub-Saharan Africa: An Empirical Typology Based on a Mail Survey.* Antwerp: Medicus Mundi International, Institute for Tropical Medicine.

Vaughan, Patrick, A. Mills, and D. Smith. 1984. *District Health Planning and Management: Developments Required to Support Primary Health Care.* EPC Publication 2. Autumn. London School of Hygiene and Tropical Medicine.

Vaughan, Patrick. 1992. "Health Personnel Development in Sub-Saharan Africa." Policy Research Working Paper 914. World Bank, Population and Human Resources Department, Washington, D.C.

Vogel, Ronald J. 1987. "Health Cost Recovery in Mali: Preliminary Report after Mission." World Bank, Population, Health and Nutrition Department, Washington, D.C.

————. 1988. *Cost Recovery in the Health Care Sector: Selected Country Studies in West Africa.* Technical Paper 82. World Bank, Washington, D.C.

————. 1989. "Trends in Health Expenditures and Revenue Sources in Sub-Saharan Africa." Unpublished report. World Bank, Population and Human Resources Department, Washington, D.C.

————. 1990. "Health Insurance in Sub-Saharan Africa." PRE Working Paper 476. World Bank, Population and Human Resources Department, Washington, D.C.

Vogel, Ronald J., and B. Stephens. 1989. "Availability of Pharmaceuticals in Sub-Saharan Africa: Roles of the Public, Private and Church Mission Sectors." *Social Science and Medicine* 29(4):479–86.

Walsh, J. A., and K. S. Warren. 1979. "Selective Primary Health Care: an Interim Strategy for Disease Control in Developing Countries," *New England Journal of Medicine* 301(18):967–74.

Walt, G. 1988. "Community Health Workers: Are National Programs in Crisis?" *Health Policy and Planning* 3(a):1–21.

Walt, G., M. Perera, and K. Heggenhougen. 1989. "Are Large-Scale Volunteer Community Health Worker Programs Feasible? The Case of Sri Lanka." *Social Science and Medicine* 29(5):599–608.

Wasserheit, J. 1989. "The Significance and Scope of Reproductive Tract Infections Among Third World Women." *International Journal of Gynecological Obstetrics* (supplement 3):145–68.

Weaver, Marica, Kadi Handou, and Zeynabou Mohamed. 1990. *Patient Surveys at Niamey National Hospital: Results and Implications for Reform of Hospital Fees.* Prepared under USAID Project 683–0254. Abt Associates, Inc.

Wells, Stuart, and Steven Klees. 1980. *Health Economics and Development.* New York: Praeger.

WHO. 1986. "Rapport de Voyage en Republique Islamique de Mauritanie." Unpublished manuscript. Action Programme on Essential Drugs. Geneva.

————. 1988a. *The Challenge of Implementation: District Health Systems for Primary Health Care.* Document WHO/SHS/DHS/88.1/Rev.1. Geneva.

————. 1988b. *Estimating Drug Requirements: A Practical Manual.* Action Programme on Essential Drugs. Geneva.

————. 1988c. *Financing Essential Drugs: Report of a WHO Workshop,* WHO/DAP/88.10. March 14–18. Harare.

————. 1988d. *The World Drug Situation.* Geneva.

————. 1988e. *World Health Statistics Annual.* Geneva.

————. 1990. "Programme for Control of Diarrhoeal Diseases." *Interim Programme Report 1990.* Geneva.

————. 1991a. *The Evaluation of Recent Changes in the Financing of Health Services.* Geneva.

————. 1991b. "The Relationship of HIV/AIDS and Tuberculosis in the African Region." Plenary presentation during the WHO/GPA/NACP manager's meeting. Saly Mbour, Senegal.

———. 1991c. *Maternal Mortality, A Global Factbook.* Geneva.

———. 1992a. "Human Resources data base." Geneva.

———. 1992b. *The Hospital in Rural and Urban Districts.* WHO Technical Report Series 819. Geneva.

———. 1992c. "Health for All data base." Geneva.

———. 1992d. *Global Health Situation and Projections.* Geneva.

WHO/AFRO. 1990. *Maternal and Child Health.* Brazzaville.

———. 1991. *The Work of WHO in the African Region, 1989–1990.* AFR/RC41/3. Biennial Report of the Regional Director to the Regional Committee for Africa. 1 January. Brazzaville.

———. 1993a. *Regional Committee Meeting, 43rd Session.* Statements by delegates.

———. 1993b. *The Work of WHO in the African Region, 1991–1992.* AFR/RC43/3. Biennial Report of the Regional Director to the Regional Committee for Africa. Brazzaville.

WHO, Netherlands Ministry for Development Cooperation, and Royal Tropical Institute. 1992. *Health Systems Research: Does It Make a Difference?* Joint HSR Project in the Southern African Region. WHO/SHS/HSR/92.2.

WHO Information System. "Summary for the WHO Africa Region." WHO/EPI/CEIS/93.1 AF.

Whyte, S. R. 1990. "The Consumers' Use of Pharmaceuticals: A Case from Uganda." Paper presented to the World Bank/DANIDA Seminar on the Economics and Policy Choices of Pharmaceuticals in Developing Countries. Copenhagen, July 2–13.

World Bank. 1985. "Pharmaceutical Strategy Paper: Consumption, Production, World Trade, and Industry Structure." D-59e. World Bank, Industry Department, Washington, D.C.

———. 1987. *Financing Health Services in Developing Countries: An Agenda for Reform.* World Bank, Washington, D.C.

———. 1990. *World Development Report 1990.* New York: Oxford University Press.

———. 1991a. "Tanzania: AIDS Assessment and Planning Study." World Bank, Southern Africa Department, Population and Human Resources Division, Washington, D.C.

———. 1991b. *World Development Report 1991.* New York: Oxford University Press.

———. 1992a. "Etude Sectorielle Régionale: Pratiques de Construction des Infrastructures Sociales dans les Pays du Sahel." Report 10294–AFR. Vol. III. Washington, D.C.

———. 1992b. "FY92 Africa Region ARIS." Annual Report on Implementation and Supervision. Main Report. Washington, D.C.

———. 1992c. "Pharmaceutical Expenditures and Cost Recovery Schemes in Sub-Saharan Africa." Technical Working Paper 4. Africa Technical Department, Population, Health, and Nutrition Division, Washington, D.C.

———. 1992d. "The Public/Private Mix at the District Level." Unpublished manuscript prepared at the consultation on district health systems for *World Development Report 1993.* November. M'Bour, Senegal.

———. 1992e. *World Development Report 1992: Development and the Environment.* New York: Oxford University Press for the World Bank.

————. 1993a. "A Framework and Indicative Cost Analysis for Better Health in Africa." Technical Working Paper 8. Africa Technical Department, Human Resources and Poverty Division, Washington, D.C.

————. 1993b. "Gestion du secteur de la santé: approches, méthodes, et outils pour la gestion des programmes sectoriels dans les pays francophones ouest-africains." Report 11953. Occidental and Central Africa Department, Population and Human Resources Operations Division, Washington, D.C.

————. 1993c. "Objectives and Evalution of District Performance: Are the Districts Really Useful?" Proceedings of consultations in support of *World Development Report 1993,* November 24–27, 1992. Institute of Health and Development, University of Dakar, Senegal.

————. 1993d. STARS 1993. Data files. Washington, D.C.

————. 1993e. *World Development Report 1993: Investing in Health.* New York: Oxford University Press.

————. 1994. *Adjustment in Africa: Reform, Results, and the Road Ahead.* A World Bank Policy Research Report. New York: Oxford University Press.

Yudkin, John. 1980. "The Economics of Pharmaceutical Supply in Tanzania." *International Journal of Health Services* 10(3):455–77.

Yusuf, Zia. 1993. "A Framework and Indicative Cost Analysis for Better Health in Zimbabwe." World Bank, Africa Technical Department, Human Resources and Poverty Division, Washington, D.C.